NOTES
from
NETHERS

NOTES
from
NETHERS

*Growing Up
in a Sixties
Commune*

Sandra Eugster

Academy Chicago Publishers
An Anita Miller Book

Except for the names of my family members,
all other names have been changed.

Published in 2007 by
Academy Chicago Publishers
363 W. Erie Street
Chicago, Illinois 60610

Printed in the USA.

Library of Congress Cataloging-in-Publication Data

Eugster, Sandra Lee.
  Notes from Nethers / by Sandra Lee Eugster.
     p. cm.
  ISBN 978-0-89733-561-4
  1. Eugster, Sandra Lee—Childhood and youth. 2. Communal living—
Virginia—Nethers. 3. Nethers (Va.)—Biography. I. Title.

  CT275.E75A3 2007
  975.5'38044092--dc22
  [B]
                                        2007027782

*for
my mother*

Contents

Introduction

My mother is always one of the last people off the airplane. Dozens of others greet their loved ones, children run happily to returning fathers, couples kiss shyly or passionately, that momentary uncertainty of reunion safely bridged, solitary travelers look around to get their bearings and then head off toward baggage. Then finally, my mother appears at the end of the corridor. She is, predictably, engrossed in a lively discussion with a fellow passenger.

My mother has been getting slighter and shorter in recent years, the hunch at the back of her neck is more pronounced. She looks small. Her cropped dark hair, well mixed with gray, is askew on her head, a product of the frequent gesture of running her hands over her head in enthusiasm or intellectual consternation. Her face is heavily lined, but its animation keeps it mobile, and directs one's attention away from her heavy cheeks and prominent nose to her bright eyes. She is utterly without cosmetics. Never once has she colored her gray strands, moisturized her skin, or plucked a facial hair. She is dressed in layers, to assist her constant taking off and putting on of jackets and sweaters in response to shifts in temperature. The loose layers are piled on heedless of how they fit together, resulting in a shaggy profile. Her perennially too-long blue jeans are rolled up at the bottom, exposing wrinkled ankle socks above tattered "boys" tennis shoes with their laces untied.

My mother does not tie her shoes.

"No," she corrected me in a recent conversation. "I *do* tie them, they just never *stay* tied. I guess no one taught me how to tie my shoes right." The result is the same, loose strings flapping around her feet, shoes half slipping off.

Thus the tying of shoes is added to the list of things my mother says she was never taught; along with how to dress well, apply make-up, or cook anything more complicated than scrambled eggs. I think skeptically of my grandmother, who was meticulously dressed in hose and heels every day well into her 90's, was famous for her beef brisket, and would never be caught with untied laces. My guess is that my mother went to some effort to avoid learning these arts.

"I could be raped or murdered on a street corner," she will declare, to my ear emphasizing the *raped* with a kind of sexual relish, "and no one would take any notice. But let me set foot outside the door with my laces untied, and the world comes to a screeching halt in its efforts to set me straight. People will dash across four lanes of traffic, hurdle walls, chase after me for *blocks* to let me know that my shoes are untied." I am sure she persists in this eccentricity largely because of the response it elicits.

She is carrying the usual assortment of paper bags, knapsacks, extra jackets, and whatever curious receptacle is currently posing as her "purse." Unkindly, my sisters and I went through a phase of calling her a "bag lady." I know that the first thing she will do, once I have greeted her, is to count her items to be sure that she hasn't lost anything. We will wait while she thinks she has lost something, and discovers that she has not.

My mother spots me, and waves wildly with both arms, burdened as they are, as if I were across a channel, not twenty feet ahead of her in a hallway.

"Sandra, Sandra, come meet Marjorie, I think she might be your neighbor!" she calls loudly. This used to embarrass me to no end, that my mother was so *loud*.

I shake hands with Marjorie, who is a pleasant but anxious-looking person, supposedly living not more than three blocks away from me.

"What is the name of your neighborhood again?" demands my mother. "I never can remember it, but I described it to Marjorie, and she thinks she knows where it is. It's on the west side, right?"

"Yes," I say, reluctantly naming the area, wondering what my mother has signed me up for. Friendship? Membership in some organization? Participation in some cause?

"Oh, I'm so glad to meet you," says Marjorie. "Your mother and I have been talking, and she's just *fabulous*. I wish my mother was half as active and interesting! I wish *I* was! And she's been telling me all about you girls, and life at Nethers! What a fantastic place that must have been to grow up in, with all that freedom, and the goats and the gardens! It sounds like paradise. I'm so impressed! What was it like, really?!"

How many times have I been asked that question? And felt the clash of knowing how different my answer would be from my mother's.

"Oh," I say flipply, "just your basic hippie commune."

Even as I say the words "hippie commune," I feel guilty. We went to such pains to avoid that phrase and all its connotations. I use it now partly for shock value. How can I possibly explain? How can I convey to Marjorie in this brief moment the truth about growing up in a communal setting, about the reality of what it is like to share a bathroom—or outhouse—eat at the same table, sweat, cook, make music, dig holes, dance, build, weed gardens, play, and argue with seventeen or twenty other people on a daily basis? How can I get across to her that the idyllic-sounding freedom was, in reality, often terrifying and disorienting? Or reveal that as the commune grew and flourished, I became increasingly unsure and constricted? That is sort of embarrassing. Here is all this groovy open-mindedness, this free school, this culture of acceptance and tolerance, and I am so worried about everything I start getting headaches and develop this freaky nervous habit of contorting my mouth that makes me look like I have Tourettes. What the hell was wrong with me anyway? To this day, I can't think about that mouth thing without cringing, and can't be teased about it, however gently my husband does it. Truth be told, it was so hard to stop that I am still afraid, decades later, that I might again start grimacing, scowling, popping my jaw and screwing up my mouth just as I did all those years ago.

Meanwhile, my mother is standing there, immersed, as always, in her own experience, and what she thinks of as mine. She knows by now that her version of my childhood is very different from my own, but she still hopes to hear me rhapsodize about it, about the innocence, the lack of restrictions, the opportunities to exercise free will and thought. I can't muster it. The effort of explaining to Marjorie, much less to my mother, what it was *really* like feels insurmountable. I am reduced to platitudes.

"A commune," sighs Marjorie. "That's so *cool*! Did everybody sleep together, and hold hands, and smoke grass all the time?"

"Well, it wasn't exactly like that," I answer. "Anyway, I was only eight years old when it started." I can see her picturing lots of big zucchini, fine dope, and easy sex in exotic combinations and locations. She is off and running, rapt in her visions of utopian hedonism and young people with long flowing hair and headbands, communing with one another. And of course, we did all that as well, and sometimes it was wonderful. But that was only part of the story.

Marjorie is a good fifteen years older than I, just the age to have gone to live on a commune herself as a young woman, or to have known someone who did. If nothing else, I can be sure she has seen the movie *Woodstock*. But her picture of communal life has little to do with what I experienced. The stereotypes of an adult's imagination are simpler and more one-dimensional than my childhood reality. I expect this from her, but it is more troubling to know that my mother's version of my childhood is every bit as stereotyped and divorced from "reality" as hers. My version of the story speaks to the intensity of growing up with multiple parents—or none, depending on how you look at it—and the sting of the ever-present, ever-repeated transience of both friends and strangers. It is about a young girl feeling lonely and alienated much of the time, despite the best intentions that surround her, a tale of chaos and confusion mixed with love and joy and good will. It is a story of the loss of the integrity of my nuclear family, of being a child adrift in an adult's idealized venture. It is a tale of what it's like to be a child among adults who are striving to unloosen the fetters of conventional behavior. My hold on what to expect from people was a little shaky to begin with, but this put it over the top. It was the late '60s and early '70s—a time of great experimentation, historically and personally, and ours was an experimental style of living. But for me, it was no experiment. It was my unchosen life. Prisoner to my eccentric mother's determination to work for radical social change while raising her three daughters in the country, I spent nine years growing up in a "utopian" community. My first eight years had been passed in a relatively traditional middle-class home in Baltimore. I had had just enough experience with mainstream life to know that I wasn't in it anymore. Where I was, was another question. I didn't grow up in a foreign country; geographically, no oceans demarcated my land from others; no mountain range or river defined its borders, yet it could hardly have been more alien. It was a world apart. The commune set me off on a long struggle to fit in, and an initially Herculean effort to "pass" in mainstream society—to at least appear "normal," that elusive quality.

One thing I have since learned is how commonplace the feeling is of not fitting in, of alienation, of being different. Deep in many hearts lies a sense of fundamental unlikeness. My efforts to "fit in" began early, and have never really ended. Why is it that at 8 or 11 or 13, it was such a struggle for me to "be myself," to "go with the flow" in the warm balm of a group of well-meaning adults? Why was I so troubled?

Maybe it had to do with how often I didn't feel what it seemed I was supposed to feel. My reactions turned out to be off-kilter and hopelessly un-hip. Captive to visionaries, I was in a constant mad scramble to get with the dream. And it was something of a moving target, because I wasn't the dreamer. Nearly all those at Nethers had chosen to be there for idealistic reasons, and they promulgated an ethos of love and tolerance that I took literally and very seriously. I didn't know that they hadn't themselves necessarily arrived at their espoused states of grace, I just knew that I fell short. Because I occasionally felt judgmental, jealous, or distrustful, I was often resentful and aggrieved, and sometimes I even lied. I *didn't* love and accept everybody, as I was supposed to, I *did* feel competitive, even though we rotated under the net to prevent team unity when we played volleyball. I *didn't* feel free and uninhibited when naked with others, even though I was still an "innocent child." I *longed* for hamburgers and milkshakes, and I ultimately felt *undermined* by the "right" to singlehandedly block a decision from going through in our interminable weekly meetings. And witnessing the home birth was a lot of things, but it wasn't wonderful. Go figure.

"I just think it's *wonderful*," declares Marjorie. Her husband awaits her, and there is a tumult of greetings between them, and leavetakings with us. Marjorie impresses on me again how much she wants to "hear all about it," and how lucky for her that she got the seat next to such a fascinating person as my mother.

We head toward the escalators, and then my mother stops short, "Wait!" she cries. "I have to count my things! Here we go—my bag is one, my jacket is two, my purse makes three, my briefcase four, my suitcase five. But I started out with six! Where is number six? What have I lost?" She starts patting herself, feeling around her flat hips and her rounded stomach. She finds her glasses in the pouch of her windbreaker, her keys in her bra, and finally remembers her money belt. My mother pulls her jackets and sweaters up to her breasts, exposing the soft wrinkled skin of her loose stomach, and finds it still safely strapped around her middle. I take her bags, laden with her familiar musty smell, and we head out. Just as we reach the doors, a man loudly calls out from behind us.

"Ma'am! Ma'am!" We turn, inquiringly, and he races up to us breathless, his face red with urgency. "Ma'am, Ma'am, your shoe-laces are untied!"

Placenta Soup

The call came just before dawn. Suzanne ran through the house, upstairs and down, banging on a pot with a wooden spoon, proclaiming the news. In surprisingly little time, we had all piled into the van, which smelled faintly of the baby goats it had transported the day before. By first light, we headed out for the three-hour drive, easily sixteen of us crowded onto the seats, or sitting cross-legged on the floor in the back where bits of hay and the occasional raisin-like turd were evident. It was still early spring, raw and gray, and those of us in the back huddled together, sharing an opened sleeping bag Alan had thought to bring along. The van's heater roared, but no warmth ever got to us. Long anticipation charged the air and kept conversation to a murmur but, early as it was, no one wanted to sleep. I held my nose a little, the sleeping bag was kind of damp, and carried its own musty stink. The floor was hard and every bump in the road was translated directly to my rear end, which wasn't abundantly padded, but I was warm and safe and only a little apprehensive about this expedition.

In their neighboring commune, Kate and Marvin had turned a shed into their own private suite. There were straw mats on the floor, a pot-bellied stove, a cane rocker, and a big wooden chest under the window, covered with a cushion Kate had made. She had also made curtains from blue calico, and hung them over the windows. The bed—a thin foam mattress laid on a platform—was large, covered by an Indian print bedspread.

The room, as we entered, was sweltering. The wood stove had been burning so long and hot, it glowed. They must have kept it going all night. A pan sitting on top was filled with boiling water, and steam rose thick into the air. Someone had put eucalyptus leaves into the water, and the tang of it caught in my throat, burning simultaneously hot and cold. Several people were already there, sitting on the chest, the bed, and cross-legged on the floor. Now that our group had arrived, clustering around the doorway, there were about twenty-five of us in the room, not counting Marvin and Kate.

Kate seemed not to notice our entrance. She was sitting in the rocker, panting rhythmically, her fingers tracing small circles on each side of her belly, in time to her breaths, "Whoo Whoo Whoo Whoo." Her brow was furrowed in concentration, and her eyes were closed. Her shirt was hiked up to just below her breasts, displaying her belly in all its enormity. It was big. It was impossibly big. It was huge. The belly button protruded like a misplaced proboscis, and the skin was stretched so tight, I imagined it would echo if I so much as tapped it, or blew on it. Surely it would sing like a great drummed cello if drawn with a bow.

Marvin, long dark hair hanging sweat-soaked in his eyes, crouched between Kate's knees, breathing in time with her, his fingers tracing their own small circles on the self-same sphere, the bowl between them, the spoon-moon mandolin-bellied bubble-hilled mound. With the water steaming, and their rhythmic circles, they were like witches stirring a brew, or magicians summoning their common alchemy. I shifted back toward the door, unsure that I wanted to see what was going on.

Abruptly, the panting stopped. Marvin stood up, and Kate, arriving like a beclouded sun, looked up and smiled welcome. Marvin ushered us in, found us chairs and perches, all the time waving around a paperback manual he clutched in his hand, clearly no longer aware of its existence. *How to Have Your Own Baby: A Partner's Manual for Home Delivery*. I found a spot in the corner, and our group had barely begun to settle in, make chitchat, and inquire into the progress, when a shift in Kate's face signaled a return to intense concentration.

Throughout the long contraction, it seemed that she and Marvin had removed themselves, shielded by a curtain of common purpose that none could penetrate. The room became dimmer and hotter. Our sweat began to mingle with the steam from the boiling water, and the air was thick. After several moments, Kate again emerged, smiling and tucking her hair behind her ear in a gesture so casual and everyday that we wondered why we were all so tense.

For hours, this continued. No one talked during the contractions, but lent the full force of our concentration to the efforts of the birthing pair. I found myself holding my breath, and unconsciously clenching my stomach muscles. Each time a contraction ended, conversation resumed as if at a normal social gathering. People told stories, shared recipes and herbal remedies, passed along tips on goat management or barn construction. A couple of people tried to talk to me, but I was utterly preoccupied with trying to keep myself calm, and planning my exit, if it became necessary. When conversation petered out, we did some singing and chanting for a while. This I found easier and more relaxing than talking. Kate remained calm and smiling throughout, our benign and remote queen.

I really didn't want to be there, but I had been hearing for so long about this "Beautiful Experience" we were all going to have, that I didn't trust my own feelings. Not going had never been an option, regardless of the fact—or partly because of it—that I knew my mother did not approve. For one thing, I had a cold, and her philosophy of illness was that you should stay in bed and fast until completely better. This was too boring to tolerate. She also had reservations about my witnessing a live birth, with some absurd notion that it might be upsetting to me, or somehow risky. However, she had not felt strongly enough to forbid my going, so I had blithely disregarded her concerns and my own quiet misgivings, and joined the others for the trip. How could I miss out on this "Far Out Miracle of Life"? I hadn't really thought it would be so bad. I had seen enough goats and puppies give birth that I knew it to be a gory but quick process, and the cuteness of the babies always far outweighed the grossness of their delivery. This, however, was different—slow and laborious, and kind of scary. But I was embarrassed to be scared, and chagrined to find that my mother had been right. Looking around the room to see if any other faces echoed my sentiments, I found I was the only one. When Tina leaned over and, with long beaded earrings swinging and breasts pressing up against the opening of her peasant blouse, said, "You're so lucky to be able to see this at your age," I nodded dimly, as my anxiety bloomed into panic. At twelve, anything that ended with "at your age" was automatically suspect. I swallowed hard and set myself to bear it a while longer.

After a time, the pace picked up slightly, and they moved Kate from the rocker to the bed. Someone added wood to the fire, water to the bowl. Stacks of newspapers were placed nearby, although I could not guess their purpose. Hours passed. Kate, no longer smiling, became grim-faced and unresponsive. Her breasts, now bared, were pressed aside by her gargantuan belly, and dangled loosely somewhere by her shoulders. Marvin, having read another paragraph in his manual, began massaging them between contractions, while both continued with their common, "Whoo Whoo Whoo Whoo," and traced their circles on her unyielding belly, always those small circles on the sides and top. Her nakedness was now so complete, and she so unaware of it, that it was frightening.

Hours stretched out behind us like a rubber strap, each minute seeming to reach the limit of possibility, then stretching forward yet again. Time stretched, as that belly was stretched, as Kate stretched to accommodate this impossible exit/entrance.

The air became yet heavier, thicker, with a bloodier odor—air so steamy Mark had to keep wiping his glasses. Slowly, between Kate's legs, the dark thatch at the center of her began to widen and stretch, first showing nothing, then slowly, gradually, contraction by contraction, showing just the glimpse of a shiny red surface underneath, also matted with a thick dark thatch. No longer breathing in any order, circles finally abandoned entirely, Kate labored. It was her great effort, and the pain, more than her absolute nudity, that seemed to me too personal for an audience, especially such a sizable one. The bloody head pressed forward and retreated, pressed forward and retreated, and nothing more. Marvin frantically read his manual, the women began to stir uneasily around me. The men panted, while the cresting, crowning, dark hair, red mucus breath became harder, faster, getting nowhere, crown, gone, more, less.

Doubling over with sudden intense stomach pains, I was struck by nausea. Fearing I would make a scene, I crouched over my churning stomach—still thankfully flat—and worked my way around knees, over legs, and out the door.

The air doused me with a shock of cold that made me gasp and curl up where I was on the path. To my surprise, it was again nearly dawn. With the good hard ground under my hip, I could see the lights from the windows of the shack, and it seemed to me they glowed red. The whole cabin was outlined in a demonic gleam, and appeared almost to vibrate with its own heat. I imagined I saw Marvin's face pass by the window, his lank hair swinging, showering a spray of sweat droplets, something desperate in his face.

Closing my eyes tightly, I turned over and faced the other direction. The night was calm and clear. Stretching out before me was the gently illuminated hillside, insects humming in a scent of recent rain. Surely it was another planet altogether. My relief at no longer having to see and smell and bear witness to what was going on in that room spread coolly through me.

After some time, I slowly got to my feet, still clutching my stomach. I found my way among the sheds and buildings dimly outlined against the pre-dawn sky. The silo door was open and, vaguely remembering that someone had turned it into living quarters, I went in, climbed heavily up each step of the homemade spiral stairs, until they left me in a loft at the top, with red-shaded windows. I lay down on black flannel sheets, and plummeted instantly into the deepest sleep, curled into a fetal ball.

Bright sun shining hot woke me. Continued pain in my belly, and a sheen of sweat on my face told me Kate was still going at it. I didn't go back. I couldn't imagine seeing again her swollen labia, sparse brown hair, that belly, those flopping breasts, Marvin with his birthers' handbook, all the piles of newspaper and tubs of boiling water. I stayed more comfortable, wandering around the fields, inspecting their barn and garden, checking out the new dome they were building. The whole place was deserted, and I avoided the shed where they all were, happy in my solitude, but hungry.

Finally, what seemed like ages later, people began staggering out, and told me that the baby was born. It was a girl and she was named Aurora. Kate was exhausted, but okay. An hour later, there was a stir in the kitchen. After some time, we sat down at the long table, and a steaming broth was laid before us with bread and cheese. Exhausted, relieved, and famished, we all ate hugely and quickly. As we were finishing, Marvin came in. Standing proud and flushed at the end of the table, he told us that Kate was tired and could not join us. She was grateful for all the good energy we had brought to her, however, and as a token of her appreciation, she had sent half of her placenta for our soup. The other half, she had already eaten herself to regain her strength, following the example of the goats and livestock.

I looked down into the spoon that was half way to my mouth. It contained the last bit of broth I had scraped out of my bowl. Suddenly the liquid looked reddish—which I had automatically chalked up to tomatoes. My instantly sweaty fingers dropped the spoon back into the bowl and went to my again-churning stomach. I felt as if I had eaten a piece of Kate, or of her baby. Certainly I had ingested a part of that long, bloody, pain-filled day and night, and now it was a part of me. Not only was the image of it burned into my memory, it lay now in my belly, soon to be part of my very cells.

Baltimore, 1960–1968

Aurora's was not the first home birth I had attended. That, having been my own, had been neither as difficult nor as troublesome—at least to me. Not that it had been entirely without complications. In our middle-class Baltimore neighborhood, home births were unheard of. It was 1960, and Mommy had had a terrible time finding a doctor or midwife willing to deliver a baby at home using "natural childbirth"—a phrase that utterly mystified me. What other kind was there?

Mommy came from a family with a tradition of lightning-fast journeys down the birth canal. Her two earlier deliveries had been nightmares of bureaucracy and mishap. Both times, the hospital attendants refused to believe her when, less than an hour after checking into the hospital, she insisted that the baby was coming *now*. "There, there dear," they had told her, "it will be hours and hours yet, just relax." Finally, some incontrovertible evidence convinced them that the arrival of the baby was indeed imminent. With Rachel, they made it to the delivery room just in time, but Erica was born racing headlong down the corridor, the obstetrician squatting on the end of the speeding gurney, trying to catch her. My sister still occasionally speculates about how this has affected her approach to life.

That was it for my mother. Four years later, she resolved to have me at home. She finally found a woman doctor willing to be an accomplice in this plan, which, according to several others she had consulted, "should be illegal!" As the story goes, when the time came, upon entering the designated room, the first thing the doctor pulled from her bag was not a stethoscope, hypodermic or fetal monitor, but, much to my mother's delight, a camera.

"So where's the picture?" I kept asking, without which the story seemed to be missing its punch line.

"Oh, I don't know," Mommy would answer vaguely, as if that were entirely irrelevant.

I didn't get it. How could she lose that first glimpse of me? How could it not matter that she had? What was the point of the story, if there was no picture? Obviously there was more to it, or something about it that I just couldn't figure out.

Having been born at home made me feel special, as did being the "baby" of the family, the youngest of three girls. My sisters were four and five years older than I. I also knew I was special, because our house had *six* bathrooms. No matter that the two in the basement obviously hadn't functioned in decades, their bowls long dry and silent.

Special too was the fact that I was one of the only three white kids (all of us girls) in my class at the nearest public school. Lanny, Leslie, and I had been the token whites in our classes from kindergarten on. Lanny, being Asian, wasn't exactly white, but we didn't notice; she was more like us than the rest of the kids. We were accustomed to having the other kids stroke and comb our "baby doll" hair, pat our skin, and compare the colors of the soles of our feet, or the insides of our mouths. I loved the attention, even loved the feeling of palms running down my hair, sticky from the melting Red Hots we all clutched in our fists as we played during recess. There was a heady kind of importance in being the class celebrities, our special skin color augmented by the fact that we three were all smart. I didn't think much of it—and my particular friendships with Lanny and Leslie developed more because we lived so close to each other, than because of the pale skin we shared. The only incident of racial hostility I encountered was when Vincent, a boy in first grade, got mad because I slipped into the last seat right under him during a game of musical chairs. He loudly protested, and in a fury, called me a Saltine, which was clearly an insult, but one I failed to understand. Somehow intuiting that it was a reference to my skin color, I promptly retorted that if I was a Saltine, then he must be a Graham Cracker. I didn't see what my mother found so funny about this.

For my seventh birthday party, I had my three best friends— Lanny, Leslie, and Angie—at my house for a sleepover. Actually, it was a "half-year birthday party," something my mother dreamt up as a treat for me in January, when I was suffering from the fact that it was an unbearable eternity until my next real birthday in July. When she suggested it, I was awestruck at the notion that I could have my three best friends stay with me for *half a year*—that meant *six months*! I asked Lanny first, and she barely hesitated a moment before declaring, "Great!" and promising to ask her mother that night. Her mother's puzzled phone call quickly brought my misunderstanding to light. My acute disappointment was quickly allayed by the excitement of the reality of the thing—these best of friends all to myself from dinner to dawn. Despite my mother's increasingly stern injunctions to "GO TO SLEEP!" we stayed up half the night talking and giggling, sharing our deepest secrets. The peak of the party, in the early morning hours, was when Angie showed us her pubic hair. This was so utterly shocking to me that I wished I hadn't seen it. Not a few wispy hairs, but a thick curly patch, clearly matching the thick curly hair on her head. Lanny, Leslie, and I, ourselves years away from signs of puberty, were all appalled, and only in that moment when we each wondered if it was because Angie was black, did our differences suddenly occur to us. Despite the shock, this moment of intimacy sealed our bond. We had done something risqué and secret, and were unstinting in our solidarity.

In the morning, hungover from the unaccustomed confidences and lack of sleep, we had cold cereal and milk in the kitchen. In some display of bravado—wanting to flaunt my parents' liberalism, and my own bold carefree self, I reached into the cereal box with my bare hands, and managed to work the word "damn" into the conversation at least twice. This was suddenly more indecent than Angie's pubic hair, and the three of them were shocked, their faces momentarily stiff as I imagined mine had been earlier in the morning. Suddenly embarrassed, I wondered what I was trying to prove. We were no more allowed to stick our hands into the cereal and swear at the breakfast table in my house than they were in theirs.

It was a small world, but I knew it well. Having turned seven, I could get to and from school on my own, could walk around the block, or, if I was feeling brave, ride my bike. I could get to the houses of my friends. I knew that Mrs. Schneider had the greenest lawn, the Digangis gave out the best Halloween candy, and Leslie's mom made the best after-school snacks (sweet smooth peanut butter sandwiches on soft white bread, none of the whole wheat, natural chunky stuff like in our house). I knew which parts of the sidewalk were too bumpy for biking, and I knew the back way to school so I wouldn't have to pass by the witch lady's house.

I rarely walked to or from school alone now anyway. Through kindergarten and first grade, Erica had walked me to and from school every day. In the beginning, I had been thankful for her company, and had clung to her. The second year, I began to resent our mother's rule that I had to hold Erica's hand while crossing streets, and had lobbied unsuccessfully for more freedom. Now that I was in second grade, and Erica had graduated to middle school, I walked with Leslie and Lanny, rejoicing in my independence. We had countless impassioned discussions about our teacher Miss Young's hairdo, and the boy down the street with the unfortunate name of Zenis—we could barely bring ourselves to say his name—and the fact that pigs have feelings just like people. I was a big talker. I talked so much at school that I was seated apart from my friends in an attempt to quiet me. I talked to my friends, to my family, and when all else failed, to myself, holding elaborate conversations among my many stuffed animals.

Every day on the way home, we'd drop Leslie off first, reminding her to wait for us in the morning. Lanny and I had difficulty finding a way to say goodbye because neither of us wanted to leave the other to walk home alone. Now, we went past her house without comment until we reached our designated spot at the exact midpoint between our two homes. We clasped our hands together in the middle, said goodbye, turned our backs, and on the count of three, let go and raced for our respective houses.

Getting home, I went up the curvy walk paved with large flat stones that sparkled in the sun, up the gray porch steps, and in the front door. I loved my house. In my eyes, it was enormous and satisfyingly ornate. There was a library downstairs, with double glass doors, and the dining room had golden grass wallpaper. There were two adjacent living rooms, and swinging doors into the kitchen. The stairs were just right for giving puppet shows, there was a pantry, an attic, and a playhouse in the back yard. It wasn't as fancy as my grandmother's house in New Jersey, but it was wonderful.

Rachel's sky-blue room was at the end of the hall. There were filmy blue curtains romantically shrouding her bed, a big blue shelf for all her stuffed animals, blue window shades and throw rugs. This room became her private sanctuary, completely off-limits to us younger sisters. It was always cool and orderly and inaccessible.

My room was up in the attic under the eaves. It had a red kitten rug, a red ladder-back chair, and even a small red rocker. I loved it fiercely. During the day, it was wonderful, and I luxuriated in the space and quiet, looked proudly out my little leaded-glass windows to the street below, happily read books on my bed under the slanting ceiling, or played with my stuffed animals. But at night, it became too quiet. I would imagine that I heard someone in the other part of the attic, and remember scary stories I had heard. More often than not, after sweating it out as long as I could, I crept silently down the stairs, holding my breath until I was back on the main floor where the rest of the family slept, and tapped on Erica's door.

Erica would let me sleep with her on the condition that I would not let my legs touch her. She complained that they were prickly and scratchy. They seemed smooth and hairless to me, but I gladly swore that I would keep my legs away from her and not move them all night. I lay straight and rigid, terrified that I would accidentally brush against her, and she would banish me to my lonely garret. But she never did.

Erica's room was full of velvet, echoing her velvety dark brown eyes. It was all in purple, down to its tiny balcony, which, curtained by an enormous wisteria vine, became a buzzing purple bower of scent and blossoms in summer. This same vine climbed up to the attic to the window of my mother's study, across from my room.

As a poet, Mommy spent a fair amount of time in this room, and I was often with her. Before I was in school, she fixed up a corner for me with a light and a big cushion. Supplied with paper and crayons, I would draw and "write" while she worked at her typewriter. I enjoyed this for the most part, although it was hard to abide by the rule that I was not allowed to talk, make noise, or distract her in any way. My mother's sacred concentration became a kind of invisible entity we were trained to respect and protect.

I tried hard to picture broken concentration. Mommy was a little bit scary when she had her concentration, because it was as if she were not there at all, or as if I wasn't. She never looked at me, and when I stared at her, or experimentally made a noise, she didn't notice. When she was writing, she would mumble to herself, trying out sounds in a low, serious singsong voice that was downright creepy. Then, after a long, long time, she would come out of her trance, and be herself again, and she would let me play on her typewriter, have me tell her the stories that went with the pictures I had drawn, or "read" my writings to her, which inevitably were sad missing-you letters to my daddy.

My parents had been separated ever since I could remember. Mommy was careful to explain to me that they still loved each other very much, but they just couldn't live together. I remember repeating these words as the years went on, presenting the situation to friends or acquaintances quite reasonably, as it had been told to me, mentioning that my parents still played together in a string quartet every other Tuesday night, and that Daddy always came for weekends and holidays. When I saw a look of skepticism or disbelief in their eyes, I resented it, but knew, somehow, that I was just reciting a story I had been taught. It took me a long time to learn to believe what I saw around me rather than what I was told about it. There was plenty of contradictory evidence. My parents did, in fact, play in a string quartet every other week, my father a fine fiddle, my mother an adequate viola, and my father did come for most week-ends and holidays. But we heard a lot more than music, sitting at the top of the stairs after we were supposed to be in bed.

Some of it was good and exciting, like the parties they used to give. Then, the clink of glasses and the sound of talk was enchant-ing. It was real talk, the building of castles of thought and idea that seemed to climb up toward us, soaring into elaborate structures. I couldn't wait to be able to understand that kind of talk. It was one of the things I looked forward to about being an adult—being able to have and go to parties like that. But just as often, from the top of the stairs we would hear the sounds of our parents fighting. I don't remember what was said, only that my mother's voice was loud and hysterical, while my father's was inaudible. It seemed the louder she got, the quieter he did, until, in a final deafening crescendo, he ceased to exist. Then we would hear the door slam, his car back out of the driveway and drive quickly away.

The end of their marriage had something to do with Macon, a large, very dark black man whom I was also ready to love. They had met him together, on the boat back from Europe following a family trip. He was an amateur philosopher, and he and my father struck up a friendship. My mother's affair with him was neither clandes-tine nor the result of a moment of overwhelming passion. Rather, it followed discussion with my father. I think he wanted to be open-minded. I know he admired Alan Ginsberg and Kerouac, and other expatriates of social convention. I never had the courage to ask him, but whatever his thinking was, it didn't work. I remember confu-sion, upset, Daddy being suddenly gone, and Macon being around. I was sitting on his lap once, and he had brought me a fascinating toy, some kind of red rubber donkey that had a hand pump, which made it move when you squeezed it. There was something vaguely disturbing about this donkey, something vulgar or even lewd in its movements, or in the feeling of pressing the warm rubber pump in my palm. But I loved the attention, and, aware of my sisters' refusals to have anything to do with this man, I cozied up to him and called him my "chocolate daddy." Instantly, I was swept by a wave of guilt and disgust at my disloyalty.

I adored my father absolutely, although I was somewhat afraid of him as well. Originally from Switzerland, he was a scientist, a university professor, an artist and a musician, and he drove a '62 powder-blue Mercedes convertible. As a painter, he was given to wearing berets and a cape. I remember him swirling in through the front door and down the stairs to his studio, leaving a trail of remote sadness rippling behind him. I picture him in those days shrouded by a black cloud, unreachable for comfort—given or taken.

He maintained a sort of partial residence with us. He still received mail at our house, which we put up on the tall radiator behind the front door. He still read the paper in his chair in the living room some evenings, or watched the occasional baseball game, a beer sitting in a glass on the floor by his chair. I would creep around him quiet as a beetle, skirting the newsprint fence, longing to be noticed.

One of my worst moments was the time I knocked over his beer. He seemed startled, as if he had not known I was there until the stream of cold liquid hit his sandaled foot. Then he jumped up, saying *"Shit,"* and kind of swatted at me with his crunched-up newspaper. I was devastated, lower than an unwelcome dog. I yearned for him, and never more than when he was there, but unreachable. When he was gone I missed him terribly, and often at bedtime cried for him. At some level, I was aware that this caused my mother fresh distress, and this knowledge was not insignificant in my continuing to do it. It wasn't exactly that I blamed her. I was too little and my need for her was too great to allow for this. But I think I held her responsible, seeing her as the villain and him as the victim. His vulnerability was always clearer to me, despite his scientific brilliance, artistic accomplishments, and academic achievements. In the world of feelings, he seemed no match for my loud, expressive, unsubtle mother.

At some point, Macon disappeared, and then for a while, Mommy pretty much disappeared as well. She didn't actually leave, but she seemed to stay in bed all the time, and didn't talk much. This was early, before I went to school. The story I told my mother from pictures I drew in my corner of her empty study during that time went something like this:

"Once upon a time, there was a Daddy sun and a Mommy sun and three baby suns. Everybody was happy. Then one day, a big black sun came, and the Daddy sun went away, and the Mommy sun went away, and two baby suns went away. And it got very dark, because there was no sun. And the littlest baby sun was afraid, but she knew that she had to shine, or there would be no light."

It was my job to bring light. I tried hard to be good, and I comforted both my parents every way I could. Once, Mommy was sitting on the porch, weeping. Great copious tears streamed down her face. I picked a leaf off a nearby tree, tried to wipe her tears away, and was flabbergasted when she began to cry harder. None of my efforts seemed to do much good. She'd make dinner, and then sit there silently while we ate. She'd take us somewhere, and not be able to get out of the car. She did lay out a fresh t-shirt and underwear for me each morning, before she went back to bed. But it was my sister Erica who eventually discovered that instead of changing my clothes, I was simply putting on an additional set each day, slowly growing more rotund and fusty. When I was returned to the conventional single layer of underclothing, I felt both cold and exposed. The soft cotton layers and increased padding had been comforting—like a hug.

It was during this time that Erica adopted me. I was four then, and she was eight. I was having a hard time with day-to-day life. I missed my sisters painfully when they went off to school each morning. The day stretched bleak and empty before me in the too-quiet house. I felt drugged with inactivity and boredom. Going upstairs to the dim hallway, I made a parade of stuffed animals, and then collapsed on the biggest one, stared at the walls, and waited, lonely and worried.

As a matter of necessity, I started reading. Everyone in the family read a lot. Erica read to me by the hour, and while she did I would become deeply lost in the story, the separation between story and reality becoming indistinct. Noticing my trance-like state and mistaking it for daydreaming, Erica would periodically stop her reading and quiz me on plot and action. It was wrenching to have to drag my consciousness up to a level where I could report accurately on what I had just heard, and I wasn't always convincing, which would disgust her, and lead her to huffily refuse to read further. What she didn't know was that I was so intensely focused on her and what she was reading that I could not pull myself out into reality enough to converse convincingly. Nonetheless, it dampened her willingness, and she often retreated to her own book, leaving me frustrated and lost in the middle of a tale. In the evenings, my sisters and mother were often unavailable behind their books, and now the days too were insufferably lonely. Being able to read was suddenly desperately important. Happy to assist, Mommy made flash cards, and patiently taught me sounds and letters until I, too, could sit with my own book.

I remember losing my shoes a lot during that time. Sensible brown leather lace-ups, they were never there when I needed them, and the greater the hurry, the greater the certainty that they would be missing. In our entirely secular household, this was the one thing that would bring me to prayer. "Oh please God, oh please oh please, let me find my shoes," I would chant to myself, searching though the disorder of the closet, the stair landing, the playroom. "Please, please, please let me find my shoes, and I will believe in you," I promised time and again. I don't know what I needed my shoes for so urgently at the time, my memory of those days is of never going anywhere. Neither do I know why their disappearance caused me such dark desperation and panic.

Perhaps it was related to the fact that I was convinced that I was mentally retarded. This I knew with an overwhelming fearsome certainty that preoccupied me, which I could neither conquer nor dismiss. Out of pity or kindness, everyone acted as though I was normal just to placate me. But they would laugh at things that I didn't find funny, and seemed to share some common knowledge or understanding from which I was excluded. No one ever told me the terrible truth, although I often tried to surprise an acknowledgment out of them. I examined my parents' faces when I came upon them unawares, eavesdropped on conversations that might have to do with me, and searched their expressions when they addressed me. I looked for the telltale flick of eyebrow, or turn of cheek that would expose a visiting adult's thinly disguised aversion and helpless disgust. I knew I was retarded. I knew that my brain did not work as it should, and my greatest fear was that they would never acknowledge it, dooming me to a fictional normality. Worse than my mental deficiency itself was their attempt to treat my condition as normal, consigning me to a life of deception. I just wanted them to admit it, to acknowledge it, to level with me. The truth, bad as it was, was better than pretending everything was okay.

We had a housekeeper then, a black woman named Viola, whom I loved. I spent hours watching her iron, or trailing behind her while she vacuumed the brown rug in the living room, dusted the art work, and scowled at the spills in the fridge left for her to clean up. She taught me to recite my name, address, and phone number. I still remember it; "2704 Queen Anne Road." During those days, there was way too much time. Each hour seemed an eternity, with only Viola for company. Once she sat me down at the kitchen table, and taking out her watch, said she would tell me when a minute was up. I sat and sat and waited and waited, and she said nothing, impassively watching the sweep of the second hand. "Is it up yet??" I must have asked three times, squirming impatiently in my chair "Isn't it up yet?? *Still* not??" It defied belief that a minute should be so long. No wonder the empty days were eternal. When my sisters got home in the afternoon, my relief was palpable.

The three of us were clearly sisters, although Rachel had bright red hair, Erica's was dark brown, and mine blonde. The unfunny joke was that we must have had a lot of milkmen. Without being able to exactly understand it, I knew it wasn't amusing because of the men who came through after Daddy was gone. Not so many, but more than in anyone else's house.

Rachel had always been self-sufficient and remote, more inclined to turn to her books or stuffed animals for company or comfort than to us. She kept her things neat and well organized, and maintained complete discipline in her attachments. Rachel made a list of all her dolls and animals, and slept with a different one each night, checking its name off on the list, so each would have an even rotation. She did not allow herself favoritism, giving the ugliest, least appealing doll or creature the same tender care as her beloved Lambie which she had had since she was an infant. Each year, after trick-or-treating, Rachel would dump out her bag of candy, sort it by type, catalogue it, divide the total amount by the number of days remaining until the next Halloween, and dole them out to herself daily. In March, Erica and I would jealously watch her unwrap her day's allotment and pop it into her mouth with relish. We knew better than to ask for any. I often longed to play in the cool order of her domain, but Rachel remained unapproachable. She did not seem to require anything we had to offer.

Erica and I turned to each other. More similar in need and temperament, we bonded early and powerfully. She protected and took care of me, kept me company, and occasionally tormented me. Once she almost convinced me I was adopted. It was only because the idea of anyone adopting a retarded child seemed so unlikely that I didn't completely believe her. At dinner, there was a rule that we had to "taste" each dish, and that if we did not eat all the food on our plates, we did not get dessert. Mommy's notion of a "taste" was very different from mine. She would glop a huge spoonful of puréed squash or mashed peas on my plate, and I would try to eat it. After gagging and choking, often alone, being the last one left at the table, I would ultimately refuse to eat it. The indignity of being sent away with no sweet, despite a genuine effort to "taste" some disgusting food, was galling. Erica regularly smuggled her own dessert to me, soothing more than my longing for ice cream. She let me borrow her feather boa, taught me how to braid my hair and how to tie my shoes. She protected me from bullies at school, and from our mother. Erica brought me up, and for years I belonged to her.

Nights when I was in her bed, before falling asleep, Erica would tell me that I could ask her anything. Anything at all, she offered, and she would explain it to me. She taught me everything there was to know about snakes and spiders, about the animals in Australia, about how to survive in the desert, how to find your way out of a forest if you were lost, how to fly and land an airplane, where rain came from, and what bones were made of. She knew everything.

Why didn't I ask her about the things that really tormented me? Why didn't I ask her about my mental status, and the other fears that kept me up nights? I had lots of worries that arrived in succession. Each occupied me wholly for as long as it took to work at it bit by bit, turning it every which way, thinking and thinking and thinking about it, until it was worn smooth and round like a sea pebble. As soon as I got one worry down to a size I could manage, it only made room for the next, which arrived rough and unwieldy. The machinery dispensing the endless supply of fears appeared indefatigable.

I spent months and months on the problem that part of the marriage ceremony involved sexual intercourse. I was somewhat over-educated about the facts of life, and under informed about social behavior, making this misconception possible. It troubled me terribly. My understanding of sex at the time was sufficient for me to wonder how you managed it with all those fancy clothes. And what about all the people watching? How did you do it standing up at the altar? I examined pictures of weddings, hoping for a clue, a hint or instructions, but there was no mention or overt sign of this part of the event. I did notice in the photographs that the faces of the bride and groom often seemed mussed after the ceremony, tinted pink, with an air of distraction or disorientation, and I wondered if this were a result of . . . ? Too embarrassed to ask, I worked on this one in solitude, until I could convince myself that I would know what to do when I was old enough to get married. I could not imagine the answer, although I racked my brains, but I knew enough to trust my future self to be able to find out before I needed to know.

I was often afraid, as we were driving from one place to another, that I would look at my mother, sitting behind the wheel, and she would have turned into a wolf. I gazed studiously out the window away from her, because I could not bear the fear. I pictured her, like a werewolf caught in the sunlight unaware of the change. I imagined that she would turn to me, her expression still recognizable behind the fur, and I would see her dripping fangs, animal eyes, and pointed snout. The terror was mixed with fascination, so I would try to catch glimpses of her reflected in my own window. In those flashing reflections, I saw all kinds of things. I saw her nose lengthen, ears prick up, and once her tongue lolled long and pink, out of the side of her fanged mouth. Swinging around quickly to face her, I tried to check again and again, but in the time it took me to turn my head, no matter how fast, she had always changed back to normal.

This fear was fueled and illustrated by the forbidden TV Rachel and I were sneaking. Our mother was working again by that time, developing educational programs for children in the slums of Baltimore. Erica was on the second shift at the overcrowded school, and didn't get home till late, so Rachel and I were home alone. Every afternoon at 4:00, we watched *Dark Shadows,* although we were officially allowed only *Captain Kangaroo* and the rare Sunday night movie. The combined ecstasy of having Rachel to myself *and* watching TV was overwhelming. The show itself scared me half out of my wits, providing material for fears and nightmares for years to come. But nothing could have made me admit to Rachel that it scared me, and nothing could have stopped me from joining her. I closed my eyes as Quinton writhed in the terrible transformation from man to werewolf, tried not to think of my daddy's cape when I saw Barnabas swirling around in his, and if there was a ring around the moon, I waited in fear.

My mother never fully metamorphosed into a terrible beast, but she did have many faces, and the scariest thing was the rapidity and totality with which she changed. She could be completely warm, comforting, reassuring, and wise. Countless times, running to her screaming after I fell down, she would hold me tight, and calmly ask, "Are you more hurt or more scared?"

That question would magically snap things back into perspective, and I would examine myself, find that all my limbs were still whole and well-attached, and realize that it was only fear. She was full of magic and, once she got back out of bed after the end of the marriage, she was energetic and busy. My mother was an idealist, with an adventuresome spirit. But when she got angry, it was terrifying. She screamed at us, and seemed only barely able to master her rage. We might be driving down the road, the three of us noisily squabbling in the back seat, drawing zones of territory and daring each other to cross the lines. When our dares were answered, we would shriek and slap each other. Mommy would suddenly swerve over to the side of the road, sending us crashing into each other. She would slam on the brakes, gravel spraying out around us, lean over the back seat and smack each of our knees hard in succession, "Whack! Whack! Whack!" Then she would turn wordlessly around, veer back into traffic and drive on. Rigid with shock, we dared not even look at one another.

From a very early age, Mommy and I frequently locked horns in ferocious battles. I remember the joy of balking out of sheer will. We were taking a walk, and I would simply sit down and refuse to move. She yelled, pleaded, and finally, walked away from me. But I held fast. She yelled a lot. She yelled when we were too noisy, when we didn't do our chores, when we were "fresh" or "disrespectful," and most of all, when we lied. As I got older, I yelled back. Some of the things she would say to me were infuriating. "BECAUSE I SAID SO!" caused a roil of internal rebellion in me. "Don't talk back to me," wasn't much better. Whatever happened to respecting everyone's opinion, and equality for all? Although I was small and my mother was loud, my stubbornness was bullish. We both were screamers. When I got her mad, she would shriek at me, her face transformed to worse-than-wolf, terrifying in its foreign familiarity.

Certainly the rage my rebellions unleashed in her scared her as well. More than once, she used more force than she meant to, jerking or pushing or shaking me. A second later, she would grab me and hug me hard, my anger still snapping on her shoulder. I hated it when she did that. I was mad too, and though I couldn't yell as loud, I could reach a level of rage that went even beyond hers. My mother did not really want to dominate me. In fact, she was rather proud of my independence of mind. Usually, when I reached the zenith of my ferocity, she acquiesced.

In an oft-related story, once when I was around four, I broke an African statue that I had been forbidden to play with. Although I felt terrible about it, the intensity of her condemnation made me bristle, leaving me more defensive than apologetic in my response. Infuriated, Mommy grabbed me by the arm, dragged me across the room, and set me down hard in a chair facing the corner of the room.

"You *sit* there," she yelled at me, "and you be *quiet*, and you *think* about what you have done."

"You can make me sit here," I allegedly screamed back at her. "You can make me be quiet, BUT YOU CAN'T TELL ME WHAT TO THINK ABOUT."

Scared by my own temerity, but triumphant, I awaited the next wave of renewed rage. Instead, after a shocked moment, she actually smiled, conceding, and agreed that indeed, I was right. She could not tell me what to think.

Our worst battlefront was the bathtub. Whenever she washed my hair, my mother got soap and water in my eyes. I had a terror of getting water on my face, and easily panicked in water. The soap stung a little, but the water gushing over my head terrified me, and I shrieked and howled and struggled. Finally, I refused altogether to let her wash my hair. When Daddy came over once a week, he would take me up to the bathroom, put me into the tub, and using a cup and a wash-cloth, would wash my hair ever so gently, without flooding my face with water and shampoo. I think my mother hated that he could do something with me she couldn't. She claimed that he failed to get all the soap out. One time, she was insisting that I let her do it, and I was refusing, and we fought, and dug in our heels, and finally, reaching a pitch of fury she could not control, she picked me up and threw me head first into the bathtub. I caught myself on the handrail, and no bodily harm was done, but we both were shaken and frightened by our rage and her power. She let Daddy do it after that.

My mother's career as a radical activist with ambitions to "change the world" began when, in 1930 at the age of eight, she formed the World Wide Peace Club. She involved herself in every good cause and purpose that came her way. As a very young woman fresh out of college, she braved every kind of anti-Semitism, misogyny and ageism to work as a labor-union organizer in the South. Passionate, idealistic, political, intelligent, and completely dedicated to her causes, my mother always threw herself fully into her work. Now that she had a family, she worked on slightly more modest projects. She was instrumental in forming an education program for inner city black kids. She held workshops and rallies and meetings in support of equal rights and the advancement of the disadvantaged. A non-believer in baby sitters, she often took us downtown with her in the evenings, to sit groggily in the back, dozing through the loud exchanges, her talking punctuated by a rhythmic chorus of support. We were fascinated and frightened by the unfamiliar lives we were seeing. We learned to sing all the verses to the old Union songs, "We Shall Overcome," and "We Shall Not be Moved," and spent many late nights in some church or community center in the slums of Baltimore, arm in arm with total strangers, swaying back and forth, singing these songs over and over.

When we had moved into our white, middle-class, largely Jewish neighborhood, my mother had taken it on as a challenge to bring integration to the area. Although struggling themselves to live on a young professor's salary, at my mother's urging, my parents co-signed a loan for the Jeffersons to be able to afford the house at the end of our block, and she convinced the Howards to buy the one across the street. At that point, several white families chose to move away, and more black families came in, until it truly was an "integrated" neighborhood—an anomaly in Baltimore, a city of many self-contained homogeneous groups uneasily abutting one another.

We, her three children, created a game called "Slave Driver" that we adored, and that we played for hours and hours on the front porch and in the yard. One of us was elected Slave Master—it was almost always Erica, who was best-suited for the role. She sat in the swing Daddy had hung on the porch, wrapped in a filmy scarf from the "dress-up basket." The rest of us were her slaves, and when approaching or addressing the Slave Master, we had to kneel on the floor at her feet, and put our foreheads on the ground until granted permission to stand up. We then had to do everything she ordered, no matter what. Many neighborhood kids shared our passion for this game.

Our liberal, radical, union-organizer mother who was devoting her life to social change, would come upon my sister imperiously ordering her submissive "slaves"—many of them children of the same black families she had convinced to move here to step beyond the chains of racism and discrimination—to fan her or bring her ice water or pick her that flower or simply stay prostrate, forehead to the ground. Can it have escaped us that this would humiliate her? Were we so angry with her?

Mommy was doing Important Work in her efforts to Save the World. She was, we boasted, too busy to attend PTA meetings, bake cookies, or engage in other frivolous motherly activities. She was different from other mothers, behaving shockingly, and responding to some code of behavior or values on a scale different from our small concerns. We longed for patent-leather shoes ("impractical!"), lemonade stands ("too much sugar!") and Silly Putty ("toxic!"). Pierced ears were vetoed as "artificial," anything pink as "silly," and most of the toys we dreamed of—dollies that "wet," or ovens that baked, were deemed "commercial," or "exploitative." There was a very strong bias against dolls and for stuffed animals. We each had an abundance of animals, small and large, and we adored them. We claimed not to like dolls, but it wasn't true. One year, wonder of wonders, Rachel got an actual Barbie doll, and Erica got Barbie's sister, Skipper. Each one came with separate packages of perfectly matched outfits, shoes, coats, and brushes and combs for their improbably long blonde and brown hair (Skipper's *grew!*). They were feminine, forbidden, and utterly divine. I had gotten so absorbed in admiring my sisters' dolls that I had forgotten about my own, lying unopened in my lap. I couldn't wait to see who I had! I unwrapped my paper, opened my box, and found . . . Ken. Ken! A boy! With short painted plastic hair, hideous shorts, and some stupid tennis racket. I couldn't believe it! My loathing for that doll was fanatical. Soon thereafter, I took all his clothes off, and marked him up with permanent black marker. It was particularly satisfying to scrawl over his naked backside, and ambiguous genitalia. My mother was enraged when she saw him, and made me scrub him in the bathtub (oh, battleground of power) in scalding hot water. Not that it did any good—to my satisfaction, he was permanently marred.

At times we were proud of our mother; at others, mortified by her. She would say just about anything. We didn't often get new clothes. It was too much trouble, and our mother bought us only the sturdy practical kinds of things that last forever anyway. When we did go shopping, we would buy a lot at once. Once, after an exhausting session of trying things on, selecting, and arguing, we finally had our choices heaped on the checkout counter. Watching each item get rung up, folded neatly, and put into the bags, we three were thrilled. Our mother wrote out the sizable check, and handed it to the disapproving saleswoman, who asked for two picture IDs. Having only her license, she was informed that they could not accept her check. Mommy began to argue. She complained and protested, working her way up through three managers, presenting countless pieces of evidence that she was who she said she was, all to no avail. "The next thing you know," she screamed as her parting shot, before hustling her three shrinking daughters out the door, leaving our precious parcels behind, "you'll be asking for a photo of me in the NUDE!" This image was a little too vivid. Mommy believed in nudity. In the house, or at the remote beach we went to every year, she would take off her clothes, rubbing her heavy breasts as she freed them from the restraint of hooks and straps. Being "natural" was a high value. But we were too aware of her sexuality.

After Macon, a few more men came through the house. The only one that stands out was Don the Englishman, who started playing the cello at the unbelievably advanced age of thirty. I would stand behind him and massage his shoulders while he practiced, and he would emit these groans and bellows of pleasure that horrified and fascinated me. I had gotten into the habit of sleeping in my mother's bed when I wasn't in Erica's. There was suddenly a conflict when Don was there, and I no longer had ready access to her bed. A chart appeared upon which I earned stars for each night I stayed in my own room. I wasn't too impressed with foil stars.

Things were pretty stable for a while. We all took dance and music lessons on Saturdays, going to Peabody for Modern Dance in the morning, and to private teachers in the area in the afternoon. Rachel studied cello, Erica flute, and I took violin. I enjoyed it, although it made my arm ache. I loved the feel of the case with its soft green felt lining, and the scent of the resin when I rubbed it on my bow. We all were good at the arts. Erica starred in a dance performance, and our grandmother sent her a huge bouquet of tiny pink (!) bud roses that were laid at her pink (!) slippered feet at the final bow, much to her delight. We also took piano lessons at home during the week, which I liked less, because the teacher smacked my fingers with his pencil when I made mistakes. We all had to practice our instruments every day for an hour, an expectation that took priority over homework.

Mommy took in a "boarder" to provide on-site baby-sitting, and to help with ferrying us all around. A tall young man named Ned, he had frizzy black hair and spots on his face, long bony fingers, and a high-pitched giggle that could be intensely irritating. He taught me the word "obnoxious," by calling me that, which hurt my feelings terribly. I wasn't much good at being teased. Far too sensitive to take a joke, and unable to stick up for myself, I could be reduced to tears in no time. And I was easily embarrassed. Once, sitting on Ned's lap, I noticed that there was something in his pocket. It looked to me like a small rubber ball, and I wanted to see it. So I asked him for it.

"That's not a ball," he answered, giggling nervously, "that's my penis."

This was more than I could believe. I mean I knew about penises and all, but he must be teasing me!

"It is *not!*" I insisted, "It's a ball!" And I started punching it lightly, feeling it bounce convincingly rubber-like against my small fist.

"No, it isn't!" he repeated. "It's my penis."

We went back and forth like this for some time, the tension mounting. And then I began to wonder. Was his "ball" getting bigger?! I looked over at Erica who was in the room as well, giggling and watching.

"Is it?" I asked her.

She nodded her head. I leapt off Ned's lap as if stung, and ran up to my room, hiding my hot face in my pillow, mortified. Later, Ned came up to apologize, but I could not look him in the face.

Shortly after this, my mother began to get restless. She longed to work on a larger scale. All too aware of the futility of trying to effect change in individuals without change in the larger system in which they lived, she had been working on an idea of comprehensive social change that would alter the context itself. Her idea was to develop a model society in a rural setting, in which a different economic system would be implemented. She called it Future Village. Central to the idea was the notion that people should be free to do work that they loved without concern for remuneration. Each person would have a guaranteed income regardless of what they did with their time. "Breaking the link between work and income," meant providing a guaranteed income, and allowing people to find and practice "work" for the love of it.

She finally decided that it was time to begin to put her ideas into practice. In addition, we were getting older, and she had always wanted to raise her children in the country. Unbeknownst to us, she spent almost a year scouting the nearby rural areas, until she found a location and a small house not far from Nethers Mills in Virginia, three-and-a-half hours away. Only then, did she tell us that we were going.

The Move

Waking up the next day, I could hear my mother moving around in the kitchen. I immediately remembered that there was something special about today, but I wasn't sure what it was. I couldn't even remember whether it was good special or bad special. It wasn't my birthday or a holiday, and it obviously wasn't Sunday, or it would have been my father I heard down in the kitchen. My father came over every Sunday to make us brunch, and each week I fought with Rachel and Erica over who got to help him cook. We were supposed to take turns, but none of us could keep track. At least neither Erica nor I could. Rachel claimed to, but she said that it was her turn about every other week, so we usually fought about it.

I loved helping Daddy. He moved skillfully around the kitchen, sleeves rolled up, whistling tunefully. He was not a big man, but he had an air of confidence that amplified his presence. His sharp-featured face was usually serious, attention focused on the task at hand. But he was also playful and whimsical. He shaped the biscuit dough into animals and figures, illustrated stories with pancakes, and built a log cabin with the bacon. He had a quirky sense of humor, and twinkled readily. Once he made me a valentine by intricately folding and cutting paper, so that I had to open a series of pockets and doors, each one leading to the next, before getting to the precious message, "Will you be mine?" I wanted very much to be his. I perched on the counter where he settled me, happily smearing butter patterns in the muffin tins with my fingers, or carefully watching over the waffle iron to catch the first curl of smoke. Sometimes Daddy would diplomatically put us all to work, setting Rachel to spoon pancakes into the pan, Erica to turn the sausage, and me to stir the orange juice. He often found a way to stop our squabbling, and it was more than the abundant fragrant food that nourished us in those weekly feasts. Daddy made ordinary things special.

Clearly it was not my father in the kitchen this morning. Where he was neat on his feet, quick, sure, and quiet, my mother was clumsy. Listening, I could picture her taking trips back and forth from the fridge, forgetting things or changing her mind. Short and dark, my mother had clear priorities about what was worth paying attention to, and what was not. Some aspects of life, like clothes, one's appearance, or furniture, were simply not important, and she spent little thought or time on them. She usually dressed in jeans rolled up at the bottom, and a man's button-down shirt hanging loose. She raked her short dark brown hair back with her fingers. Her features were large; particularly her nose, but she had bright hazel eyes and a pretty, sensitive mouth. In pictures of her as a girl, I had seen her look delicate, even feminine. In one she was wearing Shirley Temple curls, but I can only imagine how she must have hated such extravagant trimmings.

Now she banged jars onto the yellow Formica counter, cracked plates together, and swung the cabinet doors closed with a smack. Her sneakers were comfortably loose on her feet, and their untied laces clicked noisily against the linoleum floor. Nonetheless, it was comforting to hear her, and I lay there listening because of the comfort, and because of that nagging feeling that something was different, only I couldn't remember what.

And then I did.

Getting up, pulling on tights, skirt, and sweater, eating Grape Nuts at the kitchen table with my sisters, kissing my mother, and heading out the door with my Snoopy lunch box and schoolbag was all so routine, that I thought maybe the other would go away and leave me in comfortable familiarity. Meeting my best friend Lanny at the corner to walk to school together as we did every morning, I was bursting with self-importance.

"We're moving," I said.

"Where to?" she asked hopefully, on the chance I meant down the street to the empty house next to hers.

"To Country," I announced firmly.

Lanny looked at me silently, her slanted eyes narrowing further until they were mere lines in her face. She dropped her head slowly sideways, heavy hair cascading over to shade her face in a gesture too mature for her age. Lanny's long, thick, blue-black hair hung to her waist and was her beauty. At the age of seven, she was already learning to use its language.

Much as I loved her, I always had the sense of some unspeakable, unbridgeable difference between Lanny and me. There was the obvi-ous—she was delicate, dark, and beautiful, while I was lank-blonde, skinny, and looked like a boy. She spoke in a quiet dainty voice, and I was loud and thoughtless. She rarely offered an opinion unless we were alone together, where I was all talk and determination. Lanny belonged to a rich family, but it wasn't just the shiny cars in the circular drive, the maids, or the elaborate doll perched atop a forest of ruffles and bows in the middle of her perfectly made bed. There was a different kind of strange about her home. Her short Philip-pino father often stood by the door grinning and nodding as we came and went. Supposedly, he had once cornered my sister Erica and tried to put his tongue in her mouth. I couldn't imagine that, or understand why he would want to. I asked Lanny about it, and she didn't know. We tried putting our tongues in each other's mouths, but it was slimy and stupid, so we gave it up as a mystery.

"I'll probably never see you again!" I now told her imposingly, although the reality of this idea was still absent from my words. At that, Lanny straightened sharply, and as we looked at each other, it suddenly became real. After a frozen moment, we both burst into tears.

"Where's Country?" my friend Leslie asked later at school. I didn't know.

"Are you taking Chippy?" Donna asked. It was lunch break, and my friends were watching in accustomed horror as I unwrapped my lunch, disclosing a green pepper, olive, and cream cheese sandwich on dark rye bread, carrot sticks, and a glob of the cottage cheese, peanut butter, and grated carrot mixture my mother called dessert. Wordlessly, they each made a contribution; Lanny gave me half of her tuna salad on Wonder Bread, Leslie passed over three large potato chips, and Donna gave me one of her brownies.

Chippy was a chipmunk Daddy had caught for me. We had been walking in the woods one day, and Chippy had run only part-way across the path before becoming paralyzed with fear. Daddy had sneaked up on him slowly, and then suddenly snatched the tiny heart-racing animal with his deft hands before it could flee. He had made a large chicken-wire box for him, and my mother had filled it with wood-chips, adding part of a red blanket, and a small log.

My friends rarely came to my house, because they were afraid of my father's huge, strange, three-dimensional paintings that hung in deep colors on every wall, stood in corners, and loomed over the stairwell. Most of the paintings were of people. Gigantic blue faces gazed down from above, elongated eyes peered sideways, enormous orange mouths were pursed in expressions of despair or desire. There was one painting of an unhappy-looking man whose eyes followed you everywhere from his place trapped in the corner of the living room. I could never shake the feeling that he would leap menacingly from the canvas, if only he could free himself. There were nudes as well, painted in unearthly shades of green and purple, larger than life-sized. I was so used to them all, I didn't really notice them, but they scared my friends.

Chippy was such a draw that now they came anyway. His cage was in the dining room, but we weren't allowed to touch him because my mother feared he might carry rabies. The thought that one bite from Chippy could transform any one of us into a frothing, lunging lunatic like Ol' Yeller, was captivating. We stood by the wire cage, gazing at this small, harmless-looking creature, shuddering when he came near, and teasing him out when he hid behind his log.

I didn't know about Chippy.

"*Why* are you moving?" Lanny eventually asked me. We were hanging upside-down on the swings during recess, and her hair brushed the ground. I knew the answer to that one, an answer I had heard countless times from my mother:

"To break the link between work and income," I stated clearly.

"Oh," said my friend, accepting, as I did, the incomprehensible.

The fact that I was leaving made me important for a brief time. But the novelty quickly wore off, and with it, my importance. Lanny, Leslie, Donna, and all my other friends soon learned which teachers they would have for third grade, and began establishing new bonds and enmities. They started comparing summer plans, and talking about Donna's birthday party, scheduled for the day after we were leaving. I was suddenly peripheral.

Rachel was outraged. She had a wide circle of friends, participated in theatre and music outside of school, and had no intention of going anywhere. She fought like a banshee not to be displaced. Mommy was unaffected. Erica and I were somewhat curious, and reserved judgment. Daddy said he would come to visit us often, but even I knew that 3½ hours was a world different from the short frequent drive it had been.

Now that we were moving, I developed a new fear. This was the fear that I would some day have to choose which would die: my mother or my father. The circumstances of my being forced to make this choice of execution were unclear. My problem was that I could never decide which one would go. Or maybe the fear that I could.

I went back and forth, back and forth in agony. One night I would think I had it. I would feel my mother's warmth, her absent-minded joy in life, her wacky involvement in adventure, and I would know that I could never do without her. It would have to be my father that I sent to death. My father, who was brilliant and creative and wide-awake, my father, who expressed his love for me more subtly, but no less fully. When he took my hand, the world was wonderful and safe. His humor and contagious pleasure so drew me in that I could never do without him. It would have to be my mother.

There was nothing delicate about my mother. Her voice was loud, her step heavy, her presence square and solid. Even her care-taking hurt. At the beach, she always got sand in the sunscreen so it grated and stung when she spread it on my skin. But she could always tell the difference between mad and sad. She would stay with me if I needed her to, make me toast in warm milk, or hot tea with honey. Sometimes it even seemed that my mother understood the gnarled confusion I felt about people, about myself, about the world. No, it would have to be my father. My father, whose sharp nose made me want to cry sometimes for no reason I could understand, my father, who whistled symphonies, who had the most beautiful hands, shapely and capable. Capable of doing anything: building a dresser, wiring an electric box, digging a ditch, painting a painting, extracting a splinter, playing the violin, fixing broken things, tending wounded animals, kneading bread, or throwing a pot with fierce concentration flowing through every finger into the wet malleability of clay. When I got a baby tooth to that infuriating stage of looseness where it wiggled all over but was still too firmly attached to be easily pulled out, he would take out his (always clean) handkerchief and tell me to come over and let him look at it. I would stand obediently between his knees with my mouth open, and he would say "hmmmm," while painlessly feeling in my mouth. He then would bring his handkerchief back out with my tooth magically in it, bloodied at the root. No, I could never do without my father. The effort to resolve this question exhausted me. I tried to convince myself that it was irrational and wildly unlikely that such a choice would ever be mine. It was almost worse to face the reality that it would some day be made for me.

We were instructed to pack up our beloved rooms, and to bring only the things most dear to us. We were, our mother told us, moving to a tiny house where there wasn't room for much. There weren't many things that I really cared about—my great big ladybug that Daddy had given me when I was two, my favorite book of poems called *This Way Delight*, my fuzzy kitten rug, and that was about it—my deep attachments ran more to people.

I gave away most of my things, because the future was unimaginable. It was a kind of personal renunciation, as beloved toy after book went into the "give-away pile." My mother encouraged this, explaining, as she prepared the boxes for Good Will, that I would make a lot of little children very happy. I tried to summon a feeling of good will toward these imaginary children, but the truth was I couldn't care less. I wasn't giving them things that mattered; nothing much seemed to matter right then. I was just shedding extraneous clutter.

After finishing my room, I went out into the back yard. There was a bed of blue-and-pink hyacinths blooming. I lay on the ground, pressed my full length to the cool earth, placed my nose deep among the huge flowers, and inhaled. Immersed in the almost narcotic intensity of sweetness and growth, I lay there timelessly in a haze of scent, saying goodbye. Goodbye to my beloved house, goodbye to the canopy of huge tulip trees, goodbye to the stone chimney around which I built imaginary houses, and on which I brewed imaginary stews, goodbye to my friends, and my father, and my life as I knew it. As it happened, I was saying goodbye to more than I knew—my confidence, my voice, my sense of family and safety, and knowing what to expect.

The day before we left, I took Princess Rose, my one beloved dolly, to a back street, not far from our house. Princess Rose was beautiful. She had soft brown hair, and lovely blue eyes. Her face was serene and kind, and you knew she could be trusted with a secret. She was everything a little girl could hope for in a doll, and I adored her unreservedly. I solemnly placed her in the middle of the road, carefully arranged her little lace slip and velvet skirt, and combed her hair one last time. Then, without looking back, I walked away, knowing that I had done a wonderful noble thing, but burdened by sadness. My family was mystified by Princess Rose's disappearance, since my attachment to her was no secret, but I would tell no one, not even Erica, where she was. It had been a ceremonial sacrifice of which I was oddly proud, but which was so profoundly personal, that I was embarrassed to speak of it.

I was ready to go.

We moved on July 20, 1969, the date Apollo 11 achieved the first landing on the moon. We might as well have been in a spacecraft ourselves.

5

From Nurture to Nature

The site our mother had chosen for our new life was a tiny pre-fabricated log cabin. It sat in the middle of a weedy lot on a quiet, dead-end road in rural Southwestern Virginia at the foot of Old Rag Mountain. In the dim hut, barely the size of our attic back home, there was one small living room, a bedroom for Mommy, and a galley kitchen. Rachel, Erica, and I shared the other bedroom, a stuffy little chamber with a built-to-order three-bunk bed, one atop the other, me at the top. There was no getting scared in this garret; I could hear my sisters' every breath and rustle, as well as the stir and crackle of unfamiliar things outside the window.

No girdle of sidewalks contained the vegetation here; vines, weeds, and brambles clearly had the upper hand, effortlessly surmounting any fence, wall, or barrier. Only the river that ran parallel to the road stopped the growth, and then only for a brief span before it resumed on the other side. The cabin was almost airless, its six windows small and reluctant to open. It felt more like a submarine, frail shelter from the encroaching sea of honeysuckle, kudzu, and poison ivy vines that surrounded it. The single streetlight on our mile of country road was wrapped in their choking embrace, as were the tree trunks, and the telephone poles. I imagined that if I sat too long on the hill, or fell asleep in the field, I, like Gulliver, would come to myself held fast to the earth by innumerable tensile tendrils. Where vines did not cover it, grass grew knee-high, bearing little relationship to the tame green lawns of my old neighborhood. The whole place was wild, and raucous with life. There were mice in the house, squirrels in the chimney, a raccoon in the woodpile, a stray cat, countless birds, and a couple of foxes. Ants, spiders, ladybugs, and dozens of less familiar insects came and went about their business, marching in and out of the house as if they owned the place. During the day, flies buzzed, bees droned, crickets trilled, and grasshoppers vibrated. After dark, bullfrogs sang from the river, mosquitoes whined, tree frogs peeped, and innumerable other minstrels joined in to create a cacophonous chorus that was deafening and awe-inspiring. This was far noisier than any city night I had experienced.

On one side of us, Miz Minnie Minchum lived alone in a one-room trailer that sat on eight cinder blocks. Miz Minchum was spectacularly obese. I was fascinated by the sight of her heaving herself down the steps of her trailer with a basket of wet laundry to hang on the line. Her feet were improbably small and feminine, housed in enviable fluffy pink slippers. Her capacious nylon dress draped itself over the improbable rolls of fat on her torso. Her arms, protruding through sleeveless armholes, had rolls of flesh bulging at elbows and wrists. Each time she reached up to clip a huge pair of pants or a tent-sized shirt to the clothesline, waves of fat were set in motion. Small ripples cascaded over her wrist, across her elbow, down her arm and into her dress, shivering visibly across her chest and belly. At the same time, her trembling upper arms swung ponderously back and forth in a slower sideways rhythm, creating eddies and crosscurrents. I tried to watch without staring. I wanted to be friendly, but it was difficult, because I could barely understand a word she said.

"Wayah yawl feruhm?" she had asked, on our first day there.

"Huh?!" I had thought, listening in wonder as my mother answered, "Baltimore." Baltimore? What about Baltimore?

"Wheeza galayed ta hayevya."

"Thank you," replied my mother to I knew not what.

These brief exchanges always ended with Miz Minchum saying loudly, "Yawl kumbayackana!" to which I learned to nod and smile, as I did to every incomprehensible thing she said. It helped when my mother translated this as "ya'll come back now!"

On the other side of our house lived Mr. Finchum and his dog "Whitey," a shifty-eyed mutt with one torn ear. This all sounded a little too Dr. Seuss to be true, but no, Finchum and Minchum it was. Mr. Finchum and Whitey shared a ramshackle cabin that stayed upright in clear defiance of the laws of physics. While Mr. Finchum was every bit as difficult to understand as Miz Minchum, it mattered less. He was laconic anyway, and his mouth was always occupied with a sizable wad of chewing tobacco that would have limited conversation under any circumstances. Mr. Finchum's wrinkled face, creased work shirt, and baggy pants, were all the same weathered tan color. He always wore his beaten-down felt hat, brim curling up unevenly at the sides. Mr. Finchum never left his house without his snake stick, a straight, river-hardened piece he had whittled to suit, worn smooth and shiny by his palm. He had great respect for snakes, which he taught us to share. It was a good thing we didn't know at first about the abundant black snakes ("harmless, nothing to worry about, good mousers and ratters"), water moccasins ("poisonous, but too skittery to be dangerous"), and copperheads ("downright mean and ornery, ugly as sin, and dangerous as heck"). Otherwise, we would have been paralyzed with fear. Mr. Finchum hung around with us a fair amount, observing the goings-on with what appeared to be amusement.

The first day we went down to swim in the river, we dressed as we always had for the pool back home. Bathing suits—two-pieces with flounced skirts for Rachel and Erica, one-pieces for Mommy and me—and our customary bathing caps pulled down well over our ears. Not one cap was without a large rubber flower stuck over one ear; Erica's sported layer after layer of rubber petals, all in florescent yellow. Even Mommy's was bright blue with several red bows scattered across her crown. Mr. Finchum looked on in amazement. No one swam in that river, because it was so cold (freezing!), and because of the danger of leeches, unknown to us. Bathing caps were completely unheard-of, and utterly perplexing. Those Yankees, it appeared, were every bit as strange as he had heard.

We had the summer to get acclimated, and then my sisters and I were signed up to go to the local schools in the fall. In the meantime, I set out to explore. The river was nearby and fun, but most of all I loved riding my bike, so I decided to try it out on my new road. The pavement wasn't smooth and gray like our streets at home; it was shiny black, almost iridescent in the sun, and rough. Whole pebbles lay embedded in it, so the surface was sharp and bumpy. It sounded loud under my tires, and I worried a little about falling—it looked like it would hurt more. At first, I stayed within sight of the cabin, not entirely comfortable with the big spaces between the houses and the absence of people or cars. Gradually, however, I became more confident, and ventured further. It was sort of like wading out into the waves at the ocean. If you start out in the shallows, and each time go just a little further, when you finally reach the breakers, it doesn't seem so scary. As long as I told her when I was going, and in which direction, Mommy let me do as I pleased. Neither Rachel nor Erica shared my passion for biking—it was too hot, they said, they'd rather read.

I was getting to know the feel of the place, growing accustomed to the noisy silence, the variety of smells from different mixtures of water, sun, vegetation, and animal. I was beginning to get curious, and to feel less oppressed by the absence of people. One day, I went further than ever before, passing a pen that housed a huge sow lying on her side in the shade while ten or twelve sucklings drank from and napped by her huge floppy nipples ("teats" Mr. Finchum called them, to my embarrassment). After watching them for a long time, I decided to go on into new territory. Gaining confidence, I started biking faster, enjoying the motion and the sound from the road, a sort of hum, now that I was really moving.

I approached a field that sloped sharply down a steep hill. Where the field met the road, the "fence" petered out into a couple of strands of barbed wire loosely strung between a series of slanting wooden posts. Something made me look up to the top of the hill just in time to see a swarm of dogs begin running down toward me, baying and yelping. Just one or two at first, these were soon joined by several more, and then more. There were hundreds! Large ones, small ones, loose-eared, panting, barking, salivating dogs. Drawn by the noise, yet more crested the hill and poured down the field toward me in a blue wave. They bellowed, yapped, and howled, hurtling themselves willy-nilly through the fence and out into the road. Heart racing, I biked as fast as ever I could, hunched over my handlebars, legs pumping, feet flying almost too fast for the pedals. I topped the rise in the road in an instant. But I wasn't fast enough; they poured after me, surrounding my bike and yapping at my shoes as they went round and round, their breath hot on my ankles. I picked up my feet and balanced them on the central bar of my bike, coasting wildly down the next hill. I was certain that if I fell off, I would be Alpo in an instant.

I continued to pedal madly, looking back fearfully until certain that they were no longer following me. Then I stopped, slid off onto shaking legs, and crumpled to the ground in the shade by the side of the road. I was hot and wobbly, sweat and tears running down my face. After a while, I could again hear the sounds of the river, insects, and birds, over my own deafening heartbeat. I began to take stock. Was I more hurt or more scared? I was unhurt, so that left scared. No way was I ever going to bike back home, that was for sure. But what could I do? No cars went by on the street. I was far too shy to go up to a strange house as Mommy would have done, asking to use the phone, and anyway, all her warnings about not talking to strangers swirled in my head. Without Viola to drill me, I wasn't even sure I knew our phone number, or our address, for that matter. I didn't know what to do. I wondered whether I would be able to bike by the hill so quietly that the dogs didn't notice me, but I knew that the sound of my pounding heart alone would alert them. I sat there, my mind blank, that sick, post-adrenaline nausea cold in my belly.

My mother had the uncanny, if unreliable, gift of sometimes knowing when one of us was in trouble. So I wasn't entirely surprised, not long afterward, to see our car coming around the bend.

There she was, all comfort and reassurance, examining me for damage, listening to my shaky, tearful story, wrestling my bike to balance across the trunk, and settling me in the front seat. She turned the car around and headed for home.

I leaned back, resting my head on the cool cushion, and took a deep breath. I was safe. But a minute later, instead of going straight back home, my mother turned at the corner and drove up the hill. With horror, I realized she was looking for the driveway belonging to the house at the top, the house of the dogs.

"What are you *doing*?" I cried out, my gratitude instantly replaced by fear and resentment that I was going to have to go along with some crazy scheme.

"We need to talk to them," she stated firmly.

We came to a stop some distance from the house, thwarted by a sea of muck that reeked of manure. Instantly, the same snarling, baying pack I had already met, surrounded the car. I cowered in my seat, queasy at the sight of them. Up at the house, a screen door slammed, and a man came out, wearing big rubber boots. He waded in amongst the dogs, kicking and swinging his fists, yelling some unintelligible commands like "Geeyaw!" or "Shagha!" which seemed to effectively scatter them. They disappeared. My mother then got out of the car, and walked toward the man. They held a brief conversation, and she beckoned to me to come out. Begrudgingly, I got out of the car, and picked my way reluctantly over to her, shoes sinking halfway up to their tops in the stinking mud.

"Sandra, this is Mr. Jenkins, and he has invited us in for some cake."

The man nodded to me, and I ducked my head. He was big and rough-looking, close-cropped, white-blonde hair sharply contrasting with his reddened face and deeply tanned scalp.

"Ah har them dahgs warriedjathar." He said to me. I looked at Mommy questioningly.

"He says he heard his dogs chased you," she translated.

I nodded, barely able to speak, much less acknowledge my near-death experience at the jaws of his mob. He apparently expressed sympathy, if not apology, and said they had to get the smell of a person, before they'd leave them alone. I knew those dogs weren't going to leave me alone, they were going to eat me if they got the chance. I could see it in their eyes, and smell it on their offal breath. Mr. Jenkins and my mother walked side-by-side up to the house, while I trailed a few steps behind, watching my back. Once we got out of the mud field, we entered the house yard, a patch of hard bare dirt loosely enclosed by unattached sections of split-rail fence. Chickens were scratching for bugs in the dust, and a few dogs lolled about on their bellies in the shade, but they ignored us altogether.

The farmhouse had once been white, but it was now brownish red, darker at the bottom, as if splattered regularly by mud. Grayish rag curtains hung limply, visible through open windows. The porch sagged heavily at one end, and the uneven steps groaned under our feet. The screen door slammed hard behind us as we entered the kitchen, and instantly, a cloud of flies rose from every surface in the room—food on the counters, dishes on the table, the floor, the chairs. Several tried to land on my arms and head, and I swatted at them frantically. Only then, did I notice that there were people in the room. A thin woman rose from where she had been sitting at the table shelling a huge bowl of peas. She was faded into colorlessness, her face blank, seeming too exhausted even to lift a limp hand to shake as we were introduced. There were also a couple of kids, but Mr. Jenkins made the same sort of noises he had at the dogs moments earlier, and they, too, vanished silently.

Mr. and Mrs. Jenkins led us into the living room, a barren chamber with bottomed-out couches and bare walls. A rooster sitting on one of the windowsills stood up in indignation as we entered, ruffled his feathers, and jumped out with a squawk. I couldn't follow the conversation. Even if I could have understood what they were saying, I was far too busy trying to see where the children had gone, while looking out for approaching dogs, and taking care to keep the flies off me. Two flies landed on my knee, obscenely joined together, buzzing furiously. I brushed them off in disgust. At some point, there was mention of the promised cake, and Mrs.

Jenkins yelled something toward the kitchen. After a few minutes, a girl came in with a plate holding slices of white cake, and a few green napkins. I looked at her closely. This was the first child I had seen since we moved. She was older than I, I noted with disappointment, but pretty, with blonde hair in a ponytail. Her dress, like her mother's, was shapeless, and so worn as to have lost any pattern or color it might once have had. It was the soft shade that things take on at the beach after being out in the sun and the sand for a long time. Looking down at her feet, I noticed with a sort of horror that her shoes had holes in them, exposing her toes. The soles, too, were worn through, and I caught a flash of dirty skin on the bottom of her foot as she placed the plate down on a table, and walked silently back out of the room.

I had seen that cake before, sitting on the counter, naked under a layer of flies. Hadn't Mommy noticed? I wondered, watching her accept a piece, and immediately raise a bite of it to her mouth. I started to shake my head as Mrs. Jenkins handed one to me, but catching the look in Mommy's eye, I accepted it, and held it gingerly, trying to think of a way to get rid of it without actually eating it. There was none. After receiving another silent imperative from my mother, I slowly broke it off in small pieces and swallowed them whole so I wouldn't have to imagine fly turds and fly feet and broken fly wings crunching between my teeth.

After what seemed forever, we got up to go. Shaking hands and saying "Thank you," we headed for the door, but before we got through it, Mr. Jenkins offered to let me watch him feed the dogs. As with the cake, it was an offer I couldn't refuse. He said they were blue tick hounds, and that there were forty or fifty of them at last count. Apparently, he fed the pack twice a week. "They ketch enough to keep themselves going in between whiles," he later explained to me, after I had learned to understand him. "It keeps em lively—a little pang in the belly."

At another guttural command directed toward the kitchen, two boys came out, each carrying two buckets. Mr. Jenkins proudly showed us their contents. It looked like what would be already on the inside of a dog's stomach. A few big chunks of raw meat with fat hanging off them swam in a stew of old bread heels, globs of curdled milk, and was that a mouse? I held my breath, and hoped not to vomit. Mommy looked politely interested. We stood on the porch, and the boys and Mr. Jenkins waded out among the dogs now gathering in the yard, and began emptying the buckets by throwing their contents by handfuls out into the pack. The dogs instantly became a boiling, frothing sea of tooth and paw, the occasional yelp or growl bespeaking a theft or conquest. It was everything I had imagined, with myself at the center.

I couldn't watch, and turned to look back at the house. And there, just behind me, I met the most extraordinary cornflower-blue eyes of a girl. I instantly took in that she was about my age, that she had a friendly face, and that there was something like sympathy in her expression. Smiling fleetingly, she ducked out the window, and disappeared.

Once home, Mommy told us that the Jenkins had nine children—five girls and four boys. There was almost a child for every year, and, it turned out, a girl close in age to each one of us. We were invited to go the next evening to meet them, and to watch them do the evening milking.

The following day, Mommy dropped us off late in the afternoon. With Rachel and Erica there, I felt infinitely better. As soon as we drove up, it was apparent that the dogs were not around. Five of the kids were waiting for us in the barnyard, three girls and two boys. The boys had normal names; Bobby and Ritchie, but the girls had the most beautiful names I had ever heard. The one close in age to Rachel was named Ellie Lynn, the one close to Erica's age was Patty Sue, and finally, just my age was Lily May. Johnny, little Roger, Laura Jane, the eldest, and Jenny Ann were all either up at the house or out working on the farm. "Lily May," I mused. She was the one I had seen the day before. She was somewhat taller than I, wire-thin with stringy dirty-blonde hair and those astonishing eyes. She was sinewy, no fat anywhere, knees and elbows bony, calves barely swelling with muscle. As we shook hands, I could feel the strength in her tough, calloused fingers and hard palm.

Rachel, Erica, and I paired off with Ellie Lynn, Patty Sue, and Lily May, and we went with Bobby and Ritchie to help bring in the cows. Once again, I could not understand a word Lily May said, and she did no better with me. For the first time, it mattered. I concentrated, listened carefully, and tried with all my might to understand. She might as well have been speaking Swahili. As far as I could see, my sisters weren't faring any better. Still, enormous good will surrounded us, and after walking for half an hour or so, Lily May and I were suddenly holding hands, hers dry and hard as a root. We caught up with the cows in the upper field, and the girls started rounding them up with switches torn from nearby trees, whacking their backsides, and yelling "Yeehaw!" My sisters and I joined them, copying what they did, feeling like we had stepped into a Western. The cows were huge, slow, and smelly. After we finally got them moving and shooed them through the gate, we followed down the road behind them. As they slowly walked, their rears undulating, several raised their tails and added to the layer of slimy green muck covering the ground. Nobody seemed to notice. At one point, clearly wanting to show off, Ritchie and Bobby jumped up on the backs of two of the bigger cows, and pretended to throw lassos and swing hats over their heads as they rode.

There were seventy-five milk cows in all. The boys did the herding and the mucking-out of the barn, and the girls did the milking twice a day. Each girl had a set number of cows to milk, depending on her age. Lily May had to do six. Once in the barn, I sat across from her, the cow between us, with the bucket positioned under the huge udder. I watched Lily May grab two of the teats hard in her hands and squeeze them, sending strong jets of milk squirting into the bucket, hitting the empty tin with a high-pitched sound. I took a teat in my hand, and found it warm and soft, but solid and full. I squeezed it as hard as I could. Nothing happened. Lily May showed me again—a thick stream issuing effortlessly from hers. I tried again. Nothing. The cow turned her head around to look at me, seeming to say with her impassive brown eyes, "What kind of incompetent are you?" I tried and tried, determined not to fail, and at last, one tiny bead of white liquid formed at the end of the teat, turned into the barest trickle, and dribbled over my hand into the bucket. It was working! I looked over at Lily May in triumph, and she stopped her rhythmic squirts and clapped her hands, crowing in celebration.

In time, I got very good at it, though my hands ached for days after each milking.

Rachel wasn't interested, but Erica and I became regulars at the evening milking (mornings were too early, at 6:00). We became part of the routine, and sitting two to a cow with our friends, we really learned to milk. I loved it. It was so sociable, sitting across from Lily May, with just the right number of teats for us to work together. I came to love the sound, the high tone of the milk hitting the empty tin bucket becoming a deep frothy drone as it filled. We worked so fast that there was foam on the top of our pail. Then we blew handfuls of it around, or tried popping its bubbles with our tongues. There were lots of games to play. My favorite was when a fly dropped into the milk and we would have a contest to see who could drown it first. Directing a jet of milk straight on it, we'd sink it, legs flailing, only to watch it surface again, to be met with the next strong jet of drowning liquid. As soon as a bucket was filled, we carried it over to the milk shed where we poured it through a filter into a huge tin canister that later was loaded up on the truck and driven to the processing plant.

Lily May and I had nothing in common. As we learned to understand each other's speech, this became increasingly apparent. There was no correspondence between her experience and mine. We had traversed the same number of years, and yet we each to the other seemed unbearably backward. I had never even seen a cow calve, much less assist at a birth. I only knew how to milk because she had taught me. I knew nothing about the various plants and animals that were part of her everyday life. I could neither build a fire nor make a cake, and carrying a pail of water from the spring at the bottom of the hill up to the house taxed me beyond my strength. I could barely even talk! What had I been doing all my life??

Nonetheless, it was with great disappointment that I learned that when I started school, Lily May would not be in my class. I had been so happy at the thought of having a friend in this new strange place. But it was Patty Sue who was going into third grade, although she was a full four years older than I. Lily May was going back into first grade for the *third time*. It seemed that she still didn't know how to read! I, who had spent hours buried in books since I was five, couldn't fathom it. She couldn't ride a bike, had never been farther than the Etlan General Store fifteen miles away, had never seen a circus, heard a cello, or eaten licorice. Only later did I learn that the Jenkins kids barely ever made it to school at all. There was endless work to be done at the farm, and every pair of hands was needed. Then there was the problem of clothes—mild as the winters were, shoes riddled with holes were still inadequate for the wet raw weather, and they weren't allowed to wear their "muck boots" to school. Coats were pretty much non-existent, and all in all it was just easier to stay home, huddling around the stove in between doing chores outdoors. So they went maybe two months out of the year, a day here, and a day there. At sixteen, each child dropped the charade of being in school at all, and just worked full time on the farm. The school officials and all the teachers knew how it was, but no one intervened. This was just the way things were.

• • •

One morning Mommy woke us up just before dawn, and in answer to our sleepy questions, said only, "Come on, I want to show you something."

She bundled us all into the car, and drove a short distance at great speed, before parking by the side of the road.

"What are we doing here?" we asked. "Where are you taking us?"

She hushed us and told us to hurry up, there wasn't much time. Shepherding us out of the car and telling us to climb over the fence and quickly, she hurried us into the middle of the field just as the first rays of the sun reached over the horizon.

"There!" she cried. "Look at that!" And she gestured at the empty field surrounding us. Still rubbing our eyes, we looked around, confused. There was nothing there!

"Look, you three, look!" she exclaimed, and she guided our attention to the gossamer shawl laid out upon the grass as far as we could see, thousands of delicate spider webs, each saturated with dew, every drop of which now caught the sunlight and sparkled. We caught our breath, and held very still so as not to dislodge a single gleaming gem, and waited while the sun rose until every corner of the field glistened and whispered with morning, until the sun reached an angle where it no longer illuminated that secret mantle.

• • •

When September came, I waited for the school bus down at the end of our driveway for the first time, filled with apprehension. It was 1969, and I was nine years old. My sisters' school was far from mine, so I was going on my own, knowing no one. I had never even ridden a bus before. I was carefully dressed in a dark green corduroy jumper and tights, and clutched my new empty notebooks close to my chest. Would the other kids like me? Would I be able to understand them? Would I make any friends? My old friends Lanny and Leslie, my familiar, comfortable school, and well-established position there seemed infinitely long ago. It was hard to believe they even still existed.

After giving me a long, hard look, the kids on the bus largely ignored me. There was one boy who sort of smirked at me from under flirtatiously lowered eyelashes, but that was it. After a forty-minute ride, we arrived at Crigleysville Elementary. It was an ugly squat brick building sitting alone in the middle of an open field. Where the island of paved playground ended, red mud and coarse grass immediately resumed. Getting off the bus, and going into the building, the first thing that struck me was how white all the people were. The kids running in the hallways were all white, the teachers standing in their classroom doorways were all white, and the one or two parents escorting their children were white. I had never thought about that. I found my classroom and my desk, and then learned that my teacher, Mr. Crowley, was the only black person working at the school. Irrationally, this made me instantly inclined to like him. I thought we would be allies in this strange white sea. Forgetting that my skin was the same color as all the rest of the children, I was disappointed when Mr. Crowley barely glanced at me, showing no sign of recognition whatsoever. It seemed like a normal first day—we listened to the list of school rules, then we each had to stand up and introduce ourselves, and finally, we did a few math problems, and then it was time for lunch.

I took my brown paper bag and trailed along uninvited behind some kids from my class, among them the boy from the bus. As we walked down the path, two black kids approached from the opposite direction. They moved over to make room for us to pass, but the kids I was with moved over toward them, crowding them off the walk entirely, forcing them to walk into the mud abutting the path. They turned and snickered back at me. The black kids said nothing, just got past us with lowered eyes, returned silently to the path, and kept walking. I knew I should have said or done something, but I couldn't really believe what I had just seen. I sort of thought I must have made the whole thing up, or misunderstood it. Worst of all, I knew the kids I was with were testing me. During lunch, the boy from the bus came over and sat by me. After silently inspecting my lunch—for once a blessedly normal peanut butter and jelly sandwich, wholegrain bread notwithstanding—he sat down beside me, stuck out his hand to be shook, and introduced himself. His hand was sort of clammy, but welcome nonetheless. His name was Greg, he was one year older than I, and I realized with relief that I could understand every word he said.

Greg was the only one who ever befriended me. I sort of hated him—he was cruel and smarmy and proprietary, but I couldn't afford to reject him. He saved me a seat on the bus each morning, right up front behind the driver. Too grateful for his protection to object, I tolerated him flapping his leather gloves in my face, dropping snow down my shirt, and spitting in my palm. He lived in one of the little towns, and his mother was an Avon distributor, giving him a kind of urban sophistication compared with farm kids like the hapless Jenkinses. At some point, he began giving me gifts of Avon products. They all seemed to have pink caps, and to smell of the same cloyingly sweet perfume. These gifts were marred by the fact that they started only after a certain talk we had in school.

Strange things were discussed in this school—puzzlingly commonsense things like bathing and not eating dirt. We were told by the English teacher that if we bit our nails and swallowed the parings, they would stick to the insides of our stomachs, then work their way into our flesh until they began to hurt, at which time they would have to be surgically removed. Although I had never been tempted to bite my nails, this image horrified me. I imagined a sort of inside-out porcupine. One day Mr. Crowley began lecturing us about personal hygiene. He suggested that if you knew someone with "B.O." it was your duty as a friend and a citizen to alert that person to this fact. He suggested that a diplomatic way of telling someone that his or her hygiene was inadequate was to give them a gift of a bar of soap, a bottle of perfume or cologne. So when Greg started giving me creams and powders I had to wonder. He never gave me soap or perfume, but I couldn't help but think maybe he was trying to tell me something. I smelled myself carefully, and found my eight-year-old body quite free of odor, but maybe there was something I wasn't aware of.

Mr. Crowley, I gradually realized, hated me. Having imagined somehow that we would bond if not as friends then as fellow outsiders, this was both disappointing and unsettling. The schoolwork itself was too easy for me, and I had a lot of time in class doing nothing while waiting for my classmates to finish assignments. I began to watch my teacher, and it bothered him. I didn't intend to make him uncomfortable, he just interested me. His behavior surprised and mystified me, as did his tacit refusal of my support. He was mean to the kids when they made mistakes or misbehaved, and slapped them hard on the palm or the rear with his ruler. He seemed to take satisfaction in doing this that went beyond correcting the infraction itself. It was if he were finally getting a chance to give them what they deserved. This mode of punishment was new to me. Lots of kids at my old school had talked about the "belt," and the kids here were clearly accustomed to the "switch," but I found it strange beyond understanding that children should be hit at school. Mr. Crowley noticed me watching, and began eyeing me sideways while disciplining the kids. He was overly polite to me, menacingly syrupy sweet, and it felt as though he was just waiting his chance to get at me.

One week, we each were instructed to bring in a prayer. The first day, someone brought in the Lord's Prayer, the next it was Now I Lay Me Down to Sleep, then came verses from the Bible, a psalm, even "Good Bread Good Meat Good God Let's Eat" was cockily recited by a hulking teenager who surely should have been in 8th grade. The entire back row of the classroom was filled with such kids, years too old for the grade, barely fitting behind the little desks. They wore leather jackets, and stretched their long legs out into the walkway trying to trip the little kids when we went back to the coatroom.

Finally, my turn came, and I began to sing the only prayer I knew: "Baroch ata, Adonai . . ." I was good at singing, and I loved both the words and the tune to this Hanukkah prayer. I closed my eyes and sang; thinking of what Hanukkah was like—the air of festivity, the blue-and-white table decorations, the wrapped gifts sitting on our plates, the smell of latkes and applesauce. Although ours was not a religious family, we celebrated the major holidays, and they were always special and magical. Only as I finished and opened my eyes did I notice the absolute dead cold silence emanating from the teacher and the room full of kids. This was not the friendly silence of appreciation; this was the cold silence of horror. They looked at me as if I was a monster. Already a misfit, I had suddenly, inexplicably, become a freak.

From that moment on, everything changed. Mr. Crowley never had touched me, but I began to realize how much he wanted to, and to sense that some restraint had been lifted upon hearing that

I was Jewish. A bond sprang up between my classmates and their despised Negro teacher at the realization that there was a Jew in their midst. The kids went from indifference to active avoidance, getting up to leave a table if I sat down, ceasing their conversations as I approached, and turning together to stare at me. The black kids were suddenly crowding *me* off the walk. His mother forbade Greg to speak to me, but he disobeyed, and in one last effort to salvage our incipient romance, he demanded, okay, so maybe I was a Jew, but I believed in God, didn't I?? We were sitting on the swings, out of sight of the other kids. This question had never appeared on my horizon before. I had never thought about it, didn't really know what it meant, and certainly didn't know how to answer such a question. The belligerence in his tone antagonized me, as did his air of doing me a great favor by deigning to speak to me at all.

"Sometimes I do, and sometimes I don't," I finally answered, looking for some middle ground. That was the last he talked to me, and my only approximation of a friend was gone. Me, teacher's pet, class favorite, feted celebrity, without a single person to talk to. I couldn't quite understand it.

My mother was sympathetic and helpless. She suggested various unrealistic measures to regain my standing, including starting "bull sessions" about religion, and organizing the other outcasts to join together in exile—the blacks, the retards, and the farm kids who showed up two days out of twenty. The first idea was preposterous for someone like me—shy, proud, and very hurt. And the outcasts were too happy to have someone to look down upon to have any interest in allying with me. So I turned away from them all, grit my teeth, literally and metaphorically, and felt unspeakably lonely. Who needed them anyway? They were just a bunch of ignorant bigots.

In physical education I discovered that I could run very fast, and set a class record in the fifty-yard dash. Nothing felt so good as speeding away from them. Of course once the kids knew how fast I was, no one would race me. When they knew I'd beat them, they wouldn't compete. Frustrated and thwarted, I ran alone, racing the clock and myself.

6

Tranquility Farm

It was now winter. While I had been dealing with my troubles at school, the first people associated with Future Village had begun to arrive. Mommy had been working on her project for years. She had advertised in *Mother Earth News*, the *Whole Earth Catalogue*, *New York Review of Books*, *Mother Jones*, the *Progressive*, *Ramparts Magazine*, and other likely places for people who might be interested in working with her. She had been carrying on several long-term correspondences with diverse individuals who were interested in her ideas, and possibly in coming to contribute their time, thoughts, and effort to her project. Her idea was to gather a core of dedicated people who would form a "think-tank" from which the practical application of her plans would stem. As soon as we were settled in our new home, she sent out the word that we had a location, and that those interested should come join us.

Elias showed up one day unannounced, walking quietly up the driveway, and easing his backpack gently down to the ground by the door. He was everything you might have expected. In his mid-twenties, he had thick, wavy, shoulder-length hair restrained by a beaded leather headband, a full beard, and soft brown eyes. He spoke quietly, and his hand, held out respectfully for me to shake, was light and loose. He was just the kind of peace-loving idealist Mommy had in mind. They instantly found plenty to talk about, and settled in for many hours-long discussions. To my disappointment, he turned down the offer of a bed on the couch, and pitched his tent hidden behind some trees, a discreet distance from the house. He came and went unheralded, disappearing without good-bye, and returning without salutation or comment. Whenever a stranger or visitor arrived, Elias magically vanished. After they left, he would casually stroll back in, and resume whatever he had been doing. We didn't know his last name, where he came from, or what he was looking for. He never talked much about himself or his family. In fact, he didn't talk much, period. He was just quietly there, often on the outskirts of activity. Even when he was nearby, Elias's presence was diffuse, as if most of his attention was elsewhere. But I liked to be around him. His kind of calm was unfamiliar to me, as was his sparing use of words. I tried to imagine what he thought of us, a house full of boisterous girls, and couldn't.

Mitch and Bubbles came next. Two brawny black men, constantly cracking jokes, and creating a general air of hilarity, they lit the place up. Mommy had found them in Baltimore while working on one of her inner city educational programs. They didn't take her, Future Village, themselves, or anything else very seriously. They were out on a lark, just for the hell of it, for as long as it was fun. With nothing more pressing to do, they came to offer their labor for a couple of months, happy to lend a hand for whatever project was in store.

The first thing in store, it seemed, was a barn! Before we moved, Mommy had finally bribed a grudging acquiescence to our leaving Baltimore out of Rachel by promising her a horse as soon as we got to the country. If we were going to have a horse, we certainly needed a barn! And if we were going to build a barn, we might as well make room in it for a couple of people. Not Mitch or Bubbles or Elias or Mommy had ever built a bookshelf or a doghouse, much less a barn, but they were undeterred. Mitch and Bubbles fairly spouted confidence. One day getting back from school, I saw a rect-angle of string stretched out on the ground, and there it was—the beginnings of the barn. The work started with leveling off the plot, building a platform for the part that would house humans, and set-ting posts into the ground. Progress was slow. Mitch and Bubbles were chief architects, excavators, and carpenters, and they seemed to need to take frequent trips (in Mommy's borrowed car) to the hardware store thirty-five miles away to buy one more essential tool (with Mommy's money) or order more lumber. One day, a big truck came and delivered several bundles of two-by-fours, stacks of plywood and beaver board, and several serious-looking posts. When the deliveryman presented Mommy with the receipt requiring her signature, she looked a little alarmed, especially since Mitch and Bubbles were nowhere to be seen.

As winter went on, there was more rain and cold, and work on the barn slowed almost to a stop. Elias disappeared for longer and longer spells, and even Mitch and Bubbles seemed a little dispirited. Was this it? The great Future Village Project? The muddy gray weather and general air of depression exactly matched my mood by then. The cabin was smelly and insufferably small. I missed my room and my friends and my father. School was pure torture. Compelled to be solitary, I rarely spoke to anyone. Although I had always enjoyed doing things on my own, I was naturally a sociable chatterer. I was continually irritable, grinding my teeth, and fighting with my sisters constantly, especially Erica. She was trying to be nice to me—she was almost always nice to me—but I could not contain myself. I was irrationally and involuntarily furious, and she seemed the logical target for my misery. Once in the middle of a fight I picked up a handful of dry corn kernels that had been dyed bright pink through some treatment for planting. We had bought them at the hardware store with thoughts of spring, scooping them out of open bins, studying the color with disbelief. I hurled them at Erica as hard as I could. They clearly stung as they struck her arms and shoulders, and her look of pain and surprise was unbearable. I ran from the room, slamming the door behind me with all my might. Hearing a strange sound, I turned back just in time to see the full length mirror that hung on the back of the door collapse in a waterfall of shattered fragments. Horrified, I remembered the superstition that breaking a mirror meant seven years of bad luck. Although Erica forgave me and helped me clean up the mess and reassured me about the bad luck, I couldn't shake the image of her hurt face, or the wretched knowledge that I had been so mean.

My mother kept busy writing, calling, talking to everybody she could reach, trying to drum up more interest, and more participation. As spring approached, her efforts gradually began to bear fruit. Often now, strangers were in the house when I came in from school. Although she didn't let anyone actually move in with us, Mommy did let people sleep in the living room for a few days if they were just exploring or passing through after a few days of intense discussion.

One spring morning, I wandered out of the bedroom sleepily, heading for the bathroom, and there, in the middle of the living room, was a man standing on his head, completely naked. He had positioned himself in front of the new full-length mirror that had been hung, this time on the outside of the bathroom door, presumably so that he could see himself. It was in the mirror, at the base of his upside down column of nakedness, that I caught his eye. His expression was indecipherable from that perspective, but his eye was bright, and not a muscle on his body twitched. He appeared not at all discomfited by my appearance.

I could not say the same, and scooted wordlessly across the room into my mother's bedroom. She wasn't there. Her room had a door leading directly outside, and I stepped out in my nightgown and bare feet. I found her in the garden barefoot, jeans rolled up to just below her knees, digging with her hands in the dirt in preparation for planting portulaca.

"Who is that?!" I asked.

"Who is who?" she returned absently, bending to inspect the huge earthworm she had just uncovered and held writhing in her palm.

"That man," I stated, now unsure which was more repellent—my mother holding a big fat squirming earthworm on her bare palm, or an upside-down naked stranger.

"Oh!" she said. "That's Ron. He may be joining us." She poked curiously at her worm with her stubby dirt-caked finger, and watched its blind gyrations.

"What's he *doing*?" I asked.

"Trying to find a way out of the light."

"Huh?" I asked, mystified.

"They don't like light."

"Who?"

"Worms."

"No! *Ron*! What is he doing?"

"I believe he's doing his morning yoga," she answered.

"But he doesn't have any clothes on!"

"Oh sweetie, does that bother you?" Mommy asked, looking up at me for the first time. "Our bodies are natural and beautiful, and we shouldn't be ashamed of them." And so saying, she went back to her worm, and I went up to lie in the hammock. No way was I going back through the living room.

Once he was right side up, I learned that Ron was a breath-arian. A spare little man, lively as a rodent, he explained that once upon a time he had been an avid fan of steaks and bacon, eggs Benedict and cheeseburgers, baloney and sausage. But then he had had a heart attack. Following the suggestion of his spiritual guide, he had become a vegetarian, and then gradually had progressed to a fruit- and nut-arian. At each phase, he claimed to feel better, more energetic, purer, cleaner, and closer to his spiritual source. Finally he decided to try the last stage, and become a breath-arian. He exposed himself regularly to both sunshine and rain, deriving what nutrients he could as plants did.

Ron didn't stay with us after all. One morning, while standing on his head in the living room, naked as usual, he apparently got a call from California, and he left that afternoon. "When the spirit summons," he told us, "you go." Before heading off down the country road as he had first arrived, barefoot and empty-handed, he proudly reported that that month, he had eaten only six cashews and a fig.

Fletcher was the first substantial seeming person, and the first who came to stay. Tall, gaunt, in his early fifties, he was a Navy man, as every man in his family had been for generations. After growing up in a small town in the upper Midwest, to the surprise of friends and neighbors, he had married the town belle. He remained forever startled that he had won her, dry and silent as he was, in contrast to her fluttering prettiness. He revered her, and quietly devoted his life to fulfilling her every whim, striving to make her life pleasant and easy. He bent his ingenuity to making her household chores as painless as possible. Fletcher was immaculate in his habits. He never entered the house with dirt on his shoes, never neglected to clear his dishes off the table or to rinse the shaved hairs out of the sink.

Shortly after the birth of their second child, his wife died. She had never been comfortable driving, and that January day, coming around a corner too fast, she had skidded on the ice and gone off the road, crashing into the concrete pilings of an overpass. She left Fletcher with his five-year-old son and infant daughter. He was not surprised. He had known all along that this wife, this life, had not been intended for him. Like getting a lottery prize meant for someone else, he had always viewed his good fortune as an error, and had known that it would eventually be caught and corrected. He raised his son and daughter on his own in that small town with the assistance of casseroles provided by neighbor women, until his daughter Karen got old enough to take over the household duties for the three of them. Fletcher was a highly desirable bachelor, capable, reliable, sober and quiet, and a number of women did their best to attract his notice. He was forever courteous, but firmly uninterested. He had had the only thing he had ever wanted, and she was gone. He sure wasn't going to start all over again with something that could never be as good. There was some consolation in being where he knew he had really belonged all along—alone, lonely, with little to lose.

But there must have been some spark of rebellion, nurtured quietly through those long Minnesota winters that led him to our door. For a lifetime, Fletcher had followed other people's rules. First his father's, a silent authoritarian man, then the rules of the Navy ship, then the rules of the farm, and finally, the rule of fate in the death of his wife. In secret rebellion, he wrote poetry, lean pieces having to do with politics and God and human striving, and he read leftist publications, and made his own observations about the world. Perhaps he wanted to grasp one last opportunity to do something radically different. Something illogical. Whatever brought him to explore the Future Village project was a very private matter. He sold the sturdy, well-built house where they had lived for twenty years, bought a two-bedroom trailer, and arrived with his son Sam, now a hulking youth already signed up to join the Navy in the fall, and his daughter Karen, who was pretty like her mother, but with a wild edge. By the time I fully noticed his existence, he had already positioned the trailer in the field by the road, and strung up a clothesline.

Sam would be leaving soon, and he was so aghast at this sudden lunacy of his father that he would have nothing to do with any of us. Karen, however, with her pale blonde hair and up-turned nose, was fascinating. She watched hours of television in their trailer, drinking endless cans of "soda pop"—both forbidden pleasures for my sisters and me. We were only allowed ginger ale when we had stomach aches, and were limited to a half hour of TV a day, not counting *Captain Kangaroo*. Karen had obvious breasts even though she was only twelve, the same age as my flat-chested sister Erica, and her wide mouth had this funny crooked quirk that entranced me. She wasn't too clear about what she or we were doing there either, but she was mildly interested. She figured anything was better than back home.

Fletcher was hard to get next to. His far-away face was closed and indifferent, shadowed by the brim of his hat. In some ways, he seemed more like our neighbor Mr. Finchum than us. In fact, Mr. Finchum was a whole lot friendlier to me. Fletcher had nothing to say to children. Clearly I had no earthly purpose in his life. His purpose was equally incomprehensible to me. Nonetheless, after shutting themselves up together for several days, Mommy and Fletcher emerged, having forged an unlikely partnership. They couldn't have been more different. Fletcher was stiff and precise and disciplined, sharply aware of everything around him. Mommy was loose and chaotic and disorganized, creative but often oblivious. When Fletcher went out to take a look at the barn, he shook his head in disdain, but immediately took out his tape measure, and started making calculations on a brown paper bag.

Now work on the barn moved quickly. Under Fletcher's capable direction, Bubbles and Mitch shamefacedly swung into good willed action, and actually got to the point where they could rib him, and elicit the barest smile. Elias wandered back again, and was discovered early one morning after having painted a bright red peace sign eight feet high on the just-raised side of the barn. He started helping with construction, and then we all pitched in. At the end of the day, we'd all gather to sit on the raw planks, smelling of resin and sawdust. The men would have a beer, and we girls would drink lemonade, and we would just sit and listen and talk, watching the dusk gather.

Next came Peter, who had described himself in letters as a giraffe with a passion for three-leaf clovers. Unlike a giraffe, Peter was fat and hairy, and had an infectious giggle. He had grown up in Vermont. His father, a prominent doctor, was set on him becoming a surgeon. Peter loved his father, and longed to satisfy him. He got into medical school and did his best, willing himself to sit through the endless dry lectures, and to quell his disgust at dealing with human bodies. He hated everything related to medicine—the smells, the sterility, the noise.

Peter was really a musician. He explored the world by sound, the way a dog does by smell. He had to investigate every object he encountered, by striking, brushing, shaking, or blowing. It turned out that most everything could be brought to sing, if you knew how. Peter knew how. He wouldn't have minded listening to human bodies—the syncopation of heartbeats, gastric gurglings, and breath—or playing them, but slicing and stitching was simply impossible. Finally giving up, he left his father's hopes and came to us. He arrived just as the roof went over the tiny room on the side of the barn, and immediately moved in, tacking sheets of beaverboard onto the walls for soundproofing.

And then came Lynn. No one knew quite where Lynn had come from. Mommy had never heard of her, and Lynn wasn't one to ever answer a question directly. She was ethereal, yet sharply present, achingly graceful, even clad in the thick brown workboots she'd bought at the Etlan General Store. Lynn's skin was pale and smooth, her hair was red, her mouth was charming, and her features fine, but her eyes were predatory. They were fierce bird's eyes, almost yellow, which looked particularly odd, set as they were in a perfect feminine face. She was a dancer, a wanderer, and a child of the time, disguising an old leather toughness under a fragile skin. I could not decide if she repelled or delighted me, but she certainly fascinated me.

Suddenly we were many: my mother Carla, my sisters Rachel and Erica, Elias, Mitch & Bubbles, Fletcher, Sam & Karen, Peter, Lynn, and me. It was finally summer. Released at long last from that nightmare school, liberty had never been so sweet. It seemed that I was not alone in my sense of having escaped a loathsome prison. Everyone was intoxicated. We finished off the barn, an oddball, tilted structure, with Elias's huge red peace sign advertising our presence. Mitch and Bubbles moved into the loft. Rachel got her horse named Cindy, and moved her into the stall next to Peter's room. A lady up the road gave Erica a goat named Buffy, and she, too, took up residence.

All through the summer, we took walks by the stream, explored the surrounding country, and climbed Old Rag, the nearby mountain. We sat long into the evening, watching the fireflies dance among the trees by the river. There was a lot of talk. Talk about freedom and learning, about sharing and love, about community, and about "being there." It was excited talk—ideas spun out without barriers. A lot of it was beyond me. Talk about the problems with "mainstream society," with the "expanding economy," and the relentless push toward "progress." Maybe moving back was moving forward, someone said. Back to nature, back to a simpler life, back to our best potential. There was talk about the destruction of our Mother Earth, along with the baby seals and rare birds. There was talk of politics, and of the fundamental equality of all people juxtaposed against the inequities they faced, of the problems of the war and poverty and disadvantage. There was a heady satisfaction that we were grappling with these worldly ills. We weren't going to contribute to the problems by pretending they didn't exist. Mommy had always said that one thing we had learned from the Holocaust was that to fail to be part of the solution was to be part of the problem. She taught that every individual made a difference, like it or not, and that that difference could be made through action, or lack thereof. There was no opting out. We chose action! We were taking a stand, forging another way. We were going to show the world how it should be done! With love and peace and brown rice.

It was heady and fun, but I kept wondering when all these people were going to go home, and things were going to get back to normal. The evening discussions were exciting, but during the days I felt pretty lost. My sisters seemed to be in the trailer with Karen most of the time, watching TV and eating cheese doodles. I couldn't figure that out. I went in to find them, and was surprised at how tiny it was, crowded and dim. Coming in from the brilliant outdoors, I couldn't see anything at first, except for the blue glow of the TV. Gradually, as my eyes adjusted, I could see the matching pea-green couch and recliner crammed into the narrow living area, with plastic draped over their backs and arms, and there was a ribbed plastic pathway running over the mustard-colored carpet, from the entrance, through the living room and into the hallway. The fake wood paneling on the walls was dark, relieved only by a single painting of Jesus in a gold frame. The whole place smelled musty, and it seemed strange, this house on wheels, unrooted, as if it might spontaneously relocate itself at any moment. I was afraid that I would look out the window, and like Dorothy, find myself spinning through the air, or setting down suddenly in an unknown land full of strange creatures. Hadn't it already happened once? I couldn't figure out why my sisters were in there so much, glued to the television set, giggling with Karen over incomprehensible nonsense. I never remembered Erica spending more time with Rachel than with me and I didn't like it. Mommy can't have known what they were doing in there, or she would have protested.

But Mommy was busier than ever.

Finally, her efforts were taking flight. She was getting a steady stream of inquiries about Future Village, and she had the immediate dilemma that we did not have enough space to work in, much less live. And there was the problem of our education. My sisters had not had the same kind of unhappiness at their school that I had at mine, but they had been pretty gloomy too, not least of all with the hour-and-a-quarter bus ride twice each day. The obvious thing to do was to homeschool us. But where? Who?

It was Lynn who found Tranquility Farm. Bordering on the park three miles up at the end of our road, Tranquility Farm was a small idyllic estate with a tiny red house, a pond, two chestnut trees, and a flagpole. Lynn somehow finagled a year's free lease out of the owner. They had been planning to sell the place, but for some reason wanted to wait until the following year. She managed to persuade them to give it to us in return for maintenance, with the understanding that it was a one-year-only arrangement. We all thought it was magical.

Suddenly there was a flurry of activity. I turned nine. Bubbles and Mitch decided it was time to seek their next adventure, asked for a ride into town to catch a bus back into the city, and wished us a fond farewell. They assured us they would return, and sternly instructed us to keep the barn in good order. Peter, Lynn, and Elias moved into the house at Tranquility Farm, agreeing, along with Fletcher, to stay for a full year. The house was also to be a school for Rachel, Erica, Karen, and me. We cleaned and planted and planned, cut grass, pulled weeds, and patched holes in the fenced enclosure to ready it for Rachel's horse Cindy. It was August, and the thought of having to go back to Crigleysville Elementary had begun to haunt me. Learning that the vague possibility of not having to go back was becoming reality was such a relief that I was afraid to believe it.

The adults kept us away from Tranquility Farm during the last couple of weeks of preparation. We watched them bustling around full of secrets and plans, half-amused, and increasingly curious. In order to maintain some order and structure, Mommy and Fletcher decided that we would adhere to the academic calendar of the local school system. In checking the legality of their plans, they had discovered that there were essentially no regulations on home schooling, or, for that matter, on being a school. It appeared that you had only to name yourself as such, and it was done. No curriculum requirements, no attendance policy, not so much as a health inspection.

When the last night of the summer arrived, I went to bed joyfully convinced that this was actually going to happen—I was not going to be forced back to the public school at the last minute. Relieved, I slept deeply. Mommy woke us early the next morning. She told us that breakfast was on the table, that Karen would be coming in from the trailer to eat with us, and that she and Fletcher were going up to the school. We were to join them as soon as we were done eating.

Erica, Karen, and I rode our bikes, and Rachel rode Cindy alongside us. The morning was bright and beautiful, a slight mist still lingering in the apple orchard we passed. The river sounded loud and cheerful, and birds were singing. We sang too, and arrived at Tranquility Farm in high spirits, a little breathless after the last steep hill, and eager to see what awaited us. We all accompanied Cindy to her enclosure, then leaned our bikes against the side of the house, and went in through the back door, held open by Lynn. The adults were like children showing off their dollhouse, and we were suitably impressed and delighted. Downstairs they had created a "Music Room," furnished primarily with huge rust-colored cushions. In it stood music stands, Rachel's cello, Erica's flute, and my viola, all rescued from storage where they had lain forgotten for the past year. Elias had successfully bid on an old piano at an auction, and had it delivered, and Peter had set up his drums. The diminutive living room had a picture window, some comfortable couches, and Elias's bed in the corner, discreetly curtained off by an Indian bedspread. There was a three-season porch that Lynn called the "Studio." She had cleaned and polished the plank floor, found a big old mirror she hung on the wall, and Fletcher had attached a wooden dowel to the wall to serve as the "barre." In the tiny kitchen was a shelf containing half a dozen glass canisters, proudly labeled "Dates," "Cashews," "Granola," and so on. These, we were told, were for "noshing" between meals. Upstairs was the "school room," an inauspicious little chamber, with paper and pencils laid out neatly on the one table, and a handful of schoolbooks looking lost on the shelf. Up here Lynn had her bedroom, and Peter's was in the hot little attic, where the ceilings were so low he could not stand up.

It was like a playhouse, or playschool, or some delightful game in which the adults were full participants. Every morning through the fall, the four of us traveled up to school, by bikes and horse most days, or walking when we wanted a change. Mommy and Fletcher were not there every day; they were working together on the larger Future Village project. But Lynn, Peter and often Elias were there for the express purpose of being available to us. Peter worked with me on fractions, while we sat out on the porch, the light playing on the lake right in front of us. Lynn, who was better at math, did the same with the older girls, having the three of them working together on algebra. Rachel was a whiz, Erica struggled bravely, and Karen just couldn't be bothered to try very hard. As she said, she wasn't going to be doing anything that required knowledge of math, so why should she break her head over it? Karen was like that. She expended as little energy as possible. She didn't seem burdened by any sense of obligation or duty, and clearly never worried about the future. As much as possible, she did as she pleased.

"School" was pretty loosely defined. Since there were only four of us, it was easy to keep us occupied, and there was much more emphasis on enjoyment than on academic achievement. Reading was no issue for my sisters or me, we all read much of the time, so the one subject that Lynn and Peter made an effort to get us to work on was math. Rather than being our teachers, Peter and Lynn were our "betheres," a term coined by my mother. The role of a bethere was to create a relaxed, accepting, and loving environment for the students. As long as they were present and accessible, a bethere could teach a formal subject, offer to learn something with a student, or work, cook, or play.

Much of our time was spent in play. Lynn allowed us to capture her, tie her to the flagpole, and wave caramels in front of her nose. She was famous for her love of caramels, so we set out to torture her by letting her smell them, and then popping them into our own mouths. Her groans of despair were satisfyingly realistic. Then Peter came whooping out of the house to rescue her, brushed us aside like fleas, threw her over his shoulder and bore her away from danger.

I pretty much loved Peter. In addition to math, he read aloud to me. Every day we would go upstairs to the schoolroom together and read a chapter of *The Hobbit*. Then we would have a tickling match, where, screaming with laughter, I would try to escape his long hairy arms and huge hands. Peter was a comfortable person, soft like a great big pillow, and safe. It was common knowledge that Peter was a virgin, considered unimaginable at his advanced age of twenty-three. I wasn't entirely clear about what all that meant, but knew it left him closer to my side of life. He wasn't always playful. When he practiced his music daily, he was all business. When Peter set up his instrument in the music room at Tranquility Farm, it was a greatly expanded version of his original drum set. In addition to drums, he had hollow pots, dried gourds, rustling seedpods, sticks, bottles, and empty jars. With this ever-changing array, he could produce the sound of the forest or a city street, the quiet of an empty beach or the deafening sounds of planes taking off and landing at the airport. When he played, Peter would begin to sweat right away. He was a big man, and he sweated over his whole body. His torso and his thighs darkened, and his arms would begin to glisten. He moved so fast that sweat was thrown off in spray, leaving a watery trail suspended in air where he had just been. Even the sweat had a song, landing almost audibly on the glass of the window, on the floor, on papers or cushions. He didn't care if people were in the music room when he played, as long as they were quiet. The others would usually go to a different room so they could talk, but I often stayed. He let me watch him drum, quickly forgetting me entirely.

Lynn gave us dance lessons in the studio, demonstrating each movement with a perfection that I knew I could never achieve. She was a vision of delicacy, dancing with a white dove trained to perch upon her outstretched (beautifully pointed) foot, and to flutter about her head, setting off her vibrant coloring to its best advantage. She wore opals on her fingers and in her ears, and they winked and glistened as she moved. Oh, Lynn had an eye for the picturesque, and she was no fool. She was a dream-child, playing the mandolin in the field dressed in white muslin, a daisy chain in her long red hair. Her determined innocence was certainly effective on us children, and on Peter. He was clearly smitten, cherishing a hopeless love for her that she flaunted in his face. He could clearly see what she was doing, but he loved her nonetheless. At times, I hated her.

Lynn loved to tell us stories. We would sit on her bed or sprawl on cushions or the rug, with her in our midst, while she spun her tales around us.

"Suddenly I woke up, and I was choking and gasping. For some reason, I noticed the time. It was 2:44 in the morning. The numbers burned into my eyes. I couldn't breathe, or call out, and the house was completely dark and silent."

Her voice dropped. We were transfixed.

"I could feel my lungs burning and shriveling, and I was sure I was going to pass out. It went on for an eternity, and I felt the air around me, the air that I couldn't get into my lungs, getting thicker and hotter. I tried to breathe it in, but when I did, it burned and seared inside my nose. I was sure I was going to explode or go up in flames any second. But I couldn't move."

We were breathless now ourselves.

"There was a giant invisible force holding me down on my bed, pinning me completely helpless. I struggled, but couldn't move, and the whole time, this terrible stuff was filling my lungs, and all I wanted was air, simple cool air. I must have passed out, because the next thing I knew, the phone was ringing, and I could see that it was getting light outside. My throat was raw, and all my muscles ached, but I reached over to pick up the phone on the third ring. I answered it, and . . ."

Here Lynn paused, looking down into our expectant faces with those hawk's eyes of hers.

"And?!!" we cried. "Who was it?"

"On the phone," Lynn said, her tones drawn out and mysterious, "was my aunt. She told me that my cousin had died that night, at three am. He had suffocated in a fire, pinned to his bed by a beam that fell on him. He died from inhaling smoke."

We shivered with pleasure and disbelief. Our incredulity was laced with total faith, total confidence that no one, not even Lynn, could make up such a thing. Her stories were wonderful. Our favorite way to get her going was to point to one of her many minuscule scars, none of which in any way marred her beauty, and say, "How did you get that one?"

When we touched a tiny kissable mark on the underside of her chin, Lynn brightened, and settled comfortably on the bed.

"Oh that! Well, you know, my sister Megan was a perfect little goody two shoes. She always kept her dresses—she actually liked dresses!—neat, did her chores, her homework, and learned her Sunday school lessons. Everything. It was awful. One year, she got an Easy Bake Oven for her birthday, poor kid. What was worse, she wanted it! She decided that she was going to make cupcakes for all the neighbors. I wanted at least to sell them, so we could make a profit. She wouldn't think of it at first, but I started listing all the things she could get with the money. Things she would like, you know, bows for her hair, a little purse, things for her dollies, and finally she agreed.

"The whole time she was baking, fussing with her precious little pans, and the oven, I was gathering caterpillars. It was one of those years when the tent caterpillars were going crazy. They had spun their tent-webs in the crooks of branches in dozens of trees all around us, and sometimes when you walked or sat under them, caterpillars would drop down on your neck. They gave my sister fits. She just hated them. Anyway, I collected a whole pile of them, and then I mashed them up with a rock. Even I thought that was gross. When I was done, I went up to Megan, and told her I heard the phone ringing. She believed everything I said, so she went to answer it. As soon as she went into the house, I dumped my mashed caterpillars into her batter and stirred it up. She had been making banana cupcakes, and I thought my addition blended in nicely. The little black specks from the mashed caterpillars were barely visible.

"Megan came back out of the house, and said that whoever was calling must have hung up before she could get there. She could be so stupid! She serenely spooned her batter into the pans, not noticing that it had gotten thicker. She was a little surprised when I turned down her offer to lick out the bowl. Usually I pestered her for it, figuring that I could at least get something out of her prissy little habits.

"The cupcakes came out beautifully. Perfectly round, golden on top, shiny from the little orange glaze Megan had used. She was so proud!

"She put them in a little basket, covered them with a checked cloth, and actually went house to house, selling them for thrity-five cents apiece. I followed along, laughing my head off at all the neighbors pinching her cheeks and 'oohing' and 'aahing' over her little cupcakes. Sheesh! Little did they know!

"She sold them all. She came home triumphant, and started to eat the one she had saved for herself. She broke it open, and it looked all creamy and good, little black banana flecks all through it. I was pretty hungry myself, and it looked delicious. I almost began to wonder whether the caterpillars had miraculously disappeared, when I saw it. The head of a caterpillar was sticking clearly out of one half of the cupcake. Megan was already chewing on the other half, when she looked down at the piece in her hand. She saw it, and bent forward to look closely. Just as her face was beginning to crumple in disgust, our mother came to the door with the phone in her hand.

"'Lyynnn . . . Meegaan . . .' she said."

"'Yes?' I answered."

"'Mrs. Cole is on the phone. She just told me that she bought a muffin from you girls, and she found a worm inside.'

"'Not a worm,' I said. 'It's a caterpillar!'

"Megan looked up at me in horror, and I could see realization register on her face. She stood up, threw her cupcake at me in a rage, and grabbed one of her frying pans. She started chasing me with the thing, and she looked murderous enough to do damage. I was running away from her, but I was laughing at the same time. Laughing so hard that I couldn't really look where I was going, and I tripped, chucking my chin hard on a rock. It bled like hell, and my mother got scared, so I ended up in the emergency room where I got seven stitches. I didn't get punished by mom, but Megan wouldn't speak to me for about a year."

We loved it. Imagine having the nerve to do such a thing. We pictured all those neighbors taking great big bites out of those caterpillar cupcakes, and finding . . . blech! Perhaps even more exciting than the stories themselves, was the sense of having an adult all to ourselves. Lynn was only nineteen, just five years older than Rachel who, at fourteen, was the oldest of us girls. But she was clearly an initiate into a life we could only imagine. It was her complete autonomy—she seemed unrestricted by any relation or friend—and the hints of her sexuality that set her most definitively apart from us. There was something that felt almost illicit about her story telling. For one thing, this was supposed to be "school," and here we were sprawled on her bed listening to her weave tales. But it also seemed that there was no limit to what she would tell us, if we only asked. If we just hit on the right scar, or got her going on the right story, she would tell us everything. Mysterious as this woman was otherwise, when telling a story, she was uncensored. Each time she started one, I was a little afraid she would tell too much.

Through the fall, we listened to Peter drum, danced with Lynn, played records ("Abbey Road" was our favorite), read books, did a little math, gazed out the window, gathered chestnuts, roasted them, and ate them piping hot. We took walks up the mountain and along the river, and went to the Etlan General Store once a week for a school ice-cream field trip.

At some point in the winter, the charm wore off. The glass canisters in the kitchen had been empty of dates and cashews for weeks. The three-mile trek from house to school was a drag. Karen was the first to sour on biking to school. It seemed so far and boring. She got her father, who rarely refused her anything, to start driving her, and that was a temptation that was hard to resist. It was wet and unpleasant outside, and there wasn't enough to do inside. Neither Peter nor I could summon much enthusiasm for those math tutorials, and poor Bilbo had been stuck in Mirkwood forever. Elias was on one of his fade-aways, and Lynn and Peter seemed thoroughly sick of each other, and of us. Once again, things seemed to have come to a standstill.

But not for everybody. There had continued to be a slow stream of people coming to talk to my mother. They usually spent a little while with us, came to Tranquility Farm to see us in school, and talk some more. As the year passed, there were more people who wanted to stay and be part of what we were doing. There just wasn't room for them anywhere.

My mother and Fletcher started driving around with real estate agents, looking for the right house for us to expand into. They were the only ones with any money to speak of, having savings from years of working, and the sale of their larger homes prior to coming to Virginia. The idea was that they would buy a house together, and then the group would pay the mortgage, and eventually buy them out. There were two big questions: where were we going to continue to grow and expand, and how would we make money to pay the mortgage and other essential expenses?

Most communes of the day had cottage industries that kept them solvent for what little commerce they conducted outside of the group. Twin Oaks, a venerable and well-known commune structured after Skinner's book *Walden Two*, made rope hammocks, famous for their durability and beauty. Garners had chickens and sold eggs at the local market, Melody Farm sold goats' milk, cheese and skins, and so on. We tried out lots of ideas; Elias made wonderful pen-and-ink puzzles, and Rachel thought we could combine them with crossword puzzles and sell them to newspapers. Fletcher could carve neat little wooden animals that Peter thought would sell like hotcakes from the right vender. Lynn wondered about running an antique store, others suggested jam, quilts, or something to do with the chestnuts available free of charge direct from Mother Nature. But none of these ideas seemed realistic. At long last, the idea that stuck was that we would continue to do what we were already doing—namely, being a school.

When we moved away from Baltimore, Mommy had never thought school would be a problem. She hadn't expected the public schools to be so awful. It wasn't just us three anymore; there were also the children of the other people who had come to work with her. Given our experiences the year before, she felt she clearly had to continue to homeschool. Since that was already functioning, why not open the school up to boarding students, and incorporate them into the fabric of the larger project as it emerged? Students could come to work and learn. They would have many opportunities to explore their own interests, and to function as members of a model society. If charged a reasonably high tuition, ten boarding students would make us financially viable. People were more comfortable with the thought of older students, so it was agreed that I, as the youngest child, would set the lower cut-off age, and we would gradually work up to being a boarding high-school. My mother had read about Summerhill A.S. Neill's "free school" in England, and she admired his philosophy. This would be the model we would follow.

Everybody liked this idea. Lynn and Peter had enjoyed their year playing with us and occasionally working on math problems; Elias was happy not to have to be responsible for any major project; Mommy and Fletcher found that the school did not take up all of their energies, leaving time for their long-range plans. They thought that the school could sustain a home-base community for the founders of the Future Village. My sisters and Karen were pleased, and I was ecstatic. Still haunted by my shunning in public school the year before, I wasn't prepared to venture out again, and happily participated in the plans to find an English teacher, and one for foreign languages, and maybe someone who could teach Science. All our plans seemed possible, if we could just find the space for them.

Free School

Fletcher and Mommy finally found the right place, strictly by chance. Driving home from town one day, they saw a hand-written sign posted on the highway. It directed them down a dirt road, and there they discovered a house and some land that could hold us, no matter how much we grew. They took us all over on a dream, crammed into the two beat-up cars we shared. This property wasn't really a possibility, they told us, the house came with too much land, and the price was way too high. They had made a low offer anyway, but told us we hadn't a hope in a month of hopes, they were just bidding in case there might be the smallest chance, because you never knew for sure until you tried. The house had been standing empty for several years. The previous owner had died on the premises, which always made buyers a little nervous, and the market was slow. Maybe the owners were getting desperate. Whatever the outcome, they thought we should see the place.

About fifteen miles away from the cabin and Tranquility Farm, we turned onto the narrow dirt road. Gravel bounced up under the car, clanging loudly against the frame, and a satisfying cloud of dust rose behind us. After going around several bends in the road, we turned into a rutted red-dirt driveway, drove up a steep incline, and craned to see, at first the chimney, then the slanting roofs, white gables, green shutters and, finally, the house in its entirety came into view. Huge, square, friendly, and open, it sat atop the hill, surrounded by twenty-seven-and-a-half acres of shaggy fields covered in tall golden grass that rippled and shifted like the sea in the wind. On the horizon, the beautiful undulating foothills of the Blue Ridge Mountains encircled us on all sides. We rushed out of the car, and examined with delight the split-rail fence encircling the yard, the carpet of violets in the grass, the lilacs blooming in back. Karen yelled for us to come see the huge back porch. Fletcher immediately corrected her, saying it was really the front porch, pointing out the two straight rows of horse chestnut trees that had been planted to line what had once been the formal front entrance. We called it the "carriage drive." So it seemed that the back of the house was the front, and the front was the back. Perfect! The whole estate seemed magical, solid, but gone a little wild with neglect.

Inside, the house was cool, dark, and empty. It had been built in grand proportions with oak floors and moldings, huge rooms, high ceilings, and hallways so wide you could drive a small car down them. It was a luxury of spaciousness. Fletcher shook his head sadly at the inefficiency. It would be hell to heat, he said, and most of the space wasn't functional. You'd have to try, he said wearily, to waste so much space. But that it was OUR house was irrefutable, and we all knew it. Clustered around the house there were several sheds and "out buildings," and a tiny "crick" trickled along one side of the property. The neighboring farms, their fields a patchwork of different colors, had houses visible a mile away, clothes swinging on miniature lines. At the bottom of the hill by the road there was a full-sized barn with tack room, hay crib, and a large loft. There was room for an orchard and a garden and anything else we could think of. The place seemed made to order. None of us took seriously the admonition to "Remember, we might not get it."

We got it.

Hearing the news back at Tranquility Farm, we shouted with glee, ran outside into the yard and around the house three times despite the drizzle, yelling and jumping and clapping our hands. "We got it!" we shouted. "It's ours!" "Yippee!" Peter picked Lynn up and swung her around, boots and hair flying, and Cindy looked over from munching on her hay bale and seemed to be pleased at the thought of a real barn (we had told her all about it) and more room to run.

At the closing, almost as an afterthought, the agent mentioned the Jacksons. It turned out that a black family, living in the small red cabin we had noticed smack dab in the middle of the property, had life rights to their house. A remnant of the days of sharecroppers and tenant farmers, there were families with life rights on most of the properties in the area. We were assured that this was perfectly normal, and never caused problems. Mommy and Fletcher looked at each other, caught on the horn of ideal-cum-reality, and slowly nodded their heads. The land was large! Surely twenty-seven acres could accommodate us all. The red house was halfway up the hill, quite removed from our big farmhouse. Maybe the Jacksons would be the first real residents of Future Village.

Dropping all pretence of "school" immediately and without regret, all activity at Tranquility Farm ceased, and we moved camp to the new house where we did nothing but paint for two weeks, one room at a time, working long days. In our eagerness to finish the job, no one felt like driving out to get food during the day. In the fridge, we inexplicably found four heads of fresh cabbage and a jar of yellow mustard. Later we discovered the remnants of the vegetable garden, and saw the several "volunteer" cabbage plants that had yielded those heads. The neighbor-farmer who was hired to cut the fields twice a year had found the cabbages, and, hearing that the house had sold, had left them in the 'fridge for us. Kids and adults alike developed a taste for raw cabbage spread with mustard and rolled up into a thick tube, and we took breaks together out on the huge front porch, crunching companionably on leaf after leaf. We discovered that a breeze was almost always crossing our porch. Something about its position on the hill and the direction of winds brought us an almost constant refreshing breath. This was a great relief, and a welcome change from our stuffy cabin that sat low in its river valley. Although it was still early spring, it was already getting warm. We swung our legs over the railing, and surveyed the land spreading around us, watching the fields and fields of tall grass that swayed and rippled with eddies of wind. It was a sea of space and openness. This was a place that let you breathe deeply.

We kept the downstairs colors tame. The hallways were white, the kitchen lemon yellow, one downstairs bedroom blue, and the other pink. The upstairs hallway ended in a wide "T" with a row of windows high on the back wall. Without much hope, I hesitantly asked if it could be turned into a room for me. Fletcher took a look at it, and said we could put up a partition, and it was mine. I could not quite believe it. In the paint store, I hovered interminably over the color tabs, drunk on possibilities. Dandelion yellow? Spring green? Blood red? After much thought, I selected Wedgwood blue, which was about the prettiest color I had ever seen. Fletcher built a platform bed for me, right up under the windows, with a little ladder to climb up on. My ladybug had her place under my bed, I laid out my kitten rug, and assembled a bookshelf out of scraps of boards and old cinder blocks I found by the shed. My little room felt momentarily normal—reminiscent in a way of my old attic. I was content.

Karen, Erica, and Rachel, all within two years of the same age, were going to share the larger of the two upstairs bedrooms. They each picked a different color for their third of the room. Erica picked purple of course, and Rachel a robin's egg blue. Karen picked pink. They measured the room into thirds, used strips of masking tape to mark the borders, and each painted her third, ceiling and all. It was beautiful, like being inside a three-flavored pie. My mother took the other upstairs bedroom, Fletcher and Sam shared a downstairs one, and Lynn took the little room off the kitchen, which we painted pale green, on which she later painted garlands of flowers. Peter set about soundproofing one of the out buildings, which we instantly dubbed the "music shed." Up in my room, I lay on my stomach gazing out the window at the cypresses that grew at the edge of the yard, watching and waiting to see what would happen next.

So now we had a house. It looked like a house, in many ways every bit as gracious as the one we had left behind in Baltimore and much, much larger. It had walls and windows and wood floors. I loved it, and took from its space and sturdiness a measure of comfort. But in another way, the solidity of the house made the contrast with the uncertainty of my life more painful. This façade of familiarity or normality served to highlight the fiction of its structure. No sooner did we occupy the house, than it began to take on the characteristics of who we were. Without the hired caretaker, the yard full of ornamental bushes and carefully trimmed flower beds reverted instantly to wild weedy patches. Elias's unfinished project to re-paint the green trim on the gables gave the house a lopsided look from the entrance, while the family of skunks who immediately took up residence under the steps to the kitchen door rendered it unusable. Our nature removed the veneer of civility and beckoned the wild, and our house dropped her skirts and shook out her hair. There was no pretending—we were who we were.

We now had room, lots of room, and as if they knew, people kept coming, some planned, some not. It was 1970, and there was a lot of interest in what we were doing. And things got very different. We found an improbably long table at an auction, which we put in the huge dining room. Fletcher and Sam built several long benches to serve as chairs. Now that we were all under one roof, we started having meals together with some degree of regularity. This meant someone had to plan ahead, buy groceries, and schedule who would cook and clean up after each meal. Our diet was dictated by a combination of economics and health. No meat, few dairy products, lots of grains and vegetables, no sugar or refined flour. Our plan was to plant a garden, get chickens and either a cow or several more goats to provide most of our own food. I don't know who started the fad of eating with chopsticks, but pretty soon every one abandoned metal utensils for the more "natural" wooden sticks. With them, we all soon became expert at picking up individual grains of rice, eating oatmeal and even soup.

Once a week, everybody attended a community meeting. An agenda was taped to the door of the fridge, and items were added as they occurred to people. We started mapping out the garden, and thinking about fruit trees. We were to be a "Free School," which

I took to mean not having to do anything unless I wanted to, or maybe not having to pay for it—I wasn't really sure which. For the moment, "free" seemed to mean I didn't have much to do. The grownups were espousing this theory that if we, the children, were allowed total liberty to follow our own interests without pressure, to move about unhampered through the wealth of educational opportunities available from life itself, we would develop our own desires to study and learn. With sufficient freedom and opportunity, the belief held, an innate joy of learning will surface in each individual, providing sufficient drive and motivation for the acquisition of knowledge.

"One day," my mother said, "if you keep an open mind, you might find you *want* to study fractions."

"Right," I returned, and went to play a game of jacks.

It wasn't long before I realized there was another side to this freedom thing. One morning, although I did not have to "go to school," I got up early. The house was quiet. Out in the yard, I could see Suzanne, one of the newer arrivals, poking around in the weeds by the fence on her hands and knees. Several of us had thought we smelled mint there the night before, and she was trying to sniff it out. My mother was in the "office"—a tiny room with its own entrance, that she had requisitioned for administrative purposes. Crammed into the room were three filing cabinets, and two desks, each equipped with a typewriter, one manual, and one electric. The room had already taken on her personality. There were piles of papers on every possible surface, a radio blasting classical music filled with static, and a bowl on the windowsill holding a banana peel and part of an orange. Sticking my head in her door, I opened my mouth to talk to her, but she waved at me, that familiar "Shush, don't break my concentration" wave. She was writing a letter, and did not want to be disturbed. Erica, Rachel, and Karen were up in their room, either sleeping or talking, or doing some older girl thing, and I certainly did not have a place there with them. Fletcher and Sam were already out patching the chicken coop. Peter was in his shed, and Lynn was sleeping. It was so quiet. What to do? I wandered around the yard for a while, but it was lonely. It seemed so strange. Where was everybody? Wasn't I supposed to be doing something?

I suddenly missed my father with such intensity that it seized in my chest, and I could not swallow. He was never in doubt about what to do. He was always busy, sure, and safe. Where was he? I sat down heavily in the yard where I was, clenched my teeth, and waited. Breathing shallow to avoid the depth of suffocation I felt at his absence, I thought about him hard. I pictured his face, and his hands, and imagined showing him my room, where I knew he would be amused by the clumsiness of my bookshelf. It hurt more to think about him, but it felt good too, like pressing down on a bruise to test its depth. And in time, the impossibility of his absence passed, as it always did.

My mother was persistent in her efforts to get me to talk about "Daddy," as she called him. I resented her use of that title.

"Sweetie," she'd say, "are you missing Daddy?"

"Uhh uhh," I'd mumble ambiguously, shrugging my shoulders.

"You know," she'd go on, "Daddy loves you very much." (As if I didn't know!) "Is it very hard for you?"

"I dunno," I'd answer, torn between my need to resist her invitations, my longing to talk about him, and the awareness that I could hurt her by expressing how much I missed him, which I did and did not want to do.

"Would you like to call him?" she'd offer.

"No," I'd say, although I did want to, only I felt too shy and awkward.

I had seen him a few times over the past two years. He had driven down, first alone, and then with his new girlfriend, but the visits had been awful. He had looked expressionlessly at the cramped little cabin, the lopsided barn, and Elias's tent. When he had come up to Tranquility Farm, it had suddenly seemed tacky and primitive. What Mommy had presented as a magical adventure suddenly seemed like plain craziness. There was no space or time to be with him, and the tension between him and my mother was unbearable.

After sitting outside at the picnic table for a couple of hours, clearly not wanting to go inside the cabin, he got up stiffly, and climbed back into his car.

His disappointment seemed as sharp to me as my own. I never knew what he was looking for from those visits that he didn't find, but I sure knew what I didn't get. My sisters and I seemed to merge into a single faceless, wordless blob, while our mother never stopped talking. First it was just blah blah talk—How was the trip? Work? Common acquaintances? Then there was nagging talk: Would you please do this? When can you take care of that? And finally, after we had been sent away into the house, as if we would miss a single word in that tiny place, there was the angry talk. Why didn't you this and how could you have that. And then he left. We didn't seem to get anything of him. We didn't get to talk to him, or be with him, or absorb any of his lively confidence that I missed so much. He sent me postcards from his travels around the world, cards with pictures of a baby wildebeest from Africa, a mountaintop in Bolivia, or a dragon mask from China, a few lines written in his nearly illegible hand. I cherished them, and read and reread them, carrying the latest around with me in my pocket. Through that meager correspondence, I felt linked to him, but when he was there in person, there was so much else going on that he was unreachable. Somehow, I still felt tightly connected to him, and waited, just waited, to see him again. A lot of the time, I didn't think about him at all. There was too much else going on.

Trapped in Freedom

After our usual breakfast of organic oatmeal with raisins, bananas and sesame seeds, and watered-down orange juice, we each carried our dishes into the kitchen, scraped any leftovers into the trash, and stacked them in the sink. Then, people went about their business. Even after everybody was up and about, it seemed as if I was the only one with nothing to do. In the front yard, Lynn was choreographing a new dance piece, with Peter watching from the porch. Suzanne, having found her mint, was stringing it carefully on a line so she could hang it in the sun to dry. Erica, Rachel, and Karen, now perched on the little roof outside their bedroom window, were laughing. Mommy was barricaded back in her office. Inside the cool house, the living room was empty. Feeling a little guilty, as if shirking some ill-defined duty, I slipped out the side door and headed down to the barn.

Cindy was content in her new stall. She had no interest in me. Buffy the goat was lying down, and I watched her chew her cud, and looked into her strange golden eyes for a while, fascinated by their elongated horizontal pupils. She stared right back at me, expressionless, never breaking the hypnotic rhythm of her jaws. I watched her chew, swallow, and pause, then bring up a new wad that rose visibly up along her soft throat and into her mouth, whereupon she began to chew again. She was as preoccupied and inaccessible as my mother. Then I went over to the chicken shed to see the eight Rhode Island Reds that Fletcher had bought at the stockyard, having determined that the old laying boxes in the chicken shed were still serviceable. The birds were a deep rusty red, with yellow combs, kind of fat and waddly, and sort of cute. But they weren't very good company.

Moving out away from the buildings, I went up into the field, and eventually into the woods that covered Slaughter Mountain, the hill at the top of the property. I explored our piece of land thoroughly, so that by the end of a month, I knew the shape of each rise and hollow, I knew about the tadpoles in the little seeping creek at the bottom of the hill, and had ventured out into our neighbor's field to get a better view of the horse farm below. I had lain in the grass and learned the sound of grasshoppers, stifled disgust while pulling out my first tick, smelled and tasted all manner of weeds; sour lemon grass, mint, and spicy red-stemmed weeds. My feet were developing calluses and deep stains from the red dirt, because, liking the feeling of bare feet, I seldom wore shoes. I also stopped changing my clothes, finding that my jeans cut-offs and shirt sort of held my shape after a few days. There was something very comfortable about climbing into pants that were already molded to my form, and I felt no need for clean ones.

I often climbed over the zigzag fence to enter the dim whispering pine forest that bordered one side of our land. There the trees had been planted in neat rows that now made peaceful dim aisles that stretched straight ahead until the rows seemed to converge. Lying flat on the thick, soft bed of needles, looking up, I breathed deeply the sharp pine scent, and found a momentary sense of order. I felt so lost half the time. I missed my friends Lanny and Leslie, and even stupid Donna at school. I missed my routine, and my block, and the familiarity of things I knew. I even missed regular school. I had always been good at school, it was effortless and kind of fun. I had enjoyed learning math, and loved looking at the huge world map when the teacher pulled it down over the blackboard with her wooden stick, and the only hard thing about reading was being patient while others read aloud so slowly.

I was nine years old, and everything now seemed so vague and chaotic and unexpected. All kinds of things were going on back at the house, but I didn't know what they were, or who half the people really were, or what they had to do with me. Out there in the pine forest, each tree planted equidistant from the next, at least I could just see what was for a moment.

Returning from these extended ramblings, I always hoped someone would have missed me and would ask me where I had been, but they were usually all too busy to notice. There was a long-standing rule that I had to tell my mother where I was going, but I often couldn't find her. I'd look through the house, in the office, check to see that her car was still there. Sometimes I would locate her, perched on the fence in the back yard deep in conversation, behind her typewriter working on a poem, or taking a nap, her glasses still on her nose, book fallen across her chest. So I would just leave, and I found that she usually didn't notice I had been gone. Everybody but me had projects and occupations that kept them absorbed. I badly needed a job. Looking around at different possibilities, I decided to volunteer to take care of the chickens. They fascinated me, and bringing them food and water once a day seemed a small price to pay for the pleasure of gathering the eggs.

Once a day, I would make a round of the property, having located the nests of the more rebellious chickens that preferred to lay in the barn or the tool shed rather than in the official laying boxes in the shed. I gathered the eggs in the front of my shirt, eventually collecting a couple of dozen in a bumpy bulge, stubbornly refusing to take a more appropriate vessel, despite Fletcher's scolding that I would break them. I loved that huge belly of eggs, and rarely lost any.

Entering the chicken shed at any time of day was to enter a dim, dusky place. The chickens, all dozy on their roosts, perched on stands, or settled in their laying boxes. A persistent cheep, rustle, and croon filled the air. Strips of light snaking in through cracks showed that the air was thick with dust and tiny feathers. The beams of suspended sound and small particles seemed almost solid. I tried not to think about what I was breathing.

I spent hours sitting there silently, watching chicken life proceed once they had stopped noticing me. I opened the doors to the laying boxes, and the hens eyed me warily, but were too occupied to move. I loved the way each one, the moment she had laid her day's egg, would immediately stand tall in the box and crow loudly, announcing her accomplishment to the assembled company. One day I boldly slid my cupped palm under a hen as she sat. The softness of the feathers was no surprise, downy and light as expected. But the warmth was unexpected, and heavenly. I sat without moving, ignoring the cramp developing in my calf. In time, with a distinct "pop" an egg, perfect and complete, dropped directly into my hand. Bringing it out into the light, I saw that a thin film of moisture covered it. As it cooled, I watched the dampness evaporate rapidly, visibly running off the shell into nothingness, some essence of birth that was as fleeting—as ineffable—as life itself. This was glorious.

But a hen house, it turned out, was a tough place. Cocks really do crow at dawn, but chicken cruelty goes on all day long. These chickens were always hungry, with a ferocity that alarmed me, even when I fed them daily—which was not always the case. Whenever I approached with the feed buckets, they would crowd around my feet, fly up around my hands, and engage in fierce battle for the front spots at the feeding troughs. As soon as there was food at their level, they would struggle and peck one another brutally. I always tried to save some food for the weaker, ousted chickens, the ones pushed away from the troughs, but I usually only caused them more misery. Why were they always so hungry? Why so savage? No matter how much they ate, they were always frantic with hunger. This made me feel guilty and uncomfortable. What I gave them was never enough. Out of resentment, sometimes I did not feed them at all for a day or two. Their hunger and constant demanding need underscored my inability to satisfy them. Did I even want to satisfy them? I, whose hungers were so inconsistently fed. I was supposed to tend them, feral child that I was fast becoming, but I could not bear to see them comfortable in a domesticity I could not share. Sometimes I just let them wait, as I was waiting. Waiting for what? Rescue? Attention? Help? There were plenty of people around, available even, but it seemed I had to figure this out for myself—what to do with my time, how to amuse or interest or occupy myself, how to feel connected to my life.

Nobody Should (Fuck You) You Ish!

Cross came through the gate and sauntered toward the house, every bit as cool as James Dean. His closely sheared head looked freakish, accustomed as I was to the long hair of all the other men. He wore a tight white T-shirt, with a pack of Marlboros rolled up into the left sleeve and perched on his shoulder, showing off his compactly muscled arm. His belted jeans were low-slung, and he tucked them into his black leather army boots in military style. He swaggered, hips forward, shoulders dropped, thumbs hooked into his jeans pockets. I couldn't take my eyes off him.

He handled the usual polyglot greeting committee with reserve, flicking his eyes around, trying to figure this place out, trying to get a read on how the land lay. He seemed slightly dangerous, prickly, suspicious, and utterly captivating.

My mother had heralded his arrival at the dinner table the week before, while we were all gathered over brown rice and sautéed veggies.

"Hey, guess what?" she announced excitedly, "Juvenile Court is going to send us Cross."

"He picked us?" we asked.

"Yup."

"Oh, good!" I said.

"Uh-oh," said Suzanne, "how are we going to reform a JD?" Suzanne had quickly become a central member of the community.

er confident take-charge opinions, impressive array of practical skills, and commitment to the group made her a Presence.

"If we love him, and show him a different way to live, I'm sure we'll all do fine," said my mother.

The story was that in the city, Cross, who was fifteen, belonged to a group of young hoodlums who made it their business primarily to steal car keys. They lifted them from jacket pockets, off unguarded desks, or out of purses when the chance arose. After some months, they had the keys to eight or ten cars in different neighborhoods. The routine was that late each night, they would all pile into a different car, and cruise, meeting up with other kids, hanging out in the parking lot of the liquor store, or just driving around. Early in the morning, they would fill the tank with gas, and return the car to its place, no one the wiser. They amused themselves imagining the owner coming out in the morning to go to work, finding his car in a slightly different location, with the gas gauge registering full, when it might have been half empty the night before. They did this for months, and if they hadn't gotten into an accident, it could have gone on indefinitely. When the car ahead of them stopped abruptly, unlucky Cross slammed into its rear, and the police cruiser sitting across the street left them no time to get away. Cross was charged with reckless endangerment, auto theft, driving without a license, and a half-dozen other impressive sounding infractions.

He was the most harmless of criminals, a moocher rather than a thief, but one with a record—he had been caught once shoplifting a jack knife he admired. His father, a hard-working man with a beer paunch and grizzled cheeks, was thoroughly disgusted. His kid the felon couldn't even *steal* a freaking car. The best he could do was *borrow* one. The judge, a seasoned man who had seen every kind of delinquent standing before his bench, realized that Cross was not a hardened criminal, but felt that he was obligated to do something meaningful to curb his behavior. He told the social worker to find some options. The social worker had recently read an advertisement about our school. It sounded like the kind of place she would have liked to be in herself, so she called us, and drove down to meet with my mother and Bob and see the school. Bob, one of our newer arrivals, had a captivating South Carolina accent, a handlebar mustache, two peacocks, and a sheep named Ted. He was twenty-four, a tall slim man with straight hair swept across the side of his head that persistently fell down over his forehead, leading him to comb it out of his eyes every few minutes. Down south he had been teaching teenagers in a community program for disadvantaged youths, and under the circumstances was thought to be our best representative.

The social worker arrived, and, given our rule that everyone had to park down at the bottom of the hill and walk up to the house, respectfully struggled up the weedy dirt road in her pumps. She looked a little ridiculous in her suit; her nails polished a light coral, hair carefully arranged. As she came in, unable to restrain our curiosity, several of us peeked out at her as she went down the hall. She saw us, and gamely waved a hand. After they talked, Bob, having found a pair of tennis shoes she could borrow, took the social worker on a tour of the house, barn, and garden, and then she came up to the "theatre." This was part of the second floor that had been left unfinished, its wall studs exposed, and floorboards still showing. Fletcher had insulated and finished it off with beaverboard to provide us with a dance/theatre space. We had hung colored lights from the rafters, and draped dark fabric over a clothesline on a pulley to serve as our curtain. Suzanne was giving a drama workshop and Karen, Rachel, Erica, and I were doing an exercise where we had to act out the elements, Air, Earth, Fire, and Water. We took it very seriously, and now barely acknowledged the social worker when she came in and sat against the wall by the door to observe. Suzanne had schooled us well, and we were accustomed to following her directions without "breaking concentration." When she called out "Fire!" we instantly began to perform our interpretations of fire, moving with flickering, devouring movements, and portrayals of heat. As soon as Suzanne called out "Earth," we sank to the floor, leaden with weightiness. After we had gone through all the elements several times, Suzanne had us lie down on the floor in a wheel, heads close together, eyes closed, and do the same thing, using vocalizations instead of movements.

The social worker was entranced. She became so enthusiastic about the idea of sending kids to us, that my mother had to tell her we would only take one at a time, and only if, after meeting them, we thought it would work out. She did not intend to become a haven for court-referred juvenile delinquents. In the end, the court gave Cross a choice between coming to us and going to reform school and he chose us sight unseen. And here he was.

Cross captivated my ten-year-old's imagination, and I padded along behind him as much as he would allow. In him, I saw every unjustly accused hero and misunderstood good guy from the books I read. Tough as he appeared, hard as he talked, I knew he was really gentle and kind. To me, he was the embodiment of cool. All the older girls were smitten with Bob, but Cross was my idol. Unconsciously, I began to imitate him, trying to walk the way he did, slouch the way he did, squint like him. I made it my business to love him, to let him know that I didn't think he was bad.

Emblazoned on the back of Cross's jeans jacket was a huge swastika. I had just been reading *The Diary of Anne Frank*, *The Chosen*, and *Exodus*; the Nazis had crystallized in my awareness as the bad guys, juxtaposed against the good guys of the Supreme Court, which was the stronghold of sanity, justice, and fairness. My nightmares were of being chased by Nazis, discovered to be Jewish and being carted away. And here was Cross with his swastika. When I first saw it, it shook me deeply. I was shocked, momentarily frozen at the thought that I might have been wrong—that maybe he really was the bad guy he tried to make himself appear. But then I remembered: Cross had had a hard life. His father didn't love him, his mother had left him, no one understood him. It was up to us to set him straight and I was just the one for the job.

Appalled to learn that Cross had never read a book, written a poem, sung a song, or slept outdoors, my sisters and I took it upon ourselves to correct these omissions in his education. I dragged him out to admire the dew caught on an early morning spider web, and worked to teach him to sing "Old Abram Brown," a round with a simple melody about a dead guy that I thought might appeal to him.

Cross was horrified by us, and for weeks went around smacking his head with his palm groaning at his idiocy at having *chosen* this fate. He was aghast at our culture of mostly vegetarian meals ("I'm a bloody steak man!"), sunset watching ("I don't *get* it!"), and pacifism ("Give those fucking gooks what they got coming to them!"). At every group hug, sing-in, and peace talk, he could be seen shaking his head, stupefied by our values, and calling himself a "fucking lunatic" for having chosen to subject himself to our nuttiness when he could have gone to a simple reform school, and done his time in peace. It wasn't Cross's body we were assailing, it was his soul.

Our hill was graced with spectacular sunsets, long ribbons stretching in ripples of pink and blue across the whole western expanse. The entire community would often gather to watch them together, drifting out of the office, up from the garden or out of the kitchen, and joining in common appreciation of this display, clearly posted for our special enjoyment. Half a dozen of us could fit on the roof of the little cement gashouse, others perched on car hoods, pieces of firewood, rocks, or on the ground. And we sat in companionable silence, breathing in the colors, watching them intensify, and then fade softly into evening until the first firefly lit. But the whole notion of admiring beauty for its own sake, of simply sitting to receive something was novel to Cross, who fidgeted, dug his toes in the dirt under his feet, whittled fiercely at a stick with his jack knife, and twisted threads from the loose hem of his jeans while he strove to see the beauty.

My sisters and I consulted with each other about how to right the grievous, unimaginable impoverishment of never having read a single book for pleasure. Cross refused to actually read anything we suggested, but after some pestering, he grudgingly agreed to let us read aloud to him, which my sisters and I did, taking turns for hours on end. My mother recently told me that she had caught him late one night reading ahead in *Black Beauty*, when we were only half way through. He urgently swore her to secrecy, explaining that he *had* to find out what happened next in the story, but didn't want us to know, lest we stop reading to him.

Cross sat next to me in typing class, protesting the idiocy of the activity all the while, but proudly closing his eyes and touch-typing me funny one-liners, mostly about food:

"What was that brown stuff at lunch anyway?" or

"Hey, wanna go get a brewer's yeast shake and some zookeenie fries?" (we'd had to educate him on the identity of the vegetable, of course) or

"How 'bout that *oatmeal!*"

As the only paying student, Cross felt entitled to a certain respect, "I support this fucking place," he'd proclaim, "I can do whatever the fuck I want."

Cross was kind to me, something not to be taken for granted, for I certainly did not enhance his coolness quotient, but then he hardly needed that. I think I was safe for him—I didn't ask for much, and I utterly adored him. We sat out on the back porch together for hours, both astride the big railing, my legs swinging back and forth from the knee, with first a checkerboard and then a chessboard between us. We didn't talk much, but there was an understanding between us.

Cross had tattooed his initials "B.B." onto his left bicep, and a rough cross onto the skin on the back of his hand. On his other arm was a swastika. He later showed me how he had done them, dipping a sewing needle into ink, and piercing his forearm painstakingly forming a peace sign, right next to the tiny swastika that he eventually turned into a four leaf clover, finally saying, "Oh, what the fuck," at the anticipated derision of his peers, when he returned to "the real world."

We certainly were not in the real world. Cross made that abundantly clear, and there was no shortage of evidence:

It was the general practice to brush our teeth with powdered burnt eggplant, which was reputed to be a tonic for the gums, a plaque inhibitor, and an enamel protectant. Once a month, Bob would put an eggplant in the oven and cook it at a high temperature until it was burnt through, its acrid aroma permeating the entire house. After it had cooled, he would pulverize it, and put it in two jars, one for the bathroom, and one for the kitchen. It tasted foul, and left everybody's teeth with a characteristic smoky gray coloring. This we counteracted by using baking soda every few days. I could never decide which was worse, the intolerable saltiness of the baking powder or the sooty eggplant that gritted between my teeth for hours after brushing. Oh, for a tube of Colgate! I found the easiest solution was to forgo brushing altogether.

There were bricks in the toilet, and the lid was taped shut, because we had sworn off the flush toilet, opting for an outhouse instead in order to minimize our consumption of water, and conserve electricity as much as possible. We made our own candles, mixing melted crayons in with the paraffin for color, and pouring them into sand molds to use instead of lights whenever possible. We agreed we would not use the old oil-burning furnace in the basement, resorting instead to a big airtight wood stove in the living room. We planned eventually to use wind, sun, or methane gas for power, heat and light.

Peacock feathers, thanks to the pair Bob had brought with him, were in evidence everywhere. The peacocks were equally spectacular in their arrogance and beauty. Although there was no peahen around to impress, they both spent a lot of time in full display, their tail feathers fanned high above their heads as they strutted and quivered around the yard. We certainly admired their fabulous plumage, and their feathers began to find their way into the house as a favored all-purpose decoration. Lynn started braiding them into her hair; Rachel, Erica, and Karen taped them to their bedroom window; Elias went out to buy a bottle of ink and started using them as quill pens. The fact that they were too soft for this function did nothing to dampen his determination. Nothing could match the tickle of a peacock feather along one's cheek, while writing a poem or working on a puzzle. Many of us copied him.

No, it wasn't the real world, but it began to take shape. There was now some structure to each day. Suzanne, ever our organizer, made a big calendar listing the times and days of the regular classes, meals, and weekly events such as Community Meeting. Every day began at 8:00 with "music hour," during which all were invited to play or listen to music, practice an instrument, give or receive a lesson in music, or at the very least, be quiet so as not to conflict with all the music going on around. Four of us fought over the two pianos, Erica pulled out her flute, Rachel her cello or guitar, and Peter drummed. Cross would wander from room to room to see what everybody was doing, then pick a room, throw himself down in a chair or on a cushion, close his eyes, and concentrate all his energy on hearing beauty. He was terrifically earnest in his efforts. No one could have worked harder at finding beauty or meaning in unfamiliar mediums.

In the living room, one long wall was covered, floor to ceiling, with books. Several well-meaning people had donated books to us, sending boxes that we opened with great pleasure and anticipation. We got all kinds of books, from the lofty to the squalid. There were Westerns and Mysteries, Philosophy, Great Literature, History, and Biography, all of which we put on the shelves in no particular order. *Anna Karenina* sat next to *Kiss My Firm But Pliant Lips*, Thomas Mann sat next to Louis Lamour. I read voraciously and indiscriminately, gradually developing a sense of what it meant for something to be well-written, knowing that I was way over my head as I read *The Cancer Ward*, and *War and Peace*, but entranced nonetheless, absorbed by the seemingly endless variety of things, places, feelings, and situations about which I knew absolutely nothing, but which, between their two covers, seemed safe, compared to my world. Here was something I could master. With Cross in mind, I studied this shelf, finally arriving at *Lord of the Flies* as a first book for Cross to read to himself. I thought he would be able to relate.

Writing poetry was an activity we often engaged in together, sitting around in the living room, writing haiku, limericks, or free form; agreeing on a subject, and letting loose with it. Cross saw us as complete fucking aliens, but he was game. What else was there to do in the middle of "Fucking Nowhere" as he called it? Once convinced that word of his doings would never filter back to his buddies in the city, he became more adventuresome, and allowed himself to do and say things that he would otherwise not have been caught dead doing and saying. He wrote a poem! The first one was rusty, like the voice of a man who has been silent for a dozen years, or like someone speaking a childhood language he has almost forgotten. He went on. The next one came more easily, and from there they began to flow—one after the other—until it was a creative torrent. Cross wrote and wrote and wrote—wrote about himself as a tough nut, wrote about his father as a tough nut, wrote about death and hope and hopelessness and life, and as he wrote, something in him came to life, and he began to play and soften.

We roughly followed the calendar, although it was gladly and easily abandoned for a swimming trip to the river or when Fletcher needed more hands to get the new roof onto the tool shed. We all had clean-up chores, regardless of age, which some people did some of the time. Several of us kids also had a specific area of responsibility, although, like classes, those too were voluntary. Erica took care of the goats, Rachel was the accountant and chief check writer, and I took care of the chickens (sort of).

We bought three more female goats, and had them "freshened," by a neighboring buck, and now they were all big-bellied. Bob started planning the garden for spring, ordering seeds and studying the *Encyclopedia of Organic Gardening* as well as the *Farmers Almanac*. He walked around muttering about the difference in cucumbers between marketmores and lemon, and plotting when each crop could be planted to best advantage by the phases of moon. He and Suzanne were in charge of the kitchen, and they planned the menus, did the weekly food shopping, and prepared many of the meals.

My mother ran the office and took care of administrative business, and Fletcher, alone now that Sam had left for the Navy, worked steadily and silently on an endless progression of repairs and building projects. Lynn and Peter continued to spend most of their time "being-there," for us students, and offering experiences in dance and music. The emphasis, rather than being on teaching, was on learning, no matter how that came about—be it through actually doing something, reading a book, thinking or talking about it, or more didactic teaching. Thus, instead of classes, there were "times." Suzanne offered drama time, Mommy was a be-there for creative writing and typing times, and Bob was on hand for arts and crafts time. Some of the newcomers provided times in other specialty subjects. This meant that during their designated hours that particular "be-there" would be engaged in those activities, and students were invited to participate at whatever level of involvement they chose. Mommy had advertised for members better prepared to be-there for math, science, and foreign languages.

Mark, who knew French, had thick, wavy brown hair and a bushy mustache and wore wire-rimmed glasses. After finishing a Ph.D. in Philosophy, he had joined the Peace Corp and spent two years teaching English in Africa. At twenty-nine, Mark still had a bouncy walk, as if there were springs under his heels. Even when standing in one place, he bounced up and down on his toes. He played the guitar magically, and I liked it best when he played "Blackbird," while leaning against the wall in the hallway, or lounging in the brown recliner.

Alan came, a gifted red-haired pianist who had not played in several years. He was in his early thirties, tense and silent. Then came Ellen, a serious woman in her mid-twenties. Dave arrived, a handsome young man of twenty, and Laurel, a single mom in her mid-thirties with her two children, Jeanie and Clayton. Suddenly I was no longer the youngest. Jeanie at nine was a year younger than I, and Clayton was only four. Fletcher subdivided the huge upstairs landing into four tiny windowless cubicles to make more room, and everybody found a place.

The community now numbered an ever-fluctuating fifteen to twenty. It was still strange, but more okay. It never got so cold that I couldn't go outside, and I now had a dog to come along. Gnomie was both ugly and lazy, and it was hard to get him interested in much, but he provided some company. I loved my little Wedgwood blue room, and spent a lot of time up there or outside. There was an endless parade of oddball people coming and going, but there was a stable core that remained. Suzanne, Laurel and her children, Fletcher and his daughter Karen, Mark, Dave, and Ellen became the backbone of the community. I didn't worry quite as much, but I still felt lost a lot of the time.

I admired Karen, who was unconcerned about convention or what others thought, or what she was "supposed" to do or be. Unlike me, she had taken to freedom with ease and confidence. She could be heard loudly retorting, "Don't put your bad energy on me!" when Ellen, always gravely responsible, would try to get her to clean up the "quiet room" as she had been assigned. Just hearing Karen's voice, I could picture her tossing her blonde hair back over her shoulder, eyes flashing. "It's not my trip," she'd say, when she didn't want to be involved in going to town to do the communal laundry. As a last retort, she would scream out, "You ISH!", when anyone persisted in displeasing her.

About the worst thing you could call a person was, "You Ish!!" No one was quite sure where this had come from, or what it meant, but it was a powerful epithet. It was far more cutting than calling someone an Asshole, or a Creep. If "Ish" was the worst insult, "Poop" was the second worst. A Poop, more specifically, was someone who was being insufferably attentive to rules—a regular killjoy.

"Vibes" were an undisputed reality. "Good vibes" or "bad vibes" emitted by people, places, or things were spoken of as if they were as obviously visible or audible as physical characteristics. A person sending out bad vibes was strongly frowned upon, and expected to go off and get him or herself under control. Bad vibes were often associated with being a "heavy," which generally meant trying to get others to do something they did not want to do by making them feel guilty, or laying a "head-trip" on them. "Head trips" invariably had to do with a confrontation about un-kept promises, un-met responsibilities, or obligations not taken care of. Being a heavy was being "establishment," rigid, and backward.

The worst heavy of all was my mother. It was my mother who insisted on establishing some rules and some structure. It was she who maintained that there was a legitimate difference between adults and children, she who drew the clear differentiation between "staff," and "students." She claimed that with the greater responsibilities of being "staff," came greater privileges. Staff were officially required to work at least six hours a day, they had to attend weekly Staff Meetings, and were censured for neglecting obligations like cooking a meal they had signed up for. In return, they had no bedtimes, no rules about where they could and could not go, and were answerable to no one. My mother disseminated all these ideas about egalitarianism, and yet created a hierarchical structure in our very midst. She maintained that she had the right to tell me what to do, and to institute rules that I had to follow, while she was free to do otherwise. How I hated her rules! Bedtime was the worst of all, especially as, being the youngest for so long, it affected me the most. It was she who was most often called an Ish, and a heavy, and accused of laying on the ultimate head-trip—a "mind fuck."

The best thing you could call someone or something was "Fine."

"She's a really fine person," you might say, in paying the highest compliment. Or, "That was a fine thing to do."

"Beautiful" was a good word. You could have a beautiful conversation, a beautiful idea, a beautiful experience, or be a beautiful person.

If an experience was beautiful enough, one could easily become "blissed out."

"Shit" was by far the most common expression of displeasure, with "pooh" as a close second.

"Far fucking out," on the other hand, was an excellent exclamation, and used liberally, sometimes with the variation of "Farm fucking out."

At first, "Fuck you" was widely and frequently used, and satisfying in its pungency. But then Winifred ruined the phrase "Fuck you" forever.

Winifred was Suzanne's mother, and she stayed for several extended visits. She was tall and gaunt and at least a hundred years old. Her wrinkled dark brown skin was thick and very dry. She had tough gray hair, chopped off at neck level, and it stuck out from her head in stiff bristles. She smoked a constant chain of hand-rolled cigarettes, lighting one from the next, and often having two burning in the ashtray. Although she had once been the "Queen of the 12-string guitar," allegedly playing with none other than Leadbelly himself, her voice was now gravelly and masculine. She attributed this, not to her constant smoking, but to a boyfriend who had broken her voice box with a blow to the throat when he thought she was cheating on him. It was hard to imagine her as the object of jealous passion, with her leathery skin, swollen joints, and bony limbs. Winifred was always knitting thick wool socks in the brightest hues of orange and red. Into every one, she knitted a "Navajo Goof," an intentional error in the form of a single stripe somewhere on the sole, in the most discordant color she could find. The purpose of this was to prevent the gods from becoming jealous at the perfection of her creation. This to me, far from humility, seemed the greatest arrogance possible. In my mind, to fear that the gods would become jealous of one's creation was to think that one's creation was perfect, and that one was Godlike.

Winnifred broke her leg while trying to climb onto the roof to retrieve a Frisbee that had gone astray. Elias's ladder was still leaning against the house from his unfinished painting project, and Winifred got to the top of it and leaned over to grasp the Frisbee, not realizing that it was resting only on the gutter, held inadequately in place by one rusty nail. The whole thing came down in a spectacular tumble, Winifred flailing her arms and legs, still clutching the orange disc in one hand. When she landed, her hair stuck straight up toward the roof, as if it had lagged behind. She had broken her leg in two places, but laughed hysterically the whole time we were carrying her down the driveway into the car and out to the hospital half an hour away.

For the next four months, she hobbled around on crutches, looking as if she would topple over—an ancient crane on borrowed stilts. She was like a talking crow or magpie, saying the crude things everyone else only thought, at the most inauspicious moments. For relief from pain, I imagine, she spent a lot of time lying on her back out in the front yard, knitting, with her legs in the air, cast waving madly. From this central location, she was well positioned to insist, whenever someone yelled "Fuck you!" that the proper insult would be "Nobody should!" Wishing someone to be fucked, Winifred reasoned, was suggesting that they were fuckable. To say "Nobody should (fuck you)!" was the real insult.

We all continually earned good or bad "karma" on a moment-by-moment basis that sent from every action a ripple forward through an untold number of lives yet to come, and reminded us of infractions and good deeds in lives past. This was a little unnerving. It was like having a perpetual conscience with dire consequences. I wondered about all the deaths I had caused—accidental ones like stepping on beetles or intentional ones like slapping a mosquito. I wondered whether we all had equal karma—human, mammal, and insect alike, or whether there was a hierarchy of effect. If I was mean to Buffy, giving her short shrift on grain, would it have the same impact as if I was mean to Ellen? And did one have to know one was doing wrong for it to have negative repercussions? I felt perpetually guilty about letting the chickens go hungry and thirsty for days at a time. I chose to neglect them for reasons I didn't understand. Would this spell my doom in the next life?

Mark and Suzanne tried to get us to remove sexism from language, by de-masculinizing nouns. Suzanne religiously pointed out the misogyny rampant in our everyday speech. And English wasn't even the worst! In German, she informed us irately, the word for a person of unspecified gender, or "one," was "Man!" I instantly felt guilty for my interest in studying German. Under Suzanne's guidance, Chairman became Chairperson, or better yet, Facilitator. Mark taught us that Animal Husbandry should be changed to Animal Partnery. We all accepted these alterations, but when Mark and Suzanne tried to get us to remove any gender differentiation whatsoever, things got complicated. Pronouns were the problem. Suzanne insisted it was sexist to say, "she is going to the store," because what is relevant in that statement is that a person is going to the store, not that that person is a woman. When electing not to use a person's name, she said, the speaker should remain completely gender-neutral. They suggested that we use one all-purpose pronoun "co."

"Co" had the advantage of being plural as well as singular; it did not need to be declined, as it had only one form. Any ambiguities were supposed to be clarified by context. In practice, however, this was too confusing and awkward to be workable, and most of us returned to conventional grammar. I continued to feel self-conscious whenever I said "him" or "his," even when speaking specifically of a male person or animal. I felt I was not showing proper solidarity with my sisters.

Periodically, when things got wild in the house, someone would come through with the order "rough out-housing." Meaning, "take it outside!"

To which, as often as not, one of us would respond, "Nobody should, you Ish!"

The Cure

One day Lynn noticed that Elias didn't seem to be around. We looked all over, calling his name, but didn't find him. No one could remember the last time they had seen him. Checking the room he had used, we discovered that all of his stuff was gone. When he had left, and for what destination, was a complete mystery.

Lynn, too, left us, floating off to live in an old abandoned farmhouse not far away, with a man and another woman. She needed to encounter her possessiveness, she told us, spelling out that her new position as second woman, subordinate to this smooth man with a sly knowing smile, would force her to let go of her bourgeois notions of fidelity and ownership. Peter listened painfully—he would have given Lynn a whole heart with no occasion for jealousy, but she did not want that. "Too hungry for destinations to stay long in one place," as she put it, she drifted away out of principle or inertia. She was neither the first person to leave nor certainly the last. After a while, Peter found that his heart was no longer in it, and he, too, left us. We were into our second generation of community members. I was learning that every person who came to Nethers had one thing in common: one day, each would leave.

And then came Toby. Toby became my true friend.

I started off prejudiced against the skinny, pug-nosed boy, because it was his mother who first introduced mine to The Diet. This was an unbelievably restrictive eating regime, centered around raw foods, promulgated by some doctor-quack. It was reputed to cure all one's ills, past, present, and future, real or imagined. Toby's mother was as credulous as mine, and when she first came, she extolled the virtues of this Diet so convincingly that Mommy decided to try it on me.

Toby had crippling asthma, and I had a potentially deadly systemic allergy to bee stings, and dark circles under my eyes that my mother didn't like. The edicts of The Diet extended not only to what I could eat, but which foods I was allowed to eat at the same time. Every food was categorized by type—protein, starch, acid, sweet, and dairy—and you weren't supposed to combine protein with starch (eggs and toast, noodles and cheese) or acid with sweet (orange with banana) and so on. The only thing you could eat with a sweet (honey) was lettuce! The upshot was that Toby and I were restricted to special meals, and were not allowed to share in the general fare (which had never looked so good). I couldn't believe it, and looked with suspicion at this boy who had brought it. He certainly wasn't much to look at. At eleven, we were the same age. He had fair hair, a turned-up nose, eyes that looked too big, and an odd mouth. He was on the small side, not much bigger than I, although he was almost a year older. But there was a funny look in his eye. It seemed that he was laughing at somebody. Was it me? Our mothers were rapt in their discussion of grapefruits and pumpkin seeds. Toby peered across at me curiously, and then grinned.

And the whole landscape changed. His mismatched features suddenly resolved into a synchrony of open humor I'd never seen before. All at once, I knew I'd met someone I could count on. I jerked my head, "Let's go," and Toby and I slipped off. We wound up in the hay bin, a small storage room off to the side of the barn that I wasn't sure anyone else knew about. It had always been a private place of mine, and a favorite. It was sheltered and hidden, but you could still see out because the wooden slats of the wall were set an inch apart. The hay was old but clean, and four bales deep. Enough hay lay loose on top to make a comfortable nest.

I had jealously guarded this secret, using it as a retreat not too far from the house, and here I was taking in a total stranger. But Toby seemed to understand the place at once, and lay back in the straw, chewing on a stem. You couldn't lean back on straw bales without putting a piece in your mouth, no matter how corny. Toby obviously knew that.

Soon we were talking. We spoke of this and that, his little sister, my older ones, all the different schools he had been to, the different food plans he had been put on, his father. His parents, like mine, were divorced and estranged. He too saw his father regularly, but still missed him with the same central hollow feeling that I had missing mine. My mother tried constantly to get me to talk about how I felt about my father, a demand I met with determined and stubborn silence—my best rebellion. But with Toby, light falling through the slats in vertical stripes, the smell of hay dust in the air, I could talk freely, without feeling that he was going to take a part of me away. After a while—it was Toby's idea—we untied two more bales of hay, and strewed them around (and in each other's hair) to make our nest more comfortable. Why hadn't I ever done that before? It was so much cozier.

Having gained strength in shared rebellion, Toby and I no longer found The Diet so onerous. We took to walking to Woodville. Exactly a mile away, Woodville was the nearest "town," sporting a general store, a defunct gas station, a post office, and three churches. I used to go there every once in a while to get a nickel Fudgecicle bar, scrounging around in the kitchen drawers to find loose coins. Money had little meaning or value, but there were generally a few coins lying around, because coins had all kinds of uses other than commerce. Suzanne sewed them in bunches into the hems of the curtains that she made for the living room windows to weigh them down. Dimes were in demand for a favored smoking game, where we stretched a piece of tissue tightly over the opening of a glass, and balanced a coin in the center. We then passed a cigarette around the circle. Each person had to burn a hole in the tissue without being the one to cause the coin to drop down into the cup. Dimes were the most fun because, being the lightest, they lasted the longest, remaining suspended by the merest filigree of tissue fiber. I could usually find a dime to spend at the store, but it was boring to go by myself. I particularly hated entering alone, feeling the stares of all the "locals" hot on my back. And Jeanie, the one most likely to be available and willing to go with me, would begin to whine halfway there, about how far it was, how hot it was, how tired she was, and so on.

The first time Toby and I went, I was thinking about that Fudge-cicle, imagining it cold and sweet on my tongue, with that singular graininess. My mother would be mad (no sugar was allowed on The Diet) but how would she know? I had found fifty cents, so I was flush, thinking maybe I would get *two* Fudgecicles! I wondered if Toby would tell, or object. I really didn't know him very well. As soon as we got into the store, Toby went right up to the rack in the central isle, picked up a huge handful of small packages individually wrapped in cellophane, and took them to the counter. I looked in astonishment at his selection. He had at least eight packages of Hostess Twinkies. Their pale golden curls were visible under the printing on the wrapper, where they nestled in their cardboard trays like small mice. I could see their lightness, and I knew how they would dissolve instantly on my tongue like snowflakes. I started salivating. Devils food cakes too, dark brown, swirled with creamy whiteness in their middles. And Snowballs! Coconut-covered, pink and white. I had never, ever, had a Snowball. Even in the pre-Diet days, even before moving to the commune, my health-conscious mother didn't permit such treats. And here was Toby, preparing to buy a feast, an orgy, a banquet of forbidden delights, Diet or no Diet. Not to be outdone, I went to the same aisle, and snatched brownies, cupcakes, and yes, Fudgecicles, from the freezer, bringing them, too, to the counter. The expressionless woman at the register eyed us suspiciously, but we put on our most innocent faces, and smiled sweetly, showing Toby's crumpled bills, and my scrounged-up change in our hands, so she rang us up. Clearly she didn't understand the depth and gravity of our deception.

We barely got out the door and down into the field before we sated our first hunger. Hostess Twinkies. So soft. Unbelievably sweet, with that sugary filling that coated my teeth, making them rough and gritty. Toby's mouth was white at the corners when he smiled. How we ate. Finally, we couldn't hold more, but still had packages and packages of sweets. We carried these to the bottom of the hill by the house, then stuffed them up under our shirts to go in, knowing that while a bag would be noticed and arouse curiosity, no one would see that our fronts were knobby.

Toby and I stored our loot under my bed, and over the next days, after docilely accepting meals of celery and almonds, raw cabbage leaves and tofu, we went upstairs, slipped into the dim cubby, and devoured the rest of our treats, cramming our mouths as full as possible, then making each other laugh. When we ran out, we went to Woodville for more.

For the first time since leaving Baltimore, I had a companion. Toby and I spent whole days together. I showed him all my favorite places, the quiet bank down by the creek, completely hidden by an overgrown bush, the aerie up in the big pine tree right in the yard, the tiny meadow across the field by the stream, and the creepy cow's graveyard in the adjoining field, a dozen skeletons and old skins strewn in a gully. I knew he would never tell. In imitation of the older kids, all of whom smoked, Toby and I tried smoking pine needles, and mullein leaves, rolling them in the wrappers of stolen tampons, since we could not find or steal any real papers. We played and joked around and shared all the rebellious disdain for the weirdness around us that I had thought only I experienced. Knowing that I wasn't alone with it anymore, I relaxed, letting go the belly knot of loneliness. Toby was a wicked mimic, and after community meetings, we would go upstairs, and he would re-enact the choice moments of the meetings, me laughing till my stomach ached. We may not have been exactly on The Diet, but it seemed to be working. Toby was breathing, and my eyes looked less hollow. Our mothers congratulated themselves, and we snickered up our sleeves.

Toby and I started sleeping out in the hay room, spreading our sleeping bags side-by-side, able to watch the stars and then the moon glide by as we talked, and then slept peacefully. He and I exchanged friendship bracelets—knotted nylon ropes that we sealed onto each other's wrists in the flame of a match, swearing never to cut them off. I was learning to play the guitar, and I wrote a song for him that I sang to him, not caring if I sounded ridiculous. For the first time, I felt that I belonged there, and that, with his companionship, I really was on a commune in the best sense of the word.

And then, after about six months, his mother inexplicably swooped down and snatched him away with all the violence and energy of a cyclone. She seemed angry, and brooked no argument from Toby, his face pale and tight as he questioned and protested. She merely grabbed the bag he had unwillingly thrown together in one hand, his arm in the other, and marched him to the car. We didn't get to say goodbye—just one miserable look exchanged between us, and the sight of his face pressed against the window as I ran after the car, crying, "Wait, you can't go, please don't take him away." I lost them at the first curve of the road, but stood there to watch their dust rising as the car sped along the gravel to the highway.

Did I know somehow that I would never see him again? His leaving was as painful and as final as any death, and standing there on the dusty road, grit mixing with tears on my face, it seemed nearly unbearable. It wasn't possible to go back to the house where no one would share my grief, where the crowded sense of solitude had crushingly returned, resettling on me in an instant—familiar, inescapable, leaden.

Do I *Really* Love You?

I began spending most of my time outside, where I felt less alone. Spring, I learned, approached slowly day-by-day. It sneaked up for weeks, quiet and unobtrusive. If I hadn't been watching closely, I would have missed it altogether. But I noticed every bush, as it was mysteriously misted red or green under cover of a single night. I noticed when buds began to swell, and knew when, deep within a wintered branch, the slow ooze of sap began to rise in ever-renewed growth.

Once the dogwoods were in bloom, everything happened so fast that I almost had to sit out on the hill day and night in order not to miss an important event. When did the first snowdrop bloom? When did the first spring herald arrive to sing insistently from her tree perch? The dandelions suddenly carpeted the lawn, and I loved their yellow intensity, and furry fulsomeness. After the dandelions, the gentle violets looked fragile in comparison. There were so many of them! But not as many as the fireflies on a deep August night. They were so thick, and so persistently lit, that the entire hillside sparkled and shimmered. Mysterious green lights, each calling in a unique staccato for love. Flashing for love. The chorus of frogs thrumming in the darkness was calling for love as well, as were the cicadas and tree frogs.

Loath to go indoors at all, I started sleeping outdoors as well. I loved to look up from the warmth of my bag, gazing at the multitude of stars and galaxies spread so lavishly across the sky. Always, there would be streaks of light, as some fragment fell across the firmament, and I would happily count them until my eyes closed. Even when alone, I had the comforting presence of the dogs, who invariably spread themselves around and on me, with the addition of the occasional goat and sometimes an errant chicken. During the night, especially if it was fine, more and more people would come out, the row of sleeping bags growing longer as one person after another came to bed. Sometimes it would begin to rain. I would ignore it as long as possible, thinking maybe it was just mist, a passing shower, not really rain, burrowing deeper into the comfort of my covers. I was often quite wet before I gave in, and grumblingly, along with others, went inside to crash in the living room on the floor or couch.

Most nights it didn't rain, and I would awaken very early, long before the first tendril of sun touched me directly. The heavy dampness of the dawn on my sleeping bag and pillow only accentuated my dry warmth inside. I would stretch my neck to see who had joined me, and where the dogs were, then lie back comfortably, watching the light develop, to the accompaniment of bird song. Those mornings were slow and long, and tranquil before the inevitable hubbub that I loved and hated that saturated every moment of our lives together.

Our most frequent gathering place was around the dining room table. There, three times a day, we could all be found in one room at the same time. Hardly anyone missed meals. Food was just a little too sparse to encourage that, and few came late, because the food went awfully fast. Still, with all the comings and goings, at every meal, each gathering was slightly different. As I ate and listened to the clanging of dishes and snippets of simultaneous conversations, I often looked around the circle face by face. I would focus hard on one, and in the privacy of thought, I would ask myself, "Do I love this person? Do I *really* love this person?"

Clearly I was supposed to. Love was the feeling we all were expected to have for, and give to, each other. "Love one another," wasn't just a line from a song, it was our creed. More important than peace, happiness or freedom, was love. It never occurred to me not to take this literally. Every person, I had heard over and over, is lovable in his or her own unique way. Every person deserves to be loved and cherished and celebrated simply for who he or she is. As soon as someone chose to be with us, he was instantly valued. Despite the fact that they were total strangers, there was a tacit expectation that each would be immediately accepted and loved without question. It was okay to not like someone, but not to not love him. I understood that I was supposed to have an instinctive recognition of each person's goodness-at-core, despite the variability in packaging. After all, how a person looked and acted was not an indication of her inner loveability. Some people seemed okay, some great, but many were weird, and a few were awful. People kept talking about love and family, but it didn't seem like family to me. And love?

Beginning at one end of the circle, I examined each person closely. I looked at Mark, and considered what I had thought the first time I saw him. I thought about whether I would trust him with a secret, whether I liked to hug him, what he was like first thing in the morning, how he treated me when no one else was around, whether he was funny or weird or scary. There was no doubt that I loved Mark, and longed to be important to him. I liked his surprising and shocking ideas. Mark was full of radical notions. He had ways of doing and seeing things that were always original. He did not automatically adhere to popular group sentiment, but evaluated everything on his own terms. A true entrepreneur, Mark was a free thinker. Everyone was horrified when he expressed admiration for McDonald's marketing and packaging. What he admired was the ingenious effectiveness with which the company operated, from Burger College to product names. "McMuffin!" Mark would say, shaking his head in appreciation. Not that he would actually ever admit to liking the food, although we did make several trips through the golden arches in the name of research or sociological observation. Mark was not afraid to act in unconventional, and controversial ways. Although it was accepted as common knowledge that Vitamin C was a desirable supplement, when Mark simply added it to the common jug of morning orange juice, there was an uproar. Some felt he was violating individual freedom of choice.

"You have no *right*," Ellen said indignantly, "to decide what is good for me, and administer it without my permission!"

"Oh, come on," answered Mark, "*everybody* takes Vitamin C, and especially when there is a cold going around, it's in all our best interest to help curb the spread."

"That's not the point," argued Ellen. "I object to you deciding when and whether something is good for me and I am going to take medicine."

"It's not medicine!" declared Mark. "It's just a vitamin! It's completely natural! It's *good* for you!"

"So what?" continued Ellen, thoroughly roused from her usual quiet manner. "Does that mean that you are going to start mixing Golden Seal in with my tea because you decide it's good for me? Or a little arsenic, maybe? That's natural too, you know. You know, homeopaths use poisons as medicine. Are you qualified to do that? Are you going to decide that it's better for me to wear blue than red and start picking out my clothes? Who do you think you are?"

After this, Mark contented himself with setting a bowl of powdered Vitamin C on the table by the juice with a sign instructing us to mix half a teaspoon per cup to get the recommended dose.

Mark organized several group clean-ups, in which he would harness a spirit of fun and competition to get things done. We each drew a chore out of a hat, were given time limits, rotating jobs, an inspection crew for quality assurance, and prizes. During these clean-ups, Mark periodically instructed individuals to play the piano, or relax in the living room, to enhance our awareness of the breadth and variety of contributions, and the inevitable inequities of labor. Those instructed to play or relax had priority over those instructed to clean. If you were assigned a job in a place where someone was relaxing or playing, you had to go away and do a different job, and come back when they were done. The first time, it worked wonderfully. We all had a good time, and a surprising amount of cleaning got done. There was no doubt that I loved Mark.

I felt most comfortable with Ellen and I knew I was special to her. Ellen was withdrawn and silent when she first came, but I befriended her, and we spent a lot of time together. She taught me German in an individual tutorial, just the two of us spending long hours under the pines. She was endlessly patient and calm, if a little grim at times. Usually, her long straight hair hid most of her face, which was plain and often grave, but when she was concentrating, she would sometimes unconsciously push it behind her ears, and her mien would lighten. At rare intervals, Ellen would laugh, her face briefly unrecognizable. She seemed to be always available to me. I could lean against her any time, and she would stroke my hair. This was the kind of affection it was hard for me to accept from my mother, but sorely missed. Unlike my mother, Ellen came with no strings attached. If I curled up with my head on her knee, she didn't take that as permission to probe and demand. She was soothing in her passivity. We were friends, but not buddies, and yes, I loved her.

Turning to Laurel, I thought about her quiet sadness, her face that became beautifully dreamy-calm when she was drawing or painting, her vagueness and unreliability, her rare excitement. Soon after she arrived, she and Mark formed a couple, and they really seemed to like each other. I remembered her pride when they presented the musical they had written together for us to perform as our annual play. Laurel had written the story and the lyrics to most of the songs, and Mark had put them to music, but the best song was the one where they changed places and Mark wrote the lyrics, and Laurel the melody. There was tremendous creative energy between them. They brought their play to us like a birthday present, full of pleasure in anticipation of our staging it, which we did, with great enjoyment. Did I love Laurel? Of course!

I didn't love Tim. He was a newcomer, and he was trying to be like Mark, but he wasn't. His bounciness made him look silly, and he was too cheerful by far. I don't know what it was about him—he had shoulder-length curly hair, and the requisite headband, and I am sure there was a lot to know about him, as with anyone else, but

I didn't know any of it, and wasn't very interested. He was irritating and too enthusiastic. He taught math, and I never went to his class. No, I didn't love Tim.

Suzanne was difficult. Utterly self-assured, unburdened by my load of anxieties and inhibitions, she exuded vigor and determination. She was completely unapologetic, un-self-conscious, and above all, natural. Astrology was a popular topic of the day, and taken quite seriously. The fact that Suzanne and I shared the zodiac sign of Leo felt like a rebuke to me. I was a sorry excuse for a Leo, having none of the charisma, gregariousness and force I was supposed to have and she did have. But Suzanne also seemed crude, and at times inconsiderate. I didn't really like her, and didn't think she really liked me, but she was a central person, so I guessed I loved her.

Louise's limpid brown eyes were always tear-brimming. She swept tragically around the yard, as if trailing weeds, overcome with the calamity of life. Although her sadness was clearly less real than Laurel's, it was around Louise that people gathered, showering her with tender reassurances and promises of protection. I knew she was a fake, and hated that her obvious ploys were so effective. I also envied her her huge brown eyes, so profoundly full of tears. Did I love Louise? Not really.

I rarely made it all the way around the circle. It got tiresome.

I was supposed to love each and every person. But I didn't. Feeling guilty, and a little worried that someone would know what I was thinking, I considered and weighed, studied each face, mulled over my feelings, and often changed my mind. I tried to think quietly, to avoid discovery. I wasn't fully convinced that my thoughts couldn't be heard or read, and my heart beat hard at this secret exercise of freedom.

They were strangers and strange and there was all this talk about family, extended family, communal family, family this or that. Well, this wasn't my family, I was clear about that. I hadn't gained new family members, I had lost hard. My family was . . . well, where was my family? Like a duffel bag, so overstuffed that its own shape was lost, my family was unrecognizable, and grossly incomplete. It was such a mixture of loss and gain, belonging and alienation, lonely and crowded. Sometimes it was as if all these people were crows roosting in the tops of trees, and I, a flightless bird, could see them only from below, and hear their cackle.

Mother Interlude

The phone rings at 8:01 am. My four-year-old daughter has just settled down for her precious half hour of TV, a hard-wrung compromise from me. Richard is sleeping in this morning, and I have one hand on the coffee pot, as I reach for the phone.

"Hello?"

"Hi! Want to hear a poem?" comes the voice of my mother. I am glad to hear the vibrancy of her voice, and know that she has been waiting until the earliest possible moment to call without waking me. She is an hour ahead of us anyway, and on a good morning, she will rise at 5:30 or 6:00 and write poetry for a couple of hours before doing whatever else she does with her time. Clearly she has been waiting a couple of hours.

"Sure," I say, "just a second." I put down the coffee cup, and go out on the porch, pulling closed the sliding glass door as a barrier between me and *Dragon Tales*, my daughter's current favorite. I sit at the table out there, where the air is cool, and the morning birds are singing wildly. "Okay."

"I wrote it this morning. I don't know if it's any good:

> "LOVE IN THE COMMUNE
>
> Yesterday Sandra confessed
> that in fact she had not loved them
> back then when we belonged
> to our intimate community

where love, lets face it,
was the price of admission,
part of the unwritten constitution

"Apparently in our endless meetings
as we tried
hour after hour
to find consensus somewhere somehow,
she would look from face to face
and without flinching
—because that's the kind of kid she was—
she would admit to herself,
'I do not love him.'
'I do not love her.'
And she knew she sinned.

"'But darling
you must have known
I didn't love each and every one
Laurel, maybe. Maybe Mark.'

"'I knew.'

"'And that didn't help?'

"Her silence was tactful
as I fell into the ache of remembering
how much the commune
had diminished me—the Mother

"But sweetheart, Sandra
if you mean the love that
ignites our body chemistry
so that every cell
surges along with our soul
to meet the beloved
then no—we didn't love them

"But there's another kind of love
What those nutty swimmers must feel for each other
when they race towards the icy waters

of the winter ocean
what climbers feel
as they ascend Mount Everest.

"We were visionaries
even if our visions weren't the same.
Our families refused to understand.
The neighbors were hostile.
What we gave each other
was the courage
to live our visions—or try
and wasn't that, Sandra,
wasn't that love?"

The poem makes me cry, of course. And think, again, about how hard we all try to do what we think is best, for ourselves, for those we love, and how little we know about how our choices will affect us or them. I had forgotten telling my mother about my "Do I love him" meditations, but now I remember that I did, the last time we were together. There is always tension, because I have let no one in my family read any of this book, but they are well aware of its existence. My mother in particular suffers, I am guessing, from fear of a *Mommy Dearest* sort of expose, which isn't at all what I have in mind, or heart, although much of this will hurt her. So every once in a while, I try to tell her something innocuous about what I have been writing. And here we go again, the most innocuous to me turns out to have been hurtful to her, despite my best intentions.

"I love it," I say. "Of course I have no idea if it works as a poem, I'm too close to it."

"But what do you think, I mean about the love?"

"There's just one problem," I answer, struggling to find the way to say what I want her to hear. "You see, the problem was that it wasn't my dream."

Cachunk.

I hear it drop into that place of involuntary wounding, I hear her register it, take it in, *hear* it for the first time. I have tried over the years to clue her in to some of what this experience was like for me, because in her memory it was all wonderful, free-spirited, happy happy, and every time I signal that yes, yes, that was true but . . . there was more, she gets that look on her face, the lines tightening around her mouth, the eyes drooping more in their already heavily lined housing. I hate it. And here it is.

But "Yes," she says for the first time, "I see what you mean. I guess I really don't know what it was like for you. Sometimes I wonder where I was all those years."

"Me too," I think.

But what adult knows what the child's eye sees? There is nothing so unique about being hostage to a parent's dream, to living it out as if it were one's own. Children don't have dreams like that.

I was just in the park with my daughter, and saw a group of Mennonites or Amish with their layers of heavy clothing, thick black stockings, ugly brown shoes and hair hidden beneath caps. There they were in the hot August sun, playing on the slides and swings just as we were, and once I got past wondering how they could stand being so warmly dressed, I started thinking about the mark of difference that they carry, just as I did, and the meaning of it to them, and how they won't question it until later years, but are just as much prisoner to it as I or you or any child. That aspect isn't unique, it is all relative. The farther the parent's vision is from the rest of society, the greater the task for the child who wants to integrate into the mainstream world.

I am struggling, glad that my mother seems receptive this morning to hearing about my point of view. The desire to be understood by one's parents is so powerful that it gets me going even now in my forties when maybe it shouldn't really matter any more. I am thrilled, in this conversation, that my mother understood for a moment what I was talking about, and that I was able to share with her this theme, the theme of the child swept along in the current of the adult's infatuation, believing it utterly, more completely even than the parent, and trying to make sense of it, and make sense of her own failure to uphold it. As a mother myself, I see how easy it is to make the mistake of thinking that I know the meaning of things to my daughter. I don't. What does it mean to her that we had to give up one of the dogs because he couldn't stop peeing in the living room? What does it mean to her that we moved out of the house she was born in? She already has her own life and her own meanings, and it is a challenge to stay tuned in and not to construct meaning for her or in her name. Besides, don't we all hate our parents a little bit for exposing us to life and its complexities?

Mother Loss

When my mother suggested to my sister Rachel that she call her by her given name, instead of Mommy, I was intrigued. I could not guess her reasons for doing such an odd thing. Rachel rejected the suggestion out of hand, as she rejected most suggestions from that source. Although she had ultimately taken to our new life much more readily than I, she had never forgiven our mother for uprooting us and moving us away from our home. That an idea came from our mother was reason enough to disregard it. I, however, was captivated. I tested my mother's name on my tongue, and found it an unwieldy substance, with a forbidden tang.

The first time I called her by her name, I used it like a weapon in the middle of an argument. We were down in the parking lot by the cars. Mommy was forcing me to go into town with her. She had to go to the doctor, and had some notion of "Mother-Daughter Time." It was an idea that would have appealed to me if it had come when I wanted it, but this was on her time, not mine. Was I supposed to drop everything and run, just because she decided she wanted to do something with me for a change? She insisted that I go, and all the way down to the car I was making myself as unpleasant as possible. Sullen and resentful, I ignored her attempts at conversation, averting my face, and walking two steps behind her, no matter how much she slowed down and waited for me.

"What is *wrong* with you?" she finally exploded. "You are acting like such a sourpuss."

"Why are you making me go with you?" I challenged.

"So we can spend some time together," she insisted impatiently.

"I don't want to right now."

"Why not?"

"I just *don't*!"

"Well, I think you will feel differently once we're in the car," she said, working to remain calm.

"Who says I want to feel differently?"

"Oh, come on, Sandra!" now getting exasperated.

"Do I have a choice?"

"What exactly is going on that is so important that you can't come with me for a few hours?"

"What exactly is so exciting about driving with you for a half an hour there and half an hour back, all to sit in a doctor's office while you have an appointment? You are *forcing* me to do something I don't want to do. How would *you* feel about that?"

"I am *forcing* you to spend some special time with your *mother*!" she returned, angry now.

"What is so special about that?"

"Good God!" she yelled. "You are so *impossible*, Sandra."

Here was my chance.

"So are you, *Carla*!"

It stopped her mid-breath, slamming full speed into her solar plexus. The moment hung there, her face opened in hurt, wind rushing out.

What she had offered to my eldest sister in a moment of modern parenting—an effort to acknowledge my sister's maturity, and to help move their difficult relationship to a more harmonious balance—had a very different meaning coming from me, the youngest, and still her "baby."

The one thing my mother had not counted on in starting Nethers was losing her family. Although she fought it clumsily, the larger group had absorbed her family. Either you lived in a commune, or you didn't. No halfway position existed. My calling her by name was pure revenge for her taking away my family. She no longer had a right to her title. She couldn't bring me to live in this way and expect that we would have the same mother-daughter relationship we would have had under "normal" circumstances. She had to pay too, by becoming just one of many. As I felt I was.

As soon as her breath returned she shrieked,

"YOU . . . CALL . . . ME . . . MOMMY."

But I didn't and wouldn't, and never did again.

All my rage and confusion and pain funneled into that small symbolic act, and I savored her helplessness. She couldn't make me. She could yell and scream and stomp her feet, but she couldn't make me.

She finally flung herself into her car and took off, roaring down the dirt road, raising a wide cloud of dust that immediately made her invisible. I tried to ignore the guilt and regret that was mixed in with the triumph. Of course she had been right, I would have had a good time going to town with her. We would have gotten ice-cream cones after her appointment, sitting side by side on the high stools in the old-fashioned ice-cream parlor, maybe walked down Main Street to window-shop. It wasn't that I didn't enjoy her company, it wasn't that at all. I often longed for her. But I had a point to make, and I had made it. Tears stinging in my eyes, I turned back up the hill, away from the house, heading for the forest where I could cry in private.

Something was different after I used her name in that fight. She acknowledged (or I saw) the limitations of her power over me. Having declared my own private war, wanting to hurt her badly, I did. But it was ultimately my loss. My denial of her as mother became irreversible, and even decades later, the rage worn down to a tempered understanding, I still wanted a mom. But like a magician who has lost her spells, I could not change her back.

Perhaps as a result of my declaration, Carla suddenly realized that she really had lost her daughters and any semblance of a nuclear family unit. In a panic, she declared that Wednesdays would be Family Night. Each of the three biological families in the community were supposed to get together, away from the larger group, to spend "family time" and strengthen their biological bonds. Those left behind were supposed to gather as well, forming an ersatz family of their own.

Exercising her remaining shreds of parental power to their fullest capacity, Carla insisted, bullied and harangued until Rachel, Erica, and I got reluctantly into the car. Within the commune, our mother, by definition, lost some of her impact as a parent, because so much of what she practiced as a more traditional mom went against the widely held philosophy of how adults and children should interact with each other. But when she had decided that she didn't *care* about this philosophy, all pretense dropped, and she was going to make us do as she demanded, come what may.

We were headed back to the original cabin we had first moved into, where we were supposed to spend our family time and stay for the night. Rachel and Erica were particularly sullen in the face of this unexpected return of Mother in her most authoritarian guise. They were older, fully integrated into the community, belonging to the largest peer group, and were deeply invested in projects, events and interpersonal dramas. To be dragged away for a day and a night meant possibly to miss important happenings.

Before reaching our destination, Carla pulled into the Etlan General Store. With a stern admonition to "stay put, all of you," she went in, coming out several minutes later with a large brown grocery bag, which she stowed in the trunk, pre-empting any attempts to explore its contents. None of us really cared. We were listless and silent.

Arriving at the cabin, Carla took the mysterious bag into the kitchen, instructing us to "Stay Out." We sat silently in the living room, three in a row on the old couch. I looked around curiously at this place that had been the first stop in such a transformation of our lives. I had almost forgotten about it. I had been vaguely aware that we still owned it, and that my mother occasionally tried to rent it furnished to vacationing city dwellers. It seemed smaller than ever and dingy, with a moldy, un-lived in smell.

After her usual extended clatter and commotion, Carla triumphantly produced four tall, frosty, ice-cream sodas. We stared at them in disbelief, partly at the transparency of her bribe, partly at the degree of departure from normal values. We didn't want to give in to this, but fell on them nonetheless like hungry dogs. Ice cream sodas had been a stand-by for special occasions in our pre-communal days, one of Carla's few culinary masterpieces. But here in this small dank cabin, as the four of us slurped dutifully on our straws, a sharp and bitter taste floated amidst the sweetness. The familiar fizz and bubble did not bring back the old feeling. Nonetheless, we ate ourselves silly. We then turned on the old black and white TV, its unfamiliar blue light as alien as what was on the screen. We watched sit-coms, bad movies, and a brief show about seals. In a sugared stupor, the four of us sprawled immobile on the couch. Finally, at 11:00, way past Carla's famous "bedtime," I dragged myself off to sleep. In the morning, hung over, we gorged on slice after slice of toasted "salt rising" white bread with butter, reveling in its insubstantiality and salty-sweet taste, so unlike the thick chewy whole grain fare to which we had become accustomed.

This set the pattern of our Wednesday nights. Sometimes we went to the movies, or played games, or took walks, often we fought, but the one thing that never changed was the consumption of huge quantities of forbidden foods. It seemed that the effort to gather us together physically sapped her energy, and our mother couldn't bring us back to family spirit.

Without Carla there to enforce it, none of the other families followed her example. We gradually realized that the Wednesdays that went on without us had an unusually festive air. Just as we were getting ready to go, it would become apparent that something exciting was going to happen in our absence. Clearly there was a special freedom with us gone, because Carla was undeniably The Heavy. She was the one who dampened the thrill of the most exciting plans with some cautionary point, insisting that things be done through the proper channels, and without rushing. She had always been a worrier, and while the community had diffused her worry, it had not eliminated it. We had a fair idea of what the place was like when Carla was gone. We sensed the lightness and freedom that emerged in her absence, and were sorry to miss it. The place was clearly more fun when we were gone, or at least when she was. Restraint was lifted, and people were freer to do as they wished. Meals were skipped, rules ignored, risks taken, and it often seemed that some wonderful group event was just evaporating as we topped the hill on our return. We were absent when Jeff fell off the roof, when Jon got bitten by a mouse, when the chicken races were organized, and when everyone went to town to steal quinces from the tree in the square and almost got caught by the sheriff. We always missed the fun.

It was difficult to be Carla's daughter. In meetings, hers was usually the voice of dissent, and she could be counted upon to demand a direct reckoning for every conflict, a firm commitment for every agreement, with consequences spelled out if the commitment was not met. Many resented her, which was no secret, though she undeniably provided the stability necessary for our survival. People tried to catch themselves when they began expressing their resentments in front of my sisters or me, but we often heard it anyway. While their anger was much milder than my own, I automatically became defensive. I did not want to have to defend her, yet I did not want to hear other's attacks. I needed to be sure that she could withstand my own storms of rage. Her vulnerability when she was at the center of wider dissent was too clear to me. She too, wanted to be loved and accepted; she too, was sensitive and in some ways insecure, the passion of her ideals only barely outweighing a natural shyness. I hated going away, partly because I sensed shared resentment building up unchecked in our absence, and feared that it could pick up power, changing from a dust swirl to a twister, with all the power of destruction. That's the way I experienced my own feelings toward Carla, but it was discomfiting to have others echo, or preempt my rage. And I so wanted to be wrong.

14

Rosy Thyme & Sweet Violet

Every Thursday afternoon, right after lunch, we had Community
Meeting. Soon after moving, Bob had discovered a big iron triangle
in a junkyard and hung it outside the kitchen door. We used it to
announce meals and Community Meeting, classes, clean-ups, and
any other group activity, ringing it by clanging an old fire poker
around in a circle. All decisions, large and small, were made in these
meetings, and everyone was expected to attend. Where to plant the
garden, whether to buy a new goat, how to keep Bill the sheep out
of the yard (he ate the lilacs), whether to build a canning kitchen,
how often to go to town to do the laundry, how to get people to
do their chores, how to enforce the No Pissing Off The Roof Rule,
how to enforce the rule that people had to put themselves in "Isolation" when sick, how to keep the dogs from chasing the goats, how
to keep the goats from worrying the horses (especially Buffy, who
liked to chew on Cindy's tail), when to paint the kitchen, and what
color, whether to accept a new member into the community, what
to put in the newsletter, rules for use of the (pay)phone, rules for use
of the shower, rules for length of time spent in the bathroom in general, rules about making noise in the evening, rules about language
and smoking cigarettes and alcohol, rules about who could go on
what trips, and more—all material for Community Meetings.

The existence of these rules was weird. Ironic really. A lot of folks
came to Nethers exactly to escape rules, only to find that even on a
commune, some rules were necessary. There were even a handful

of meeting rules. Every participant was to have ample opportunity to speak, and no one was to be pressured to contribute if he or she preferred not to. People were not to interrupt, allowing the person who "had the floor" a respectful opportunity to express his or her views—at length, if need be. These rules did nothing to mask the inevitable tensions of so many different personalities packed into tight quarters. No one was supposed to launch personal attacks, but no topic was too trivial to evolve into a battle about a personal conflict, and even the most benign agenda item could suddenly erupt into full blown emotional conflict. Our meetings were really about us, and our relationships with each other.

My mother Carla was too controlling. She always had the final say, consistently held the most conservative position, and somehow was the only one who could autocratically declare something out of the question or imperative, regardless of group opinion. Despite the unconventional path she had taken in her life, my mother had never shed her fundamental middle-class values. True to her upbringing, she expected children to not talk back, abhorred profanity and slang, and was intolerant of deception or dishonesty. She was, in short, the antithesis of cool, insisting bull-doggedly on responsibility, accountability, clarity, and commitment.

Bob was irresponsible. He had many talents, not least of which was a gift for shoplifting. For a while, there was a competition over who could get away with the most spectacular heist. Cross appreciated this contest, and had a lot to offer us by way of technique. Learning could go both ways, and Cross was glad to be in the position of expert for a change. He and Bob were a match, each trying to outdo the other. Bob won hands down by stealing a bridle, hiding it under his coat, and gallantly presenting it to Cindy, Rachel's horse, as a gift. He declared that his next target was a saddle. At this point, Carla, who had been pointedly ignoring the whole thing, insisted that he was being irresponsible and reckless, corrupting Cross, and placing us all at risk.

Dave was downright lazy. He made of show of doing things— always something out of sight of the house—but he never produced anything. He could predictably be found lying on his back gazing at the sky, at the site of whatever it was he was supposedly doing, sort of waiting for it to take care of itself.

Mark was impatient. He wanted things to get done now, and expected everyone to drop what they were doing and join him in what he had decided was most important. Suzanne was unrealistic. She didn't understand why we couldn't build the canning kitchen, a kiln, and paint the outside of the house this month, and was already trying to figure out how many one-by-six boards to order for the kitchen platform. Fletcher was uncompromising, Alan oblivious, Laurel unreliable, Ellen compulsive, and Tim, our newest member, was dishonest. Mostly, we were all intensely together, having to find sufficient agreement to sleep, eat, work, learn, and be-there under one roof. And the time we were most focused on being together was during Community Meeting.

It was in Community Meeting that Suzanne confronted Alan for using the term "bitch" in a misogynistic and derogatory manner, a discussion that, after the obligatory dog joke developed into a prolonged and heated debate about the differences or lack thereof between the sexes. At another meeting, Carla's request that we not use so much profanity in general, especially around visitors or prospective students, evolved into a harangue about freedom of speech vs. freedom of hearing. The concept of "second-hand smoke" had not yet been introduced, but the notion of being poisoned by others' voluntary emissions was old news to us. Ellen complained about Bob piling things that needed to go up at the bottom of the stairs where she kept tripping on them, which developed into a quite personal assessment of each person's industriousness or lack thereof. Bob confronted Laurel with the fact that the last three times she had signed up to cook a meal she forgot and was nowhere to be found, and in general could not be counted on, which generalized into a prolonged discussion about personal responsibility, and who was lacking in this fine quality. Anything was fair game for Community Meeting. When discussions got particularly heated, Carla would get the "peace pipe," which was represented by an object—a candle, a feather, or a scarf—

and the only person who could speak was the one holding it. This usually slowed things down enough for tempers to calm.

I dreaded these meetings, and they lasted forever. Opinions were impassioned, and tempers ran hot. Few meetings adjourned without at least one person yelling "Nobody should!" and stomping out with a door slam. The outbursts were frightening, even when they were my own. I found the personal nature of the confrontations upsetting, dreading the day that I would be the object of one. And it was hard to bear my own strong feelings and opinions. I became as heated as anyone, and more than once felt disheartened by the puniness of my influence. Freedom apparently did not mean getting what I wanted. It did mean that I had to tolerate other people's points of view, even if they were stupid, and that I often did not get my way. Others' opinions, it seemed, were obnoxiously equal to mine.

No standing policy or condition could be changed without a consensus to do so. This meant every minute detail was discussed until a meeting of minds was found through flexibility and compromise (or until everyone left the meeting). If a consensus could not be found, the change did not occur. Any member of the group, regardless of age or standing, could "block consensus," declaring a flat refusal to negotiate or agree to a middle-ground solution. This final "NO" was a weighty power, and generally exercised only under extreme conditions.

One particular Thursday, people drifted in and sat or lounged, roughly in a circle, occupying the various chairs and couches or pillows on the floor. Three sat on the window seat Laurel had built, one in the big brown recliner—the most coveted spot. Many people were touching—legs casually crossed over others', one person's head in another's lap, shoulders gently meeting. Bob and Jeffrey, a temporary member just beginning his probationary month, sat spine to spine, providing backrests for each other. Laurel had her head in Mark's lap, Dave was rubbing Suzanne's foot. People often brought crafts projects into the meeting to help them concentrate. Right then, Suzanne was crocheting, Tim was threading beads onto a loom to make a new headband, and Rachel was knitting. Carla disapproved of these manual occupations, thinking that they distracted from the meeting, but here she had been unable to assert her influence. She had brought it up at several Community Meetings, and consistently no one else seemed to care. We were a colorful chaos of bright peasant blouses, T-shirts and jeans cutoffs, uncombed hair, wild beards, African print caftans, and headbands.

Before each meeting began, we had an "opening," intended to enliven our energies and allow us to focus. One popular opening was a trust game where we all stood close in a circle, and each person in turn went into the center, closed his or her eyes, and simply fell in any direction, knowing (hoping) that he or she would be caught by the tight ring of people, held up by a multiplicity of hands, and then passed gently around the circle. When I was in the middle I felt dizzy, not really worried about being dropped—I was small and light—but disoriented by having so many unidentified hands catching me at the small of the back, the elbow, the forehead, wherever I landed. It was an eerie feeling.

Sometimes the opener would have us all go lie on our backs in a long line on the grass in the back yard, and gaze up at the clouds, shouting out the different images we spotted as they shifted, stretched and wisped away. On a rainy day, we would learn to sing a new round, do a dance with concentric circles moving in opposite directions, or we might lie down in a ring on the living room floor for "Ha Ha Herman," each person resting his or her head on the belly of one person, with the head of the next person resting on them. Then the leader would say "HA!" bouncing the head on his belly. The next person said "HA! HA!" the third "HA! HA! HA!" Somewhere around the fourth or fifth person, someone would get the giggles, and we invariably dissolved into free-form laughter, heads bouncing this way and that on bellies large and small, hard and soft.

This time, Mark told us we were going to see how many people we could fit in the telephone closet. A small foyer at the top of the basement stairs created this tiny space, two feet square. Here we had installed a pay phone, a stool to sit on and a pen, hanging on a string by the side of the phone. The walls were covered with writing; phone numbers, messages often never delivered, and doodles made during long conversations. We started piling in, each person standing as close as possible to the next, arms in the air to make more space, piling three high on the stool, with Jeanie squishing in under it. Jeffrey managed to brace himself high in a doorjamb over our heads, calling himself Spiderman. Clayton consented to being lifted to sit on the phone itself, and we actually closed the door, with fourteen people squeezed into the space. For that brief moment, in the warm tight press of bodies, feeling all the different textures of skin and clothing, different smells and temperatures, I felt us as one organism, a lively unruly beast—well-meaning, unpredictable, very much alive. We came bursting out, laughing and gasping for air. Russell, one of the first out, managed to hang himself up on a hook in the hallway by the collar of his shirt, and dangled there, head flopping, toes just grazing the ground. Mark, Alan and Suzanne together lifted him off and carried him into the meeting. Settling back into our original places, some picking up their crafts projects, we began the meeting.

"Who is facilitating today?" Carla asked.

"Ellen," Suzanne said. Ellen had just been accepted as a full member. Since her arrival three months earlier, she had become slightly less serious. When at rest, her face was still sober, framed by her long straight hair parted down the middle. But now, when animated by interest or humor her face took on a new lightness.

"Who's taking minutes?"

"I am," Bob said.

"Would you read the minutes from last week, please?" Ellen asked.

I was never sure why we adhered to this archaic formality. It seemed to serve primarily to remind people of how stuck we had gotten the last week, instead of allowing us to forge ahead on the new positive energy engendered by the opening. Why not let the past be the past, particularly as nothing ever got settled, so the past was always brought back into the present anyway.

Nonetheless, hands passed the notebook around to Bob. It was a thick three-ring binder, with a nature photograph on the cover, depicting a waterfall and a stream in the woods. The pages inside were filled with writing in many hands, most of it illegible. There was more doodling than writing, intricate abstract designs, and rough sketches of people, signs of the many hours spent there.

"There aren't any in here!" Bob said.

"Who took minutes at the last meeting?" Ellen asked.

"Alan was supposed to," Bob said, after consulting the notes from two weeks before.

"Alan? Where are the minutes? Didn't you take minutes?" Ellen asked.

"Yes, I did," Alan replied.

"Then where are they?"

"They're not in there," Alan said.

"I know that," Bob said, "I already looked. Where are they?"

"You can't see them. I took mental minutes," Alan explained.

"Well, we need to read them," Ellen requested patiently.

"You want to read my mind?" asked Alan, affronted.

"Not particularly," Ellen answered. "Why don't you read your own mind, and tell us what happened?"

"Oh. Okay. Well, we talked about a lot of stuff, and nothing got decided."

Ellen persevered. "What did we talk about?"

"Oh, clean-ups, and the rats, and the fact that people have been using too much water. And Carla complained that people are making too much noise after quiet hour."

Ellen sighed. "Well, okay, let's start with a check-in, and then we'll have the agenda. Who wants to start?"

A "check-in" was our custom of going around the room and giving each person a chance to say a few words about how they were feeling. We were not supposed to respond to each other, just to allow each person a moment to say something about what was on his or her mind, or "where" we each were.

"I'll start!" said Tim. "I've been thinking how cool it would be if we built a duck pond! I've found a spring up the hill, and I was thinking we could dam it up and flood that whole little valley, and it would be really far out. So I'm pretty excited!"

Alan was next to Tim, and we all looked at him expectantly. "Mmmmmph!" said Alan, in his typically communicative manner, still rattled over the minutes incident.

"Ummm," Suzanne pushed her wire-rim glasses higher up on her nose, and put her long blonde hair behind her ears, "I'm feeling pretty good about things. I feel really in tune with you all, and I appreciate all the positive energy going around. Uhh," she wrinkled up her nose, "I guess that's it."

Dave continued to knead Suzanne's foot as he spoke. "I just want to say that you all are really fine people, and all the love around here is far out."

"Well," said Ellen, "I am a little frustrated, because I've been trying to caulk the windows so the house will be better insulated, and the last person who used the caulk gun didn't clean it, so I can't get a good seal with it, and it's making a mess. I wish people could be just a little more careful about cleaning tools so the next person can use them. Otherwise I'm fine."

And so it went, each person having his or her say and "clearing" so that they could focus their energy on the meeting itself, and the matters at hand. After the check-in, we started on the agenda.

About an hour or so into the meeting, Fletcher suddenly appeared. Several people were surprised to see him. His tardiness wasn't so unusual, what struck us was that he had come at all. Although indispensable in solving all practical problems, Fletcher took little interest in the personal aspects of group life. Since Community Meetings were heavily dominated by interpersonal matters, he avoided them, instead going about his business, making decisions and acting on them without troubling about other people's opinions or feelings. Fletcher's productivity was fantastic. In ten short months, he had already winterized the Theatre, soundproofed the Music Shed, fenced off one completely new garden, and fixed the fence on the old one, repaired the porch steps, fashioned countless handles, hinges, hangers, and fasteners, and completed innumerable other jobs. He was outside most of the time, coming in only for meals, and to read before going to bed. In some ways, he didn't really seem to belong to the group. Now, standing in the doorway to the large living room where we were all gathered, Fletcher looked as if he had gotten off the plane in the wrong country. He stood rigidly upright in his worn blue workshirt and pants, with the air of quiet reserve common to those accustomed to long hours of solitude.

A silence fell at Fletcher's entrance, and for one sharp moment it was hard to fit him into the same picture with Jeffrey, the person nearest to him. Jeffrey was now lying on the floor, his head in Suzanne's lap. He had to tilt his head back over Suzanne's legs, looking upside down toward the door, to see the newcomer. In this position, his beard pointed straight at the ceiling, and his spine arched, exposing his pale belly and the dark line of hair descending into low-slung jeans. He was wearing an old, too-small T-shirt he had tie-dyed in a vile combination of orange and green. His bare feet sported astonishingly long toes, which were now splayed widely, frog-like. He was all loose relaxation, yielding readily to the same gravity that Fletcher proudly defied.

Fletcher picked his way over and around people to the shabby green velour couch we had gotten at an auction. Most of us avoided this couch, as it was incredibly hard and prickly. It served primarily to house the amazing number and variety of brilliantly colored pillows Suzanne crocheted. Suzanne crocheted during meetings, during meals, in the evening, outside, in the out-house, and in the car. She had several baskets of wool and supplies scattered throughout the house, so she always had a pillow to work on. She never went beyond pillows, though we had more than we could ever possibly use or want. They now served every purpose, from launchable weapons to something to put under one leg of the table to stop it from wobbling. I wondered sometimes what would happen if she continued forever, imagining the entire floor becoming a cushioned sea, bumpy and bright.

Fletcher carefully moved six or seven pillows to make a space for himself, picking them up gingerly with his rough fingers, and piling them high at one end of the couch. He sat down, his bony knees protruding sharply. Gradually, our conversation resumed, and Fletcher quietly turned his hat in his hands while we discussed clean-ups, and the fact that people were not doing their jobs. Tim complained the he didn't feel supported in his efforts as jobs coordinator, and asked for a "go 'round" on that topic. He had a tendency to become overbearing in his authority and made me, at least, less inclined to do chores by constantly reminding me. We went around the circle, each of us in turn giving Tim feedback, and telling him, as nicely as we could, to get off our backs. Then we began talking about the garden. Mark had taken over the garden from Bob, and he had developed a spring planting plan, and was asking for volunteers to dig post-holes for a new fence to keep the goats out. Posthole digging was a laborious, frustrating, and unpopular job, especially in our hard and rocky Virginia soil. No one volunteered.

The garden was a source of great irritation to Fletcher. He was a sensible man, gifted with a hammer and nails, skilled in all kinds of practical matters, and committed to efficiency, logic, and economy. The garden violated all three of these qualities. Despite Mark's painstaking plans, diagrams, and calendars, the rows whimsically took off in all directions, changing crops without warning or reason, and wasting a tremendous amount of space. Anyone who had a yen for Jerusalem artichokes or beets, corn or chard, planted their chosen crop, often neglecting to mark what they had put in, creating a garden of constant mystery and speculation. Was that healthy patch of growth, weed or vegetable? Flower or foe?

Fletcher had little interest in Mark's beloved notions of pest repellence through plant pairing that came out of the *Organic Gardener*. Bean beetles were reputed to hate radishes, so beans and radishes were interspersed. Onions were sweeter if planted next to lettuce. Potato bugs hated the smell of parsley, and so on. As Mark lectured us about the importance of thinking before sowing (and eventually reaping), Fletcher started fidgeting. After a bit, he abruptly stood up, returned his hat to his head, walked to the door and said, "Well, at least we won't have to worry about meat this fall, I've got a pair of young pigs in the truck." And he went out the door.

"WHAT??!"

In a confusion of questions and surprise, Tim ran after Fletcher and brought him back into the room. Standing again in the doorway, he impatiently fielded our questions, batting each one back as quickly as it came.

"What pigs? Pigs from where?"

"I got 'em at the market."

"But what will we do with them?"

"Feed 'em, and take 'em to the slaughterhouse come winter."

"But where will we keep them?"

"I got a pen set up by the lower garden."

"How old are they?"

"Some months."

"What are their names?"

"Hell if I know."

"What do they look like?"

"Come see fer yourselves."

"We're not going to eat them, are we?"

At this, Fletcher turned, and stomped out the door. We could not restrain ourselves, but straggled after him. There in the back of the red pickup were, indeed, two smallish pink pigs. Their eyes were bright, their noses long, their ears were wide and supple, and their soft pink skin was almost translucent. Sure enough, silly little corkscrew tails curled up on their rumps. They snuffled at our eager hands, and their noses were moist and gentle. I touched one under the belly, right by its leg. It was warm and suede-soft. They were very cute.

Without anyone having noticed, Fletcher had put up a fenced enclosure at the bottom of the hill with a lean-to, roofed with scraps of corrugated tin. We escorted the pigs down to their new home en masse, showing them, and inspecting for ourselves, the feeding troughs, the straw pile under the shed, and all the nice roots for digging. I found two shriveled old apples from the tree across the fence, which the pigs gobbled greedily, splitting them easily in their back teeth, and chewing with obvious enjoyment.

"Uh, the meeting's not over," Carla said. "Fletcher, you should have brought this up with the community before acting on it."

"What's a coupla pigs?" Fletcher asked.

"Well, let's discuss that," said Carla.

"You discuss," said Fletcher. "You want me to get rid of 'em, you just tell me." And he headed for the tool shed.

We reconvened in the living room. The discussion began.

"First of all," Carla said, "I feel strongly that Fletcher should have brought this decision up to Community Meeting before just going out and buying the pigs. I wish he would join us."

"Well," said Russell, "Fletcher told me that he didn't go there with pigs in mind. When he saw them, and the price was good, he just decided it was a good idea. I think it's far out."

"I agree with Carla," Suzanne offered. "I mean, I don't know what I would have said if he had brought it up first at the meeting, but it doesn't feel right that we are deciding what to do *after* the pigs are already here."

"Well, I think it makes perfect sense that he got them," Jeffrey said. "When something comes your way, it is important to seize the moment. I mean it's like karma or something. If you turn your back on it, you're like saying 'no' to what the universe is offering, and that's not cool, man."

"Whatever Fletcher should or shouldn't have done, we still have to decide what we are going to do with the pigs now," said Ellen, always practical.

Several people made noises and nods of assent.

"Okay," said Carla. "You're right. So what do people think of the idea of us raising pigs for our own consumption?"

"It seems to me," stated Mark, "that Fletcher's move was a stroke of genius. We've always planned to grow most of our own food. We have the garden for vegetables, the chickens for eggs, and the goats for milk. Why haven't we thought of this before? It's totally in sync with our goals."

"But we don't eat meat," declared Suzanne. "Or at least not much."

"I do!" Mark said and continued, "No really! You're right, we don't eat meat, or at least not much, but isn't that just because we can't afford to? I mean how many of us are, like, really vegetarians?

Who here doesn't eat meat when they get the chance?" He looked around the room. Nobody said anything.

"But how can we raise an animal and then kill it to eat it?" asked Suzanne. "We are all against war and capital punishment and killing. I mean we don't even kill the spiders that we find in the house, we take them outside, and then we're going to turn around and kill some poor innocent pigs?"

"Every time you eat a hamburger, you're eating an innocent animal that was killed," Tim pointed out.

"I don't like hamburgers," Suzanne said.

"Okay, a chicken salad sandwich then," Tim continued. "Do you think the chickens rushed up to the block and voluntarily stretched out their necks? Did they ask to die so they could be your lunch?"

"Pigs don't have feelings anyway," Jeanie offered. "Not like we do."

"Yes they do!" "How would you know?" "What are you talking about?" cried Erica, Ellen and Bob simultaneously.

"Look," Dave said, "if we had a trout stream on the property, wouldn't we fish and eat our catch? The Indians did, and we learned from them that it isn't a matter of whether or not you kill to survive; it's how you do it. You must ask the animal spirit for permission before you take its body. You must balance your need with its need, and honor it with respect. Then it's a really cool experience of oneness between man and animal."

"Yeah, but nobody here is talking about survival," said Alan. "No one is going to die if we don't kill these piggies for our dinner. But you're right about the fish. I think we would fish without any discussion or difficulty, and why do we think that it would be okay to kill fish, but not pigs? For all we know, fish are more aware than we are. They might have lives and children and feelings like we do, and then we come along and violently put an end to it just because we want some fish and chips."

"I don't believe fish have the same kinds of feelings that pigs or dogs or humans do," asserted Erica.

"I'm thinking about the health standpoint," said Carla. "I have to believe that a pig raised on our own homegrown veggies, and foraging for its own food would be healthier to eat than one raised on a pig farm and pumped full of hormones."

"Yuck!" interjected Karen.

"Yeah!" said Ellen. "And happier too! Just think. We could give these pigs a really happy life before sending them to slaughter. You know what's going to happen to them anyway, we might as well keep them and give them a good life, and then benefit from them as well."

"I just think it's wrong to kill an animal for food unless you really have to," I contributed, stifling my discomfort at speaking out, trembling a little as I spoke, and trying to keep the quaver out of my voice. I hated how nervous I got when I spoke. I was shy in public, and expressing my opinion in front of a group of people was pretty hard.

"Well I think nobody has any business eating meat unless they can stomach the process of raising and killing an animal. Where do you all think those neat cellophane-wrapped packages in the store come from anyway?" said Mark.

"Time for a go 'round," said Ellen, reasserting her role as Facilitator. Periods of unstructured talking were punctuated by an occasional "go 'round" in which each person in turn expressed his or her opinion. It was the job of the facilitator to determine when a go 'round would be useful, to remind everyone of the rules, and to keep things moving.

Ellen continued, "There are a lot of people we haven't heard from yet. Do we keep the pigs for meat or send them back? Mark, why don't you start?"

"Keep them!"

"Alan?"

"Don't keep them."

"Suzanne?"

"Keep them."

"Laurel?"

"Don't keep them."

"Karen?"

"Don't keep them."

"Tim?"

"Keep them."

"Carla?"

"Don't keep them."

"Dave?"

"Don't keep them."

"Jeffrey?"

"Don't keep them."

"Sandra?"

"Don't keep them."

"Russell?"

"Keep them."

"Jeanie?"

"Pass."

"Erica?"

"Don't keep them."

"Jeffrey?"

"Keep them."

"Rachel?"

"Don't keep them."

"Mary Jane?"

"Don't keep them."

"Bob??"

"Don't keep them."

"Okay," said Ellen. "I say keep them. But we clearly have some more talking to do. Could we hear from some of you who haven't said anything?"

"I just wonder," Mary Jane spoke quietly. She was a visitor in her third week, a sensitive, delicate woman who said little. "Is this the kind of example we want to set for the kids? I mean we are all supposedly pacifists, but raising and slaughtering other lives isn't living as a pacifist."

"I think the example of being practical is just as important as the example of pacifism," said Rachel hotly. "And speaking as one

of the 'kids' as you like to call us, it doesn't make sense for you
to go setting examples that aren't realistic. In fact, I don't see that
you set any more examples for us than we do for you. Just because
you're 'adults' or 'staff' doesn't mean you have so much influence
over everybody."

"I don't see how we could ever send those pigs back," Laurel said.
"You know what it is like in those pig factories. The animals have
no freedom of movement, no personal attention, and no love. How
could we possibly send them back? If we do that, we're subjecting
them to the same fate anyway; we're just not taking responsibility
for what we are doing. It would be cowardly!"

"I don't see it as cowardly to refuse to participate in the barbaric
and stupid practice of eating burnt flesh," rejoined Dave. "Would
you go ahead and shoot someone, just because you knew somebody
else might do it? That is the stupidest thing I've ever heard!"

"Why are you talking about shooting somebody?" returned Laurel. "We are talking about pigs here, and the fact that your actions
are going to determine the fate of these pigs. You are just too holier-
than-thou to take note of your own impact on these lives. What you
are saying is a total cop-out."

"Cop-out!" yelled Dave. "You're the cop-out, you . . . ."

"Okay you two," broke in Ellen firmly, "let's stay on track here.
Maybe we should do another go 'round to see where we are."

The discussion went round and round, and on and on, and it was
with dismay that I realized that the prevailing sentiment was shifting over to keeping the little pigs for our later consumption. I had
thought our decision not to slaughter the innocent animals was a
sure thing, but go 'round after go 'round, fewer and fewer people
in the circle protested, most won over by the arguments relating to
kindness and health. Was it really violence to eat pork? But it wasn't
just "pork." It was those two young little pigs. I remembered the
moistness of their noses, the way their warm curious breath blew
in and out as they sniffed my fingers. I remembered how friendly
they seemed, and good-tempered. They appeared to be enjoying
their ride in the back of the pick-up, and looking to us with happy

anticipation for more fun. I hadn't ever given much thought to the matter of eating meat. What I liked and didn't like mattered, and whether or not there was enough. But I had never considered it as a philosophical issue. I didn't know what was right or immoral. I understood the logic of the various arguments, but it didn't change my feelings. I just knew that I would never eat one of those pink little bodies, and that it felt totally wrong for us to raise them with love, and then snuff their spirits out of existence, cook them and eat them. Several hours later, mine was the last voice of dissent.

We had been at it so long that tempers were short. People were shifting uncomfortably in their seats, and looking out the windows at the fading light, obviously thinking with longing of other things they could be doing. Russell had gotten so frustrated with Ellen that he had taken a cue from Alan and called her a "bitch." At that point, she had told him to leave the meeting because he had broken the rule against personal attacks. Then he yelled, "To hell with you all! Nobody should, all of you!" before marching out of the room, slamming the door hard behind him.

Anyone could go at any time, but leaving the meeting meant leaving the decisions up to those who chose to stay. Sometimes it seemed like a game to see who could hold out the longest. It was easy to feel hostile when one person prolonged the meeting by not coming around to the common view. And this time, I was the one who was holding out. There was no short cut, no decisive moment of vote—we had to discuss and consider and compromise until everyone in the room could agree to something. If there was a deadlock, then things stayed unchanged. But one person alone wasn't a real deadlock. When it came down to one person, it became a matter of power, character, and pressure.

The discussion had run its course, and everyone had had his or her say. This wasn't an issue we could compromise on: either we were going to keep the pigs, or we weren't. If we didn't all agree to keep them, they would go. Of my supporters in the Don't Keep Them camp, Bob and Karen had wandered off without ever having said much. Suzanne, Carla, and Alan were convinced by the arguments that the pigs, doomed from birth to die for the table, would fare better with us than without us, and that they would be a source of healthy meat. Mary Jane didn't feel that strongly about it, and Erica had gone out to do the evening milking. I was the last hold-out. As the final go 'round progressed, each person stated his or her willingness or desire to go along with Fletcher's plan. Meanwhile, feeling deserted and surprised to be alone in my position, terribly exposed but unable to concede, I grappled with my conscience, and my loathing of taking a public stand. I didn't want to block consensus. But I could not agree to kill the pigs.

Clayton, at the age of four, was the only member of the community who had been denied the right to block consensus, and this only after he had abused the power several times. Clayton single handedly prevented one person's acceptance as a new member, vetoed changing the color of the kitchen, and put the kibosh on a group trip to West Virginia, all for the exquisite joy of thwarting a room full of mostly adults.

It wasn't like that for me. The mere thought of blocking consensus made me chilled and sweaty. I hated having a dozen pairs of eyes turned on me with the narrow probing beam of flashlights. But then, isn't the very structure of consensus antithetical to the person in my position? Designed to equally distribute power, it served instead to highlight the fact that personal power is not equal. What was missing was the awareness that a sensitive person, or a child, would not be able to withstand the pressure of adhering to an unpopular, but strongly held, conviction, in the face of public group opposition. At ten, I felt caught between the two equally intolerable alternatives of compromising my beliefs and facing the controversy of singlehandedly insisting on an unpopular outcome. Blessed (or cursed) with strong convictions, I seemed always hampered by a need to avoid conflict and a loathing of being the locus of dissent. And isn't that my old bugaboo—or one of them. Perhaps influenced by watching Carla stand against group opinion time and again, and sensing how it affected others' feelings about her, I couldn't tolerate being the one in that situation. Too concerned with fitting in and being liked, and too fearful of criticism, I couldn't block consensus. The equality that was supposed to confer upon me a sense of empowerment, undermined me instead, and left me feeling like a little shit, because I didn't have the courage to stand by my opinions.

I had shifted my position so that I would be at the end of the circle, gauging the group sentiment before making my final contribution. I couldn't block consensus, I just couldn't. But the thought of those lively little creatures corralled into the slaughterhouse was equally intolerable. Finally, it was my turn.

"Okay," I said. "I'm still completely against it. I just think it's totally wrong to kill something just to eat dinner, unless you have to. But I'm not going to block consensus." I paused, grasping at a thought just as it occurred to me. "What I'm going to do," I said, "is stop eating any meat myself from this moment on, in protest of your decision."

"That's hypocritical," Russell said. "Just think of all those carrots you slaughtered for the carrot cake at lunch, and the calf that died for the leather on your shoes, and all those little chickens that will never chirp or peck, because of your breakfast muffin. And think of all the animal products hidden in foods. Gelatin is made of goat's hooves; there's lard in piecrusts, and bouillon in soups. You can't possibly avoid all of that!"

Taken aback by this rebuttal, I said I didn't know. I just wasn't going to eat any meat. Russell snorted. Thus began seventeen years of strict vegetarianism.

• • •

"What are we going to name them?" asked Suzanne.

"We can't name them, and then kill them!" protested Alan. "You just don't name food! Do you name the beans, or the onions when you plant them?"

"But these aren't vegetables, they're animals, just like the dogs and the goats."

"Only we don't eat the dogs or the goats," said Bob.

"Well, we certainly could eat the goats, and lots of people in different cultures eat dogs. Nebula, for instance, would be a great delicacy in China," stated Jeffrey.

"Ugh!" said Dave, who, finding the rest of the house too lonely, had wandered back into the meeting. He was the owner of Nebula, the black lab.

"This is ridiculous!" said Mark. "Whether we, for whatever illogical reasons, choose to eat or not eat a certain animal doesn't have any impact on its animalness! I say every mammal deserves recognition of its individuality by having its own name."

"There are an awful lot of Marks in the world," said Rusty.

"All right, all right," sighed Ellen, "lets do a go 'round and see where we are. We may not even have a disagreement. Name or No Name?"

A quick go 'round showed unanimous agreement that the pigs be named.

● ● ●

"So! What are we going to name them?" asked Suzanne.

"Charlotte and Wilber," suggested Laurel.

"But they're both girls!" protested Jeanie.

"Charlotte and Wilbette?"

"Ribs and Roast," suggested Alan.

"Yuck!"

"Gross!"

"Eeoo!"

"Parsley Sage, and Rosemary Thyme," said Mark, an admirer of Simon & Garfunkel.

"Rosy Thyme and Sweet Violet," said Mary Jane quietly from the corner by the radiator, her fine pale face framed by an overabundance of rich brown hair.

"That's it!" we all agreed. "Rosy Thyme and Sweet Violet."

● ● ●

Why did I volunteer to tend the pigs? They were such foolish creatures, but somehow the concrete numbering of their days gave them
a pathos they otherwise could never have possessed. And I felt responsible for their fate, my reticence—or cowardice—having sealed their
doom. But I was also outside of it, exempt from guilt, as I had rid
myself personally of the excess of eating the flesh of other beings.

The best thing about the pigs was their unflagging enthusiasm.
They were never in a bad mood, were never tired or grumpy. On
bright days, they basked lazily in the sun, on rainy ones, they rolled
gleefully in the mud. They were really quite clean, defecating
demurely in one sheltered corner of the pen, and constantly rolling
on the straw to scratch and clean their pink selves.

Most fun of all was how they ate. No one could have enjoyed
food more. They would spot me coming down the hill with the
slop buckets, and begin to squeal, trotting up and down by the
fence in happy anticipation. Reaching their pen, I let them smell the
buckets to intensify their anticipation before I poured the slop into
the trough. Once the food was in the trough, the pigs, side-by-side,
fell to with gusto. They munched on apple cores, grunted happily
over potato skins, swallowed wormy tomatoes without a glance.
They were in heaven! Leftover squash, cold oatmeal, bean sprouts,
and moldy barley were all gobbled up with great delight, their little
piggy eyes squinting in ecstasy.

We started keeping a bucket for the pigs under the sink, right
next to the compost pail. I would hover in the kitchen while meals
were being cooked, making sure that any delectable morsel would
make its way into the right bucket. No, they didn't enjoy eggshells
or coffee grounds, but Wait! I knew someone who would snarf up
those cucumber peels. That may be rancid yogurt to you, but it's
tiramisu to a pig. I started serving myself extra large portions at
meals, taking great pleasure in scraping the leftovers from my plate
into the slop bucket when I, like everyone else, cleared my plate
and stacked it in the kitchen. Every now and then I would pour in
a glass or two of milk, and I started making it my business to clean
out the fridge once a week.

Because they loved it.

Burnt toast, pumpkin soup, peanut shells, wilted carrots, fermented rice, sour plums, hard old bread heels, orange juice, soy dregs, whey from cheese-making, broccoli stems. They loved it all.

There was only one time that they turned down food.

Bob was a wizard in the kitchen. He managed to adorn our simple fare with an elegance that made it palatable: a few raisins and sesame seeds in the oatmeal; a sprinkling of fresh herbs on top of the brown rice; wonderful aromatic homemade granola roasted slowly in the oven, covered with honey and oil, lumpy with luscious dried fruits and nuts.

It was hard to get elegant within our constraints. We spent very little on food, buying in bulk, and counting heavily on the garden and the goats. We used as few processed foods as possible. No white flour, nothing canned or frozen, basically no meat. Cheese was a fabulous luxury, much coveted, and the prime "unsnackable." Snackables were boring things like sesame seeds, rice, potatoes, and oats. At the breakfast table one morning Karen related her dream of sneaking into the kitchen and getting out the wheel of sharp cheddar we had just ordered from Vermont. It was supposed to last a month, and in her dream she had bitten through the wax covering, and gouged out the dark yellow flesh with her fingers, stuffing it by handfuls into her mouth, the soft substance wedging damningly under her nails. She had been terrified that Bob or Suzanne would come down, turn on the light and find her there, crouching in the dark by the fridge, telltale yellow crumbs clinging to her lips. We all howled with laughter, because any one of us could have had that same dream.

One of the most basic tenets of our diet was that we did not eat sweets. White sugar was viewed as poison, and whatever simple sweets we had were made with honey, which was expensive, and in limited supply. Chocolate was unknown.

One day, however, Bob decided to make pudding. Carob is supposed to be a chocolate substitute, but only a fool would take it as one. Carob has a burnt, grainy taste, no matter what you do to it. But Bob, the Wizard, set about making carob pudding. He asked Erica to keep Christie's milk separate one day, as she was the goat known to have the creamiest milk. I selected for him, upon request, eight of the freshest brown eggs from the Rhode Island Reds. A new fifty-pound tin of the best clover honey was opened for the occasion, and a rare whole vanilla bean purchased.

Bob went to work. First, he made a beautiful custard that was in no way harmed by the addition of a little cornstarch to help thicken the thin goat's milk and counteract the consistency of the honey. He had painstakingly mixed the carob powder with warm milk, dissolved, strained, stirred, warmed, and coaxed it until it became smooth and supple, no lumps in evidence. He mixed this into the custard at the very end, and it went from pale and creamy to dark and luscious, looking smooth, glossy, and very puddingy. Bob carefully poured the mixture into a bowl, shooed away his audience, and set it in a safe place to cool and set while he made dinner.

Everyone knew about the pudding. It was big news. We hurried through the meal, and the evening dishwasher cleared the table with an unaccustomed number of helpers, while Bob prepared to dish out the dessert. He carried the bowl to the table, and we watched jealously as he served, eyeing each spoonful to be sure that no one was cheated. The pudding had set perfectly. Once the bowls were passed around, we grabbed our spoons with chatter and excitement, and dug in. I carefully lifted a spoonful, watching it jiggle pleasingly as I raised it to my lips, and into my mouth.

The taste, already savored on my tongue in anticipation, was . . . indescribable. Somewhere between rust and sour curds. The texture, so smooth to the eye, was gritty underneath, giving the impression of a mouthful of fine dirt. The milk had turned, and had a rotten overtone. One by one, our mouths puckered, faces grimaced, and heads turned away from Bob, who was phlegmatically spooning pudding into his mouth as if nothing were amiss. Finally, no one was eating but him. He looked slowly around the table, eyes narrowed to slits, set his spoon carefully down by his bowl, and said, into the waiting silence, in his thick Southern accent, "Well now, *that's* pudding."

We stared at him in disbelief, until he finally relented, and made a face so horrible, so exactly what we were all restraining, that we shrieked in relief, and trooped together into the kitchen to dump it all out into the slop bucket.

Rosy Thyme and Sweet Violet greeted my appearance that evening with surprise. I'd figured they, at least, could enjoy what we had been denied. They were willing and ready for anything. Or so it seemed. I poured the pudding into their troughs while they pranced enthusiastically, and then stood back to watch. Rosy snuffled inquiringly, with uncharacteristic caution. Sweet Violet stuck her snout in, and nosed around for a minute, and then they both turned their backs and trotted away! They left! They rejected food! The next morning, the pudding was still untouched, and I had to rinse out their troughs with buckets of water before I could feed them breakfast. We never let Bob forget it; carob pudding became a euphemism both for elaborate preparations and great expectations turned to mud, and for a substance so noxious that even the ever-ravenous pigs rejected it.

• • •

The one thing they loved almost as much as food was to run.

One day, a call went out, "The pigs are loose!" Up on the neighbor's field, we could see Fletcher flailing his arms, and yelling, with Rosy Thyme and Sweet Violet running back and forth around him. Rosy dashed right in front of him, and Fletcher lunged, sure to catch her, but she twisted her backside at the last split second, and his hands closed on nothing. Surely there was a smirk on that porcine visage when she turned her head back to look at him.

A number of us ran to help. After many leaps and unsuccessful snatches, we eventually formed a large ring surrounding the two pigs. Now we had them! They stood in the middle, bellies heaving, a glint of fun in their eyes. Slowly, slowly, we closed the circle, mak-

ing it smaller and smaller. As if on signal, Rosy Thyme and Sweet
Violet took off at the same instant, in opposite directions. Rosy
headed straight for Fletcher again, and Sweet Violet ran toward
Ellen. And they broke through! Sweet Violet was aided by a last-
minute flinch from Ellen, and Rosy Thyme sassily ducked between
Fletcher's legs as he stood in a wide stance, arms outstretched to
catch her. Two tries later, we managed to grab Sweet Violet and
hold her, despite her horrific squeals and shrieks. With Sweet Violet
back in the pen, the fun went out of it, and Rosy Thyme let us catch
her too. She was entirely unabashed. Fletcher, however, stalked
moodily off to get tools to reinforce the fence.

I was aware of the irony that I was fattening the pigs for slaughter. In being too cowardly to block consensus, I had, in fact, determined their fates. In assuming responsibility for their deaths, I figured the least I could do for them was to ensure the quality of their
short lives. Sometimes, making peace with one's own actions is sufficient, and sometimes it isn't. I personally took a higher ground,
absolved myself of guilt (or tried), and allowed things to take their
course, when I had the power to alter it. At the time, I felt cowardly. I thought I should have been able to tolerate the discomfort
of blocking consensus. I didn't really understand why I couldn't.
Now, it's easier to understand. I was desperate for acceptance and
approval, but the criteria altered with the ever-shifting cast of faces.
Not yet able to trust my own feelings or opinions, I was in a constant scramble to avoid disapproval or censure, and was reluctant to
act without substantial vocal support.

They got less cute as they got older. I still loved to watch them,
but gradually, I visited them less often. Having learned the lesson of
comings and goings that defined my life, I drifted away as the time
of their departure approached, detaching myself in anticipation. In
September, while it was still warm, I passed on the feeding duties
to Tim, and arranged it so that I would be away visiting my father
when they were taken in. I thought briefly about staying with them,
maybe even accompanying them to the slaughterhouse. But I was
not so sentimental as to believe that it would make any difference

to them, and the melodrama of such a gesture did not appeal to me. They were, after all, only pigs. I heard later that they trotted happily up the plywood ramp on to the same red truck that had brought them, neither balking nor hesitating. Maybe they thought we were taking them for a Sunday drive.

When I got back, I went down to the basement to see them. Lining the bottom of the freezer were a number of packages, wrapped first in white paper, then in plastic. One, I could see, was labeled "Loin." I touched it, remembering Rosy's flank, her pleasant skin, so dry and soft. Was this she? It was cold and very hard.

A month later or so, around Thanksgiving, Suzanne busied herself with special effort and grandeur in the kitchen, and produced a Pig Roast. She had basted the skin carefully brown, and placed a line of pineapple rings down the back. With everyone for once seated quietly at the table at the same time, she brought it in and set the platter down in the center amidst uncharacteristic silence. It was impossible to look at the corpse without remembering the pigs' antics, and their cheerful faces. After she had cut it, pale fleshy slices falling side by side, a few people bravely held out their plates. One or two cut bite-sized pieces. But only Fletcher ate, chewing his way methodically through a large slab. After he left, someone quietly removed the nearly whole roast, and we gathered around bread and tofu. That was the last time anyone tried to use the meat. It gradually became buried under bags of green beans and peaches, huge blocks of butter, and jars and jars of milk. That freezer may still be in that basement, and if so, it is likely that, at the bottom, Rosy Thyme and Sweet Violet are still there too.

Now, at the end of the story, I see that I should have blocked consensus—that my voice was not mine alone, but was a voice for the whole group, as evidenced by our inability to actually eat the pigs. In trying to straddle, in trying to hold to my own convictions, bolstered by my own private protest, without becoming the focus of resentment or conflict or disagreement, I thought I had found the perfect solution, when in fact, it did no one any good, least of all Rosy Thyme and Sweet Violet.

Daddy

Since our move to the country, my father had continued to visit us regularly, but less frequently. Every time he came, it was a new disaster. It was a kind of agony for me—seeing the place as I imagined it must look through his eyes. The days of his visits always seemed dreary and gray, the beauty of the landscape eclipsed by cloudy weather or muddy roads. Only when he arrived did I really notice the ramshackle outbuildings, the clothes flung onto the lawn and then left out in the rain, the dilapidated split-rail fence, the half painted porch. All the walls and boards and tools and posts and trees seemed to be slanted or leaning or warped. Nothing was straight or square to the ground. The gate stuck when he opened it, the doors squeaked, and as often as not, there was a goat in the hallway, or the smell of skunk or sour milk, or a chicken running around in the yard, or a huge puddle in front of the door. And inside the house somebody was inevitably yelling obscenities or chanting and burning incense, or there was a game of water tag going on, with the likelihood that Russell or Suzanne would pounce unexpectedly from behind a door and, not realizing we had a visitor, douse us with a bucket of water. It was bedlam, and there was no concealing it. But I only really cared when Daddy was there.

I had an extra sensitivity to him. I wanted to shield him from the worst shocks of communal life. I hoped to spare him upset, I think, and discomfort. My father was hardly a weak man, yet I felt he needed me to protect him. He had beautiful hands, and they were always very clean, nails carefully pared, pale half-moons visible at every cuticle. My father liked to do things right, and he valued his creature comforts. He took good care of his possessions, which were always high quality, and lasted forever. He wore leather shoes and soft wool sweaters unadorned by the burrs or hitchhikers that I routinely carried. I wore the same clothes every day for weeks. I didn't see any compelling reason to change them unless I spilled milk on them, or broke an egg, or got muddy from the dogs. As long as I was comfortable, I didn't see any reason to dress differently. But when Daddy came, I suddenly was aware of the holes in my shoes, the ragged ends of my cut-offs, my uncombed hair. My sister Erica untangled my rat's-nest hair for me every couple of months—brushing it daily was too much trouble. I tied it back with a rubber band, which hurt to take out, so I just left it in all the time, except during our untangling sessions. Erica was painstaking in her gentleness, and she always told me how pretty my hair was, and drew a line on my back with her comb to show me how long it was. She made me feel beautiful like a princess, and I would always swear to comb it more often, but I immediately returned to my old ways. I didn't have the time for such frivolous concerns.

From the moment he arrived, a frown permanently creased my father's forehead, and he looked more and more pained as the visit progressed. He was intensely uncomfortable on the commune, and could not conceal his uneasiness. Whether it was the liberal views our lifestyle represented, the air of open sexuality, or just the plain mess, clearly his visits were unsettling. Of course I was never sure how much had to do with the general surroundings, and how much had to do with Carla.

She continued to monopolize him when he was there, leaving only for brief moments, seeming to expect that the five of us would spend happy time together like a normal family. Once I watched her try to take his hand as they started off on one of the walks she insisted he take with her every visit so they could talk in private. Daddy tolerated her hand for a moment, and then pretended to need to adjust his glasses, after which he put his hand in his pocket, ignoring her reaching fingers. Why did she do that? Didn't she realize that he didn't want to hold her hand? Their walks seemed interminable, and somehow in the interim, something of his always got ruined.

Once my dog Gnomie got hold of his new gold-framed glasses in their leather case, and chewed them to bits, case and all. The next time, Daddy drove down in his second wife's brand-new green Toyota Corolla. It wasn't until he went down to the parking lot to leave that he discovered the goat sleeping placidly on the roof of the car. As he shooed her angrily off, Buffy's sharp hooves added to the already plentiful dents on the roof and hood. These events seemed to give him an outlet for venting his anger, and he would make a sharp exclamation, throw his things together, and leave in a cloud of fury.

He always looked so unhappy. Watching him climb back into his car for the three-and-a-half-hour return trip so soon after arriving, I hated to see him go off alone like that. I would cry, feeling empty and lost and angry myself. I was disappointed, and missed him again, seconds after having seen him. He was so not there. I hated Carla for being so demanding and selfish and I hated him for being so gone and I hated my sisters for not seeming to care that much, at least not as much as I did.

Finally, toward the end of one more horrible visit, trailing up the hill behind Carla and Daddy, I decided I had had enough. Somehow I managed to get a moment alone with my father. Walking along holding his hand, I knew I had to speak now.

"Daddy," I said, my heart beating hard.

"Yes, Baby," he answered, as he often did.

"Couldn't we come to visit you, instead?"

He stopped and looked down at me sharply, obviously a little surprised.

"Would you rather we did it that way?" he asked.

"Oh, yes," I answered.

"You don't like me coming here?"

"No."

"I see."

He said nothing more to me, but I knew, from the warm pressure of his hand, and the way he kept his elbow tight so I had to walk close beside him, that he was pleased. Very pleased. This made me feel wonderful. Pleasing my Daddy was an unparalleled experience.

He and Carla must have discussed it and, although she clearly hated the idea, he held firm, bolstered, I was sure, by knowing that I had asked him to do it. When the next time for a visit came around, he called to find out when we could come. Rachel and Erica, both fully fledged teenagers, didn't want to go right then, there was a sweat planned, and a new male visitor had arrived. He was younger than usual, close to them in age and thus exciting to be around. I decided to go visit Daddy by myself.

The first time, I was a little scared. Eleven suddenly didn't feel all that old. Carla took me to the bus station in town, giving me a long fierce hug and pinning me with her eyes for several seconds before releasing me. She stood outside the bus until it pulled out, trying to talk through the glass, finally waving hard as we drove out of sight. I had to change buses in the City, and Carla had arranged with an old college friend of hers to meet me there, and help me find the new bus. I wished she hadn't. The prospect of changing buses was a little daunting, but it was nothing compared to having to make conversation with a total stranger for forty-five minutes. Caroline actually turned out to be easy enough. She had brought me a copy of *Trumpet of the Swan*, which, unfortunately, I had already read years earlier. That led us to a discussion of books, which went pretty well, and before I knew it, I was on the bus again, knowing that my father would meet me at the other end.

On his own turf, Daddy seemed transformed. He was unguardedly delighted to see me, swept me and my shabby knapsack into the car, and whistled as he navigated skillfully through the heavy downtown traffic until he reached his wife Carol's office building where we were to pick her up before heading out to their home—an old farm house forty-five minutes out into the country.

I had met Elaine a few times when she and Daddy had come to Virginia together. A slim woman with poofed-up hair and cat's-eye glasses, she was quiet and nervous. Over the years, she had regularly sent tins of (fabulous) cookies and bags of gifts for us with my father when he came to see us. This had never ceased to amaze me. I didn't remember exchanging two words with her, and yet she bothered to be so nice. She always seemed pleasant, but she was a stranger to me although they had been living together for ten years.

Daddy did not want me to sit in the back seat, so when Elaine got into the car, I moved into the middle and sat on the little box that housed the gearshift. In this way, the three of us could sit together. Although the uncushioned seat got pretty hard after a while, and I couldn't move my legs much, I was completely happy. Daddy got me to tell them all the news of the commune; how many baby goats had been born, their names and personalities, what we were boycotting in addition to the obligatory California grapes and iceberg lettuce, how we were handling the invasion of Japanese beetles, who the newest visitors and students were, what my sisters were up to, and so on. He never said a word about my mother, for which I was grateful. I told him my favorite Joni Mitchell song, and he asked me to sing it for them, which I did, proud that I knew all the words, even if I had pitched it too high and had to squeak on the high notes.

Getting to the house, I climbed stiffly out of the car and looked around. On a piece of land of almost equal size, this property could not have been more different from Nethers. The driveway, graciously lined with maples on either side, had recently been covered with new gleaming white pebbles, and stretched straight down a gentle slope to the garage. As we drove down, the pond came into sight on one side, the house on the other. Around the pond were weeping willow trees, gracefully trailing fingers into the water by the big dock. The white house, newly painted, was a two-story farmhouse, with a swing on the porch, and a glass sunroom Daddy had added for his studio, all shaded by a majestic red maple tree.

The barn was tidy and smelled of new hay, machine oil and clay. The full-sized tractor Daddy had bought to keep the fields cut looked clean and was clearly ready to start at the first try. As was the lawnmower, the rototiller, and the snow blower. Everything was organized, tidy, and everything *worked*. Every tool you could imagine was hanging in its proper place in the smokehouse, next to shelves and shelves of homemade preserves, pickles, tomato sauce, jams, and applesauce.

Entering the house, I felt cool Mexican ceramic tile floor under my feet, and the air smelled of serious cooking, leather furniture, and books. As soon as we were in the door, Daddy asked me if I would like a bath. It seemed a little odd, but suddenly the thought of warm soapy water sounded wonderful. It had been a long trip, and I couldn't remember the last time I had taken a bath. The downstairs bathroom had an old tub with claw feet, and Daddy ran the water himself, pouring bubble bath in at the beginning, so it immediately began to foam and fragrance rose into the air.

"Put your clothes outside the door," he instructed me, "and call me when you're ready for me to wash your hair."

I would have been too shy to do this, but he made it sound so natural that I thought my shyness silly.

I stepped out of my clothes, slightly embarrassed by the dirt and bits of straw that dropped out of my shoes as I took them off. I wasn't wearing socks, and my toes were brown with grime. I balled up my clothes, and, opening the door as little as possible, stuck them outside the door. In that moment, I heard a peaceful murmur of voices in the kitchen, classical music from the stereo, and smelled something enticing.

I climbed into the bath, and leaned back in the unaccustomed luxury. It wasn't just the luxury of a fragrant bubble bath, it was the luxury of calm and quiet and order. I could feel something relaxing in me as I lay there, a knot I hadn't known I was carrying in my stomach. I sank lower in the water, to where I could hear the crackle of the bubbles popping against my ears, and thought about nothing.

The water was tepid, and horrifyingly brown when I sat up again. I pulled the plug, and started soaping myself, scrubbing at my arms and legs with a washcloth, and getting to my back with a brush that hung on a hook by the tub. Then I worked on my feet. I got the brown stuff off my toes, but my heels and soles would not come clean. They were stained red, the color of our Virginia dirt, seemingly permanently. Giving up, I ran new water in the tub. Then I climbed out, stuck my head out the door, and called for my father before jumping modestly back under the new bubbles.

Daddy came in, sat on the edge of the tub, and washed my hair, just as he had when I was small. He was efficient as always, and completely relaxed, as he did it, telling me what we were having for dinner, proudly listing the vegetables that had come out of the garden, most of which I had never heard of—leeks? Salsify? After the last rinse, he told me dinner was almost ready, and showed me a bathrobe I could put on. He lay several towels down on the floor to soak up the puddles I had made getting in and out of the tub, and picked up my shoes from the floor, holding them gingerly away from him, as he went out.

After dinner, Daddy and Elaine took me up to "my" room together. It was pink, simple, and very clean, with a single bed, a dresser, and a Navajo rug on the floor. It was very cold. Exhausted, I immediately climbed into bed, still wearing the bathrobe because nothing in my bag seemed clean enough to put on my newly bathed skin or the crisp white sheets. I fell asleep immediately.

The next day, on our way in to his office, Daddy diplomatically asked me whether I would like some new clothes. "Sure," I answered. Taking the next exit, I realized he meant right away. At the store, he picked them out for me himself, outfitting me from top to bottom. I was torn between delight and humiliation—by now having figured out that I must have either smelled bad or looked appalling, or maybe both. I knew how the goats smelled when I went into the barn from the fresh air, and the chicken shed. I knew that I often had smelly stuff on my clothes—milk or eggs or dog spit, but I never thought I smelled bad. This was a new kind of self-consciousness.

My two-week visit flew in a whirl of new experiences. I went to work with Daddy during the day, and sat in a corner reading and watching him. He was a university professor, and lots of people came to see him, and he talked with each one easily and with apparent pleasure. I had never seen him talk so much. I'd had no idea he could be so sociable, almost garrulous. He seemed to actually enjoy it. Every once in a while, he would bring a person over to my corner and introduce me as his youngest daughter, with obvious pride. This took me completely by surprise. I always knew Daddy loved me, but I had never thought there was anything about me to be proud of. On the weekends we worked together on the farm. He let me sit by him over the wheel while he drove the tractor, mowing the fields. We dug a trench across the yard to bury an electric line, and we tilled the garden. I had never worked so hard, or gotten so much accomplished so quickly.

When we were done in the late afternoon, we went up to the house where Elaine handed us each a tall frosted glass; his Compari and tonic, mine tonic and lemonade. We sat in the swing and took off our shoes, and then swung together as we sipped our drinks and ate peanuts. Then we both went in to shower and change, and we all sat down to dinner together. Elaine had always created a feast, exotic to my tastes, full of cream and cheese and nuts and sherry and fresh herbs. It was too rich, too spicy, and I inevitably got indigestion, but I absorbed its elegance greedily. They let me taste their glasses of red wine, which I found foul, although I would never admit it. We went to a concert (I fell asleep), and they had a dinner party where I met all kinds of people who looked interested while they asked me questions about life on the commune, but rarely paid attention long enough to hear the answers. It was a little confusing.

The whole time, part of me was wondering what was going on at home—certain that I was missing something important and exciting. Had the goats kidded? Was the newsletter printed? Who had come or left or gotten into an argument or fallen in love? I felt completely out of the loop. I would call my mother, and hear the usual tumult in the background through the phone, which was located in the hallway, but I couldn't tell what was really going on. When I hung up, Daddy's house was so quiet it made my ears ring. It was hard to be there, it was hard to be away.

When I got on the bus to go home, all my new things in a bag by my side, I felt replete. I had lived this quiet, cultured life, participated in sophisticated conversation, and seen a lot of different things. I felt fundamentally changed, and thought I could handle the confusion of communal life with new maturity. I was eager to get home to see everybody, and terribly sad to say goodbye to Daddy who, so unlike Carla, gave me one brief hard hug, and turned away, not waiting for the bus to pull out. I wished he had.

When I got back to the Main House, I looked around with new eyes. The degree of chaos and the amount of dirt was alarming. I didn't even make it through the door clean. The dogs, barreling out to greet me with much wagging of tails, jumped up and swung their tails against me; I was immediately muddy again. I tried to keep my new things nice, I tried to keep myself clean, but after a few days it was too hard. I stopped seeing things in such harsh relief, and I relaxed into the familiar disorder.

And so it was. I began to go back and forth. The disparity between these two worlds was incomprehensible. Each time I went from one to the other was a tremendous jolt. Each time I made the transition, there was a window of moments when I felt I could see absolutely clearly, perceiving the good and the bad in each place, the advantages and the costs. Of course I spent plenty of time trying to decide which was better, which I preferred, but found that I could not choose. It always seemed to me that if I could just combine this aspect of the one with that part of the other, selectively picking and choosing, I could design the ideal combination. Sort of like with my two parents. As it was, it was like having lived in two countries, and finding that, while completely conversant with each, I was never whole in either. Something was always missing, which meant that rather than having two countries, I had none.

Carla, to her credit, allowed me to go to stay with my father as often and for as long as I wished. My father and Elaine, too, incorporated me into their child-free life with no complaint, and often on short notice. I would suddenly call Daddy up to tell him I would be arriving the next day, stay as long as I wanted, and just as suddenly, decide that I needed to be back home, NOW, sometimes catching the bus that same day, leaving Daddy to make arrangements for me to be picked up, as there was always someone around to do it. My sisters came once or twice, but failed to see the charm, more assimilated as they were into communal life and all its goings-on.

So I was like an honorary only child, periodically taken into an adult world where I was treated with politeness and respect, and nobody acted obviously abnormal. But there was a tension there, too. The importance of doing things right was burdensome, and my father's unspoken criticism of the commune and my mother was painful. Every once in a while I would come out with something shocking, like exclaiming "Farm fucking out!" when Daddy showed me the nest of starlings tucked away in the gutter. He never said anything, but he would look at me with displeased astonishment and I would positively shrivel with humiliation. Sometimes it seemed a lot more relaxed and easier to be at Nethers.

The going back and forth was excruciating. Carla just reminded me of a phone call I once made to her, the day before leaving my father's to come home. Apparently I was weeping inconsolably.

"But sweetheart," she said to me, "you can stay longer if you want to."

"But I don't!" I answered through my tears.

"But then what's the matter?"

What she didn't understand was how hard it was to go back and forth. How irreconcilable the two felt. I looked for ways to bridge the two worlds. Daddy gave me a Grundig radio, which I kept by my bed, and which by some quirk almost picked up the same classical radio station that he listened to. I tuned into this static at night, and lay in bed imagining what he and Elaine were doing, knowing that if they were at home, they were listening to the very music I could barely make out through the crackling.

One November, at a loss as to what to get him for his birthday, I decided to crochet a bedspread for my father. I began with an impossibly long chain of single loops. It grew slowly, widening one row at a time. One skein of yarn produced six rows back and forth, so each time I neared the end, I would ask the next person to go into town to bring me back a skein of yarn in any color. I hadn't told Daddy about this project, and I savored his surprise in anticipation. As my bedspread grew, it became my robe, and I was able to hide beneath it. I refused to break it off into manageable pieces, preferring to have it spread over me, the growing weight welcome and familiar. I began to work on it during Community Meetings, and they became much less difficult. I sat, covered by my industriousness, finding my own freedom in the labor, and protected by the talisman of my father. He would have had little patience with the sorts of things that went on, and no one there could have made him uncertain or scared or upset as they did me. Wrapping myself in his bedspread seemed to lend me a little of his confidence and perspective. It made it possible for me to stay still for hours at a time, able to tolerate the intensity of opinion and emotion that inevitably emerged, able to remember that it wasn't always that important.

Somehow it was harder to stay connected to Nethers when I was at Daddy's than the other way around. There was something so Alice-in-Wonderland bizarre about the commune that it became like something I had read in a book, or dreamed, or imagined. The division between fantasy and reality was not so sharp at Nethers, and that gave it an unreal quality, as did its isolation. Sometimes I wasn't completely sure it existed at all until I returned and walked up the drive to see the house, massive, solid, and very real indeed.

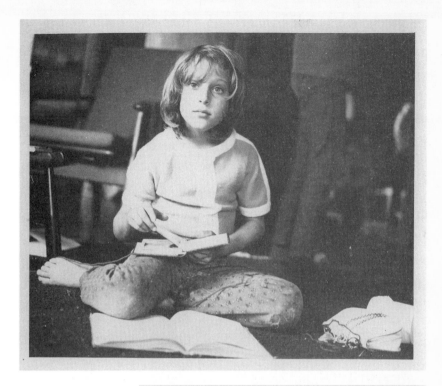

ABOVE:
Sandra, right
after the move to
Virginia, 1969

RIGHT:
Sandra and
Erica on Old Rag
Mountain, 1970

RIGHT:
Carla and Ned
in front yard of
the cabin, 1969

BELOW:
Elias' peace
sign on the
barn, 1970

Carla and Sandra in an apple tree, 1969

Gabe, Andrea, Sandra, Tim, student, Suzanne on the way to the Laundromat, 1976

Cindy (horse), unknown boy, Rachel, Erica and Sandra (in loft),
Ned, in barn, 1969

View from the porch of the Main House, 1971

Rachel, Sandra, Erica on the roof of the barn, 1969

Karen, Erica, Sandra, Ellen, Carol, Jeffrey, Laurel planning the geodesic domes, 1972

Student, Carla, Suzanne, Jerry, Ellen, student, Mark, Laurel in the back yard, 1974

Carla and Sandra participate in "Bull Session," 1976

Wood cutting party with visitors, Sandra standing with saw on the right, 1976

Sandra, student, Toby, Erica, Rachel, Jeanie, Suzanne in the front yard, 1971

16

Who Are You, Really?

Nethers had a transformational effect on people. Black sheep, successful professional, juvenile delinquent, genius student, artist, misfit, drifter, and rebel came and went at Nethers, all living cheek by jowl, subject to roughly the same freedoms and limitations. They came to find themselves, to escape others, to pursue ideals, or to develop some. It was 1972, and everyone was experimenting to see who they were, trying to be more spiritual or less controlling, to rid themselves of notions, assumptions, and prejudices, to transcend unwanted fetters and express themselves honestly and fully. There was an infinite variety of peculiar ways to express oneself. No matter how well-groomed, carefully dressed, or well-spoken a person appeared upon arrival, you never knew what was going to emerge after a week or two. People unfolded through a series of metamorphoses—larva to chrysalis to nymph. They grew or shed legs or tails, changed their skins, and transformed themselves in some relentless quest for their natural shape. Sometimes, the most "normal"-looking people changed into the most bizarre, as if exceptionally good packaging indicated particularly peculiar contents. I found this tricky, as I learned over and over, that my first impressions of people were not very informative at all. It was eerie to think that everybody was so different from the way they appeared. Was everyone walking around behind a mask? Was I?

It was common for people to go through a stage of exaggerated profanity, as if a store of vulgarity had amassed, and pressed for release. Four-letter words shot out of their mouths like cherry pits. Sometimes a startled look followed cartoonishly, and it was hard not to laugh. Some got overly polite, so nice that they seemed fake, constantly talking about sisterhood and love and "groking" this or "grooving" that. That usually lasted only until something got on the person's nerves, as it inevitably did, and then the civility instantly evaporated. It was nice to discover that, for all the variations in "authentic," just about everyone could and would, at some point, play. We played guessing games, charades, chase games, water fights, tag, all-out day-long games of territory and capture that eventually involved every person on the place. In play, all differences in age and temperament became irrelevant.

•••

A common arena for self-expression was mealtimes. Meals were important, partly because we were all a little bit hungry a lot of the time. Economics dictated a certain sparseness in our kitchen, and we were all very physically active. Eating together under any circumstances is a curious intimacy. For us, it was the one time we all gathered without the structure of a project or an agenda. Everyone showed up three times a day, unless they were sick, fasting, or away. Our interdependence was highlighted at the table, as we relied on each other not to take more than one share, and not to do anything gross in the common pot. It was the place where we were most obviously and directly affected by each other.

Marvin was an angry man. Beneath a thin veneer of soft-spoken quiet, his anger ran visibly close to the surface. He scared me. But he was trying to become "conscious." He wanted to reach a new level of awareness, so his every movement was considered, his every word thoughtful. Including eating. Marvin had heard somewhere that each mouthful of food, liquid or solid, should be chewed one hundred times before swallowing. This provided the greatest nutritional value, he had learned, and also offered a rare opportunity for meditation.

Hearing this over breakfast, I tried it with my oatmeal. By the time I got up to fifty, there was only a sweet thinning liquid in my mouth, and my jaws were tired from going round and round without resistance, so I gave it up.

Marvin was not so easily dissuaded. He had found his window to awareness, and he was going through. Thenceforth, at every meal, he chewed each bite one hundred times. At first we tried to tease him out of it, but he remained impervious. He became increasingly isolated at mealtimes, as he was no longer able to participate in conversation. Meals were generally quick affairs, slap bang, quickly downed, and off, nothing to linger over. If you didn't eat pretty quickly, you wouldn't get your share anyway. But not for Marvin.

Marvin's solution was to pile his plate high, and to go to the far end of the long table where he could chew in peace. His eating took forever, and became increasingly annoying for those doing kitchen work. Pretty soon, we were putting lunch out before he had finished breakfast. He protested whenever we took something off the table from the previous meal, stating between bites that he wasn't necessarily done with everything until he was finished. Then, we weren't able to clear off the lunch table until nearly dinnertime. Marvin became a near permanent fixture at the table, his jaws working in rhythmic circles. Even when not eating, he remained apparently inactive. He no longer worked, he rarely went outside, and he did not participate in conversations, meetings, or activities. He just sat there. His eyes became glazed, his movements slow, and he stopped responding to most things. He may have become more conscious, but he was scarier than ever.

I began to imagine him as an eating machine without sentience. I thought I could see him slowly expanding, puffing up a little, meal by meal. I could have sworn that his head got smaller, his eyes tiny, his arms and legs less mobile. He began to remind me of the ticks that latched onto the dogs' ears and sucked and sucked, swelling until their grotesquely bloated bodies forced them to drop off and lie helpless on their backs, tiny little legs waving uselessly. Sometimes, something went wrong, and a tick would just keep on sucking and sucking until it actually burst, producing a quick spurt of dark red blood. I found myself sitting further and further away from Marvin, fearing something like this could happen to him. When he finally left us, too harassed by all the distractions from his eating, he could still walk, but he was considerably larger. His face was blank, and he continued chewing a bran muffin as he left.

• • •

Everett, on the other hand, couldn't eat fast enough. He had lost half of his intestines. Or so he said. And indeed, a long, ugly, scar ran across his equally ugly abdomen. He claimed that after his surgery, for medical reasons, he could eat only high-protein, highly-processed foods. He couldn't digest any of the whole-grain, roughage-rich fare that made up our entire diet. In a rare departure from normal practice, we had actually hired Everett to come stay with us for a time. He was an engineer, and we were in the middle of designing the solar-heated house, a technical puzzle even Fletcher couldn't solve singlehandedly. We needed Everett, and did not feel free to offend or disbelieve him.

Chewing hard on my brown rice with soy sauce, I eyed Everett's plate, mounded high with at least a dozen scrambled eggs. He was wolfing them down mechanically, huge clumps of the glorious buttery yellow vanishing rapidly. Any hope that he couldn't possibly finish all that was lost, because, supposedly, he also had to eat huge quantities of food. With only half his intestines remaining, he carefully explained, his digestion was so inefficient that he only derived a fraction of the normal amount of nutrition from the foods he ate.

At the next meal, watching him spoon up a pot full of white (!) macaroni with cheese, while I made my way through plain doughy whole-wheat noodles, I realized that not only was Everett eating gargantuanly unfair things and quantities, but most of it just passed on into the outhouse, where not even Rosy Thyme and Sweet Violet could have enjoyed it. What waste. I started seeing him as some sort of unappealing conduit running directly from in-house to out-house.

The first outhouse we had built was placed close to the Main House for convenience, right next to the tool shed. A simple one-seater with no windows, it was purely utilitarian. We were too busy with other building projects at the time to do more with it. As soon as the hole filled up, we dug a new one right next to the old, and then gathered six or seven people to move the house. We lifted it up, and moved it over the new hole. The contents of the old one, now exposed in the bare daylight, were disgusting. We covered the remains with dirt and left the pile to decompose under a piece of plywood. And so it continued. Every few months, we would dig a new hole next to the old, progressing gradually in a circle around the tool shed. It seemed to me that the frequency with which we had to do this increased markedly with Everett's arrival, and he never volunteered to help.

Eventually, we built a beautiful new red outhouse that changed the standard forever, and started a property-wide competition. The new deluxe outhouse was placed on the side of the hill facing the mountains, and it had windows. The view was terrific. To add to its charms, we had an ongoing outhouse graffiti notebook, in which each visitor left a message, a thought, or a poem.

The new outhouse was also a two-seater. Well, not really a two-seater, it was a two-goer. Some held that the natural, and therefore most effective way to "go" was while squatting. Others appreciated the comfort, and the contemplative moments offered by "sitting." So we accommodated both schools in one house. For the squatters, there was a wooden dowel handle strung on nylon ropes like a tow for water-skiing. One was supposed to straddle the hole, and use the towrope to keep one's balance. I tried it once, and peed on my foot.

Four or five outhouses existed on the property by that time, serving the various dwellings sprinkled around the hill, and a serious contest for classiest latrine began. Dave won when he took a comfortable wooden chair, sawed off its legs, and cut a hole in the middle for a lid, attaching a handle for easy removal. As a toilet seat, this was luxurious. He even had some of Suzanne's crocheted cushions on it, although they made me a little nervous, as I was afraid I would drop one down the hole. A little footstool raised one's legs, offering some of the advantages of the squatting method, without the discomfort, or the discomfiting sensation of having one's rear hanging, as it were, in the air. It was almost worth walking fifteen minutes up the hill just to use this outhouse.

One day, not long after we built the deluxe outhouse down by the Main House, one of the oldest holes by the tool shed caught fire. Some visitor apparently had flicked his cigarette butt down on the mound and the methane gas, now pure and concentrated, had ignited. It made a gigantic flare. Since it was the middle of winter, we didn't put the fire out, figuring that allowing it to burn off was the safest option. It burned for three days. It was fascinating to see a heap of dirt on fire.

One evening we gathered around the fire with green branches, hating to see such an opportunity wasted. Was it our imagination, or did the marshmallows taste funny?

• • •

Brian had seemed outwardly "normal" until one day, we were out walking through the fields, while he talked animatedly. The grass was knee high, and grasshoppers flew up thick beneath our feet at each step—rustle, whirr, whoosh. Dozens of them jumped out from under us, and with a great buzzing of wings, landed a few yards ahead. Some were brilliant green with little red eyes, some small and brown, some fat and yellowish. Without hesitation or comment, not pausing in his talk, Brian caught a big green one in his fist. He looked at it for a moment, then grasped it by the head with his left hand. Still talking and walking, he methodically pulled off the wings and legs, one by one, then twisted the body from the head with a deft snap, and popped it into his mouth. When I stopped in shock, he threw back his head and laughed, teeth glinting against the blue sky.

"Try one!" he said, holding out the body of his next intended snack—still writhing in his fingers. "They taste just like roasted corn, and they are wonderfully nutritious!"

I backed away, revolted.

"No, really!" he insisted, holding the squirming, dismembered insect out to me. "They are amazing, almost a complete protein! We should research a way to market them! You know, a cheap source of nourishment for third-world countries."

I backed away further, shaking my head.

Brian's pleasure in my distress made him grow larger, arms and legs swinging now in wide primate circles, hair grown suddenly full and lustrous, crackling with vitality. All at once, he began leaping forward, grabbing grasshoppers by handfuls, no longer stopping to tear off their limbs, but stuffing them whole into his mouth, leaving heads and wings trailing from his lips, as he chewed and swallowed, eyes bulging round, making a great noise of smacking and crunching.

I slowly slipped into the protective rustle of the tall stalks. Brian, now rolling in the tall grass, hooting as he clutched all about him for his fleeing prey, did not notice my departure. The stalks closed over my head, the rustle closed over my ears. Seas of green leaves dangled in a gentle curtain. Lines of stalks stretched ahead for six feet, then blended into a restful regularity of random shape and movement. Restful like water, like sand, like any multitude of moving variability. But this one was made for me. Secret and safe. Once I was far enough in to be invisible, I lay down in the narrow space between rows, my shoulders just brushing the leaves on each side. Cornstalks stand on handfuls of root fingers that seem to clutch at the ground. From these fragile handholds rise the tall abundant stands of green and yellow.

My foothold sometimes felt as fragile. It wasn't only the unpredictability of how people acted—it was something about repeatedly having to retreat from them to feel safe. As a small child, I had loved Grimm's fairy tales, not least of all because they terrified me. It had always been such a relief to look up from my book, away from the talking head of the mare nailed bleeding to the barn door, or the brother who had become a goose, arms growing into feathered wings on the page, to feel safe again in the relative normality of my surroundings. I would see the familiar ugly brown carpet, the shoes piled by the door, and feel reassured, ready to return to the thrill of the story. Now I lived in a Grimm's fairy tale—the fantastic was the norm. But fantasy is only enjoyable when it is contained by the expected. Otherwise, it is the acid trip run amok, or psychosis, where every mirror is a door, inanimate objects speak, and things are never what they seem.

I wanted to be normal. I didn't know what I wanted. I didn't know who I was, but I expected the adults to know who they were. I found their antics funny and annoying at best, and deeply unsettling at worst. I retreated into my cornfield, where the rows of identical plants were straight and regular, and I could reel in my imagination, coiling it like a rope that has no use. The last thing I needed was my own elaboration on reality—I had to be steady and straight, face turned to the sun, clutching my handful of dirt.

Age Conflicts

The difference in status between "staff" and "students" was a matter of constant conflict and agitation, and a repeated topic for an eternity of meetings. The official stance was that students were invited to share responsibility for community decisions and projects, but retained the right to withdraw from adult responsibilities and "just be children" for as long as we needed. Staff members were required to attend weekly Staff Meetings, and work a minimum of six hours a day, while students, beyond discharging their assigned chores, were welcome to work as much or as little as they pleased. The price of this privilege was the loss of equal standing. I chafed deeply against the ingrained prejudice against children that I so often perceived. Equality—a core value that got a lot of air time—didn't seem to apply to us kids. To me, it felt that the automatic assumption was that younger meant less capable, less intelligent, less qualified to make decisions, less aware, and less responsible. When a kid was praised for doing something positive or mature, the very fact that praise was deemed necessary made it seem fake. The real meaning was "You did a wonderful job in spite of being such an inferior person."

On the other hand, several staff members confided in me as if I was an age peer. Having always suggested maturity beyond my years, this was nothing new. Adults had been unburdening their hearts to me ever since I could remember. In my now-familiar bus trips to Baltimore to visit Daddy, I had become accustomed to hearing the life story of my seatmate. As a painfully shy person, I had learned that an unfailing strategy to deflect attention from me was to get the other person to talk about him or herself. It was astonishingly easy to do this. I liked it, but I also hated it. Much as it was hard for me to talk about myself or to share anything significant, I desperately wanted to. It was disconcerting that it took so little to divert people. I guessed they really weren't that interested after all. It didn't help that I knew I was exacerbating my own loneliness. I may have been shy, but I liked talking about myself as much as the next person. I just needed a little encouragement, and it was burdensome to carry all those confidences. Truth was, I didn't *really* want to know the cause of Louise's huge limpid tears, and the turbid romantic jealousies of the teenagers were tiresome. But it made me feel special to be the bearer of such private matters.

So I was grownup enough to have equal decision-making power to the adults, to carry their confidences, to work and be responsible, but not to set my own bedtime. It didn't seem to add up. I couldn't figure out where I stood. I looked at Laurel, who was thirty-eight, and thought it amazing that she was more than three times my age but I obviously knew every bit as much about life as she. What had she been doing all that time, I wondered? Laurel, with her cloud of dark curly hair, was very talented, but mostly she just seemed sad. She was always on one diet or another. I remember her eating only cottage cheese for weeks, then switching to some red liquid diet. She spent a lot of time wandering through the kitchen, pointedly not eating. I never really understood why, because her weight never seemed to change and she looked perfectly fine to me anyway. She dressed in oversized gauze shirts in muted shades of mauve and moss green and cream. A couple of times, I came upon her in strange places—sitting at the top of the basement stairs, or crouched against the side of the house by the back porch—one hand clutching a bag of Oreos in her lap, the other cramming her mouth with cookies. Assuming that the look of panic and shame I saw on her face was concern that I would want some of her contraband, I discreetly left, feeling that I was at least as mature as she! I would have at least offered to share, had our roles been reversed.

Truth was, none of us students, with the possible exception of Rachel, wanted the obligation of working six hours a day as required of staff, or the obligation of all those extra meetings. What was so important to us was that we not be defined by age or role, but more as individuals.

Ironically, when I visited my father, I gladly did that much work and more, and my father and Elaine treated me fully as an adult. They did not impose a bedtime on me, poured me a glass of wine along with theirs, and fully expected me to hold my own in adult company. They assumed I would be able to amuse myself for hours if they were working, and gave me the choice of whether to go into the office with them or stay at the farm by myself (one ten-hour day alone there cured me of any romance in that notion). They took me with them to whatever concerts, plays, or parties they had on the calendar, regardless of content. I adored being treated as an adult, and never complained for fear it would remind them that I was really a child. This pseudo-adultism was a balm to my constant resentment at being treated like a child at home. But it came at its price.

For one thing, I was hungry all the time. My father and Elaine never ate breakfast, and it didn't seem to occur to them that I, at eleven or twelve might need to. For my part, I was apparently unable to utter a word to the contrary. After their mugs of coffee and mine of mint tea, Daddy and I went out and worked together around the farm for several hours. I wondered that he didn't hear my stomach grumbling in protest. Around 1:00, my father called a halt for lunch, and the three of us sat down every day to homemade sourdough bread, cheese, and homemade pickled hot peppers. At least this was serve-yourself, and I could take a thick piece of bread and slather it with butter, cheese and jam, in self-conscious contrast to Daddy and Elaine's spare single pieces of bread and demure slices of cheese. After lunch, we went back out to work; digging a trench across the yard to bury a cable, digging young maple trees up out of the forest and replanting them along the driveway, tilling, planting, weeding or harvesting in the huge garden, rebuilding the chimney, fixing the plumbing, patching the roof of the barn, pruning the trees in the orchard, pouring cement, or mowing the fields with the big tractor. I was a hard worker, stoic and uncomplaining, and much stronger than I looked. And I loved it. Just being beside my Daddy all day was nourishment, plus I knew I was useful and he needed me.

But by 6:00, when we quit and went back to the house, I was famished. Elaine would be in the kitchen cooking, and I would offer to help, more out of hopes for handouts than any real desire to. But snacks were few and far between. Her cooking seemed elaborate and complex, and I was so *hungry*. When she finally got the dish assembled and into the oven, my hopes would lift, and then plummet when she announced, "Perfect! That'll be done in an hour and a half." When we finally sat down, an eternity later, Elaine neatly spooned out our portions at the stove, and set the plates before us at each place. The servings seemed meager at best, and I often found the food odd and unpalatable. I would again fill up on bread or salad, timorously ask for a second helping of dessert, and go to bed uncomfortably full, only to begin again the next day. My father and Elaine did a lot of entertaining, and were famous for their bountiful provisions. It wasn't lack of generosity that made them underfeed me, it was that they were so out of touch with what I needed, and I was unable to assert myself.

And then there was the bed-wetting. Every time I went to my father's, to my mortification, I wet the bed. Night after night I awakened just moments too late, to feel the warm wet trickle seeping down my leg and onto the hygienically clean mattress beneath me. I would leap out of the bed in a panic, tear the sheets off the bed, shivering in the frigid air, asking myself "Why why why does this happen to me? I'm eleven (twelve, thirteen, fourteen) years old, this never happens at home." Bundling the bedding together, I would take it to the basement, put it into the wash, and go upstairs to find new sheets, trying to move soundlessly around the house so as not to be heard. I always meant to get up early to dry the sheets and spirit them away undiscovered, but never managed it, and usually found them neatly folded outside my door in the morning. No one could have been more discreet, but I burned with shame.

At home, the age-related conflict most fiercely and frequently debated was the question of bedtimes. Carla was a fanatic about sleep. She brought research report after newspaper article to meetings, presenting data on the amount of sleep necessary for different age groups, the consequences of not getting enough sleep, the fact that one can't make up for lost sleep on a simple hour-for-hour basis, the differences in quality of sleep during different phases of the night, the effects of room temperature, presence or absence of ambient light, noise levels, and the condition of one's stomach. She became a veritable sleep expert.

One of the favorite sayings about freedom was that it gave us the opportunity to assume greater responsibility for ourselves. How, we argued, would we have a chance to do this if we weren't given the opening? Again we tried all kinds of things. We chose a committee to establish personalized bedtimes for each individual, based on age, circadian rhythms, and lifestyle. That didn't work. We changed from strict bedtimes to sleep guidelines for all (technically optional). We were supposed to have a brief meeting every morning where people reported on their personal decision about the time they went to bed the previous night and how it had affected them. Guess how long that lasted!

It was an odd thing to focus on. It seems likely that it would have regulated itself without artificial means. There wasn't a TV or movies, no one was going out anywhere, there was no drinking or drugs, so staying up late meant reading or talking to someone or playing a card game, or listening to records on the ancient, scratchy mono record player with its built-in speaker. We would have easily regulated ourselves. Erica had to get up early to milk the goats every day, those of us who habitually slept outdoors awakened very early naturally, and with the exercise, hard work, and healthful food, we were all pretty tired at night. Still, for me it was the power issue. I think it made my mother frantic to see her children running around the house after nine pm. We were too obviously out of her grip.

The students did divide easily into "younger" and "older." Most of both boarding and "home community" students, now numbering eight to ten, were teenagers. At eleven, I was the eldest of the three or four younger students. I, however, felt myself infinitely superior to Jeanie, ten, and Clayton, five, the two "home community" children younger than I. I did not want to be associated with them, any more than the older home community kids wanted to be associated with me. I longed to belong with the older kids, but I slipped through the middle.

Although equality among students was certainly part of the philosophy that Carla and the staff purported, it was a hard sell. Competition was actively discouraged (we rotated under the net when playing volleyball, a game in which I had surprising standing, possessing a deceptive serve that landed, time and again, right in the space between the front and back players), comparisons were considered specious, and each student was to be celebrated for his or her uniqueness. With no grades or other standards of evaluation, there was no basis for intellectual or performance-based competition. Nonetheless, there was a clear hierarchy among us kids. This was based largely on personal charisma and success at breaking rules. Sex, drugs, staying up late at night, and smoking cigarettes were all powerful status symbols. Sex was totally uninteresting to me. Use of drugs was universally and completely banned, the one infraction that resulted in instant expulsion if caught, and, being out of the loop, I heard about drugs only as rumors long after the fact. And I still thought cigarettes were disgusting. So that left me squarely nowhere. I watched the flirtations that went on around me, and heard about conspiracies to do risky or forbidden things, and felt terribly left out. When Danny, a boarding student, whispered in my ear that I was a "fox," and he would be crazy about me if only I were a few years older, it was momentarily thrilling, until the reality reasserted itself that I wasn't a few years older, and he wasn't interested in me at all. My sense of not quite fitting in was pervasive. I was universally accepted, and very much loved generally, but my "place" felt solitary. Since Toby had left, I had been terribly lonely for a companion, but no one had replaced him.

What did I have against Jeanie?

We came from similar backgrounds. Both our parents were divorced, our remarried fathers equally remote in their tasteful lives of intellectual pursuit in clean, orderly homes. Our mothers were physically present, creative, and more than a little weird— mine more than hers. One would have thought that Jeanie and I would be good friends. But we weren't.

Jeanie's greatest crimes were that she was a year-and-a-half younger than I, and a bad sport. She had long brown hair, emerald green eyes, and luxuriant eyelashes. I knew she would be beautiful when she grew up, which was more than I could say for myself. Now, however, she was a whiner and complainer, a bad loser, and we shared no interests. Nonetheless, I depended on her. She always wanted to be with me, so I could spurn her if I had a better option, or turn to her if no one else was available. She also was unapologetic about being a child, and played happily with her dolls, talking excitedly about the trip that was planned for her to go to an amusement park with her father. I would have *loved* to go to an amusement park, but nothing would have made me admit it. And I could just imagine my father's snide comments about such a place. A lot of the time I actually enjoyed playing with Jeanie, but I felt she lowered my standing. She was younger than I, and less integrated into the community, but at least she was almost always at hand. But then that changed, too.

I tried so hard to be part of the group. Jeanie, on the other hand, had the courage to decide not to be. After the first couple of years, she elected to go to the local public school. To me, this was unthinkable, but I secretly admired her for it. There was a lot of unspoken condemnation of her rejection of our lifestyle, and her embracing the mainstream others had traveled so far to escape. From our very door, she chose to board the yellow bus of convention. She was a traitor, a rebel in her own right. I watched her go down the hill in her corduroy jumper, swinging her books, and knew she was choosing a path onto which I was afraid to venture. I had already been out of regular school for four years, and I thought it was far too late for me to fit back into that world of classrooms and grades, ball games, dances, dates, and normal kids from normal homes. I was too far afield, too far behind or ahead. A misfit in every way.

I tried to imagine what it would be like to be in regular school. The first difficulty was the notion of having to be inside for six or seven hours at a stretch. I remembered those little desks, and imagined how imprisoned I would now feel, stuck behind one of them. Then there was the problem of clothes. Seeing Jeanie in jumpers and saddle shoes was like a caricature. I hadn't realized people actually still dressed that way. I had grown so accustomed to my uniform of jeans—long or short depending on the season—and T- or flannel shirt, that I mistrusted my ability to adapt. I sneaked a look at Jeanie's books when she left them in the living room. I had been on a Fowles kick, reading *The Magus*, *The Collector*, and *The French Lieutenant's Woman* in rapid succession. That was something I did routinely. After reading one book that interested me, I would hunt down others by the same author, and immerse myself in them. Thus I read *For Whom the Bell Tolls*, *A Farewell to Arms*, and *The Sun Also Rises* over the course of a month. Steinbeck kept me busy for a while, as did Maugham. In Jeanie's bookbinder was a copy of an abridged version of *Misty of Chincoteague*. The glossy cover of the slim paperback showed the inevitable wild horse, neck arched high. They couldn't seriously be reading that for school, could they? It seemed so. I had loved the story, to be sure, but it seemed like decades ago that I had read it. On the other hand, looking into Jeanie's math book, I didn't get past the first page of numbers and charts before shuddering and putting it aside with a feeling of dread and helplessness. This stuff sure didn't look familiar. The history book read as soporifically as I had remembered it, as did social studies. No. I had no more place in that curriculum than I did in that social world. I didn't know which was more intimidating. Jeanie didn't talk much about school—at least not to me—so I had no idea whether she had successfully traversed the distance from commune to fourth grade—she who seemed much closer to normal than I. Did she fit in? Had she found a place? Could I?

Jeanie would come back from school sometimes, late in the afternoon, carrying her books, and I would have spent the entire day on the living-room floor playing Canasta or solitaire. Looking up at her, heavy-headed from sitting inside so long without moving, I would wonder: what was I missing out there? Would I ever get out? And if I did, could I survive? It irked me that for all my greater cool, I was more of a coward than she was.

Silence and Screaming

Other than the occasional visit to our sister communes for the birth of a baby or the raising of a barn, our contact with the outside world was very limited. The one affair that reached past the self-imposed isolation into our very midst was the war. Initially, my awareness of the war was hazy. I generally knew we were at war, and that it was the subject of great unrest both at home and nationally. Peace symbols and anti-war slogans were common and highly visible. I was somewhat hurt when Carla took my two sisters to Washington, D.C. to join one of the big peace demonstrations, excluding me because I was too young, but then I got caught up in the excitement of staying home without them. War of any kind at any time or place was a hard concept to absorb, and as long as it stayed remote, this one was not markedly different. But then it came closer to home.

Between 1971 and 1972 with the introduction of the lottery system, three of our members were suddenly confronted with the draft. Bob was the first to be called up. He got an impossibly low number. There was a lot of talk about what he should do. Together, we reviewed the exclusion criteria, and discussed various possible scenarios. Bob went home to visit his mother in Charleston, and the next time we heard from him he was in jail. He had decided that the way for him to be a conscientious objector would not be to run to Canada or fake some kind of ailment, but to voluntarily go in to the draft board to openly state his position and his refusal to go. This he had done, and as he had expected, they had incarcerated him. He had told only Mark what he was planning, and Mark had kept quiet, so it was a shock to us. It seemed so unbelievably noble, and absurd. It was impossible to imagine Bob in prison! The whole thing, war and all, was preposterous. We tried sending him care packages, but, life being what it was, immediate, absorbing and fast-moving, we didn't keep it up very long.

Then came Dave. Dave and Suzanne had recently become very much a couple. They were infatuated with each other, and the thought of being separated was intolerable. Dave stayed up for three nights in a row, and drank pots of coffee before heading in for his exam. The officials were not particularly concerned with his rapid heartbeat and excessive sweating, but his spectacularly infected left ear lobe apparently was reason to give them pause. Suzanne had pierced Dave's ear with an unsterilized sewing needle three weeks earlier, and Dave's ear had been red, hugely swollen and full of pus ever since.

It was Fletcher who finally figured out that Elias had been evading the draft all those years. This explained Elias's jumpiness, his secretiveness, and his disappearance when there were any unexpected arrivals. How stupid we felt not to have realized, and how sorry that he hadn't asked for help. Not that there was much we could have done. One thing about Elias: you got the impression that he could take pretty good care of himself.

Everybody knew somebody who went to Canada, who could qualify as a Conscientious Objector, who got off one way or another. It became part of the standard greeting, any time a man of draft age came in, to find out how he had avoided going to war, and to tell how our men had. No one personally knew anyone who went to Vietnam. There was a division of opinion about whether we were leading the revolution by keeping everyone out of the war, or copping out by not protesting more directly.

A man came through and talked to us about "tiger cages," showing us slides of tiny prisons made of slim poles roped together. It took a long time for me to understand that he was talking about people being imprisoned in these bizarre cubicles. I had gotten immediately outraged over the mistreatment of tigers. To learn that it was people being kept there was almost too hard to get straight. Thinking of Bob ending up in such a place where neither his talent for shoplifting nor his easy Southern humor would aid him, made it more possible to imagine him here in a cage of our own making. At least in prison he was fed and, presumably, not tortured. But the whole notion of the war was absurd. The idea of people killing one another, imprisoning one another, torturing and starving one another didn't make any sense to me. Barbaric doesn't get close to describing the situation. It was simply unimaginable.

Greater awareness of the war led us to more sober examination of our lives, and an effort to be more loving and tolerant with each other, to be gentler, to focus on the positive. We suddenly had many group hugs, rings of people, arms tight around each other, faces close to those across the circle. I loved the differences in hair color and texture, how the lights and darks mingled among heads bent together. I loved their different smells. Laurel smelled of patchouli, Erica smelled warm and musty like hay, Mark smelled of garden earth, Suzanne smelled of cooking. We began a series of Meditation Meetings, which were introduced by Jeffrey, who had been a practicing Quaker for a time earlier in his life. He introduced these meetings to us as "a time to come together in silence to invite a compassionate awareness of and openness towards each other, where we speak only when moved by the spirit to do so." They introduced a new tone of quiet serenity that was so enjoyable, that we decided to try a whole day of silence.

We gathered in the living room at dawn, having agreed that from this sunrise to the next, no words would be exchanged among us. Singing was encouraged, humming allowed, but no spoken communication. It was considered bad form to write notes, although it was acceptable when necessary.

Without words, everything got done as usual. We had art time, and dance time, the usual card games and games of jacks went on with more than the usual amount of laughing, but no talking.

Laurel and I were working on an independent study in which we had read Homer's *Iliad* and then decided to read Alexander Pope's version. We were both completely taken with this nearly endless poem, finding Pope's verse dense and satisfying. We usually read aloud to each other, taking one stanza at a time and discussing it until we were sure we got it, then going to the next. I had in mind to move to *Paradise Lost* when we finished this one. We tried reading silently together, but it didn't work so well. Without speaking them aloud, the words remained meaningless, locked into silence. The piano was played almost non-stop, as were a number of guitars and recorders. Meals were oddly awkward. The summons of the big wrought-iron triangle that hung outside the kitchen door was newly deafening in the surrounding lull. Eating took forever without the familiar clatter of conversation. To ease an increasing sense of discomfort, Jeffrey went over to the bookshelf, grabbed a fat book and, selecting a page, began to read a Cummings poem from an anthology. When done, he passed the book to Ellen on his left, and she immediately took his cue and read aloud a poem by Whitman, and passed it on. The rhythm and tone of the different voices speaking well-crafted, shapely words into an attentive silence was so pleasant that we stayed at the lunch table taking turns reading poems long after we had finished eating.

In the late afternoon, we gathered in the living room for Community Meeting. We sat together for some time looking at each other and the surroundings, and listening in the startling quiet to a panoply of sound that apparently had been there unnoticed all along. The fridge hummed in the kitchen; goats' bells rang out by the sheds somewhere; a flock of birds sitting in the cypress by the back door positively shrieked their news; the highway droned in the distance as some truck labored to get up the hill; water dripped from a faucet in the bathroom or the kitchen. The sounds were innumerable and constant, and it was odd to think that they had always been there, were always there, drowned out by our own noise and bustle. The sudden noisiness of the silence reminded me of when I lay down after running, and unexpectedly heard the rush of blood in my own head. My blood was streaming along all the time, without my noticing until I stopped to listen.

Time with no speech became unpredictable. It was somehow pegged to sound. Moments that would normally pass unnoticed lengthened alarmingly. Others slipped by unusually quickly. I thought about the Trappist monks who spent years in silence. One had visited us once, a man who had lived in silence for seven years. He was big and slow-moving, and had the softest, most melodious voice. What little he said made you want to listen. Unable to conceive of not talking for seven years, I had quizzed him about it. "How did you know what to do?" I asked. "How did you make friends? What if you needed something? What if you had to say something important to someone? What if the phone rang? What if there was an emergency?" He listened patiently to my questions, and told me that the people he felt he knew best were ones he had never talked to. Then he leaned close to me, and confided that he had worked in the barn with the cows, and had talked to them every day, so strong was his need to speak, which had convinced him he was not really cut out to be a monk.

After a short while, people got nervous just sitting in silence together. Eyes started sliding off sideways, and the effort to not talk became oppressive. The silence sat less heavily outside, and most of us gravitated to the outdoors. People were newly conscious of each other. Some were visibly disturbed, discomfited, some indifferent. I was partly relieved. Relieved at not having to try to find the right covering. It was what I imagined wearing a uniform would be like. For a day, I didn't have to worry about finding the right clothes. My words were thin and flimsy clothing anyway, shielding only briefly my deep sense of nakedness. It was also a relief not to hear others talking. Sometimes the efforts to hash out conflicts, confront feelings, be honest and open and to share, to consider other's viewpoints and express my own were overwhelming.

The people I admired most, partly because they were so alien, were silent. I felt too rambunctious and noisy. I admired Dave's silent calm, and strove to emulate it. Dave was an enigma to me. He was mysterious and dark, and seemed able to remain separate amid the hubbub. I longed for something of his cool. One night I was sitting out on the back porch with him. I was agitated and upset, close to tears. I tried to tell Dave what was bothering me. Whatever it was, it was probably incomprehensible, too convoluted, or just beyond Dave's capabilities.

Before I had even finished, he stood up abruptly, pointed to the sky, glimmering with brilliant stars, and said, "Whatever it is that is troubling you, just look at the stars, and it will all be okay," and went into the house. But it wasn't. Disappointed, I left, feeling resentful and deceived. I was beginning to think that not much of anything lay under all that sultry silence. Could it be that Dave was silent because he just had nothing to say?

He was certainly beautiful, his Native American blood making his skin a dusky brown. His hair was luxuriant and Indian straight, as was his nose. Dave gave wonderful hugs. Hugs so big you could make house in them. But he rarely spoke. I thought I was boringly chatterbox-transparent, too easily giving in to all the words around me, words that were sometimes an affront, often an intrusion. Why did everything have to be said repeatedly? Why did everything have to be discussed endlessly? After experiencing the day of silence, I decided that I would become quiet. Native talker that I was, I wanted to be in charge of how close people could get to me. Over time, I schooled myself to stillness and quiet. It was a matter of rebellion, of refusing to participate. Only by not talking could I resist being absorbed. I did not know that in squelching my natural communicativeness, I was turning off a primary valve, re-routing a major artery. My self-imposed silence cut too deep. I engaged in years of holding back from speaking my mind, until it became less clear to me what my mind was. The confident opinionatedness I gave away with my words would take me years to reclaim.

To end the day, we gathered in the evening to break the silence together, most of us reluctant, now that we had made it through twenty-four hours. Our favorite way was through vocalizing. Someone started singing, any random tone "Laaaaaa." Others joined in, and then a new harmonizing note was added "Maaaaaa." We sang quietly at first, then gained strength as we took pleasure in our own sound as it swelled to a full chorus. A dozen tones joined together and entwined in the air between us. The sudden resurgence of voice felt like touch after solitary confinement. I leaned into the sound as into a warm embrace, gladly adding my own.

● ● ●

The one person unable to keep the silence was Melissa. And even she didn't exactly talk. I suspect that Melissa was actually crazy. At the time, she was just very weird, even by our standards. She must have been fourteen or fifteen the year she was with us. Because of scoliosis, she wore a back brace that extended along her entire torso. Thick metal ribs began at her hips, ran along her spine on both sides and in front, and ended in a high girdle around her slender neck, tilting her chin up sharply. I saw the brace once; it laced on either side, through thick leather flanges. It was huge and cold and horrible-looking, like some primitive instrument of torture.

Melissa was tortured. Within her metal cage, she was wildness itself. She had long beautiful dark hair that was always tangled, and huge blue eyes that she sometimes rolled in dramatic grimaces. She leaned against the bars of her prison with frightening intensity. But never was she so frightening as when she left it. Very occasionally, Melissa would go without her brace. When she did, she was all suppleness. Pliant, almost boneless, she was terrifyingly flexible. She threw herself around like a rag doll, limbs double jointed, seeming not to notice or care when she slammed into walls or furniture or other people. As uncomfortable as the brace looked, I sighed with relief when she returned to it.

Melissa was beset with spasms of uncontrollable rage. We all sought to help her in different ways, trying to find harmless releases for her. Her favorite one was to scream. On a regular basis, at some time during the day, Melissa would begin to get jittery. After fidgeting, moving around, and shaking her head, she would eventually get up and, in a trance-like state, head for the door. Someone would jump up to accompany her. The only restriction we placed on her was that she couldn't do it in the house. She had to go outdoors. As soon as she got off the porch, stumbling with the urgency of a bursting bladder, Melissa would begin.

She would clench her fists, close her eyes tight, open her mouth amazingly wide, and emit bone-chilling shrieks and screams. High pitched and purely agony, those screams must have traveled miles in the thin Virginia air. She would scream and scream, each breath sheeting out in a solid layer of sound that seemed to hang in the air before settling slowly to the ground like a tarp. Each time Melissa ran out of air, she would pause, eyes still closed, and solemnly inhale deeply. For a fleeting instant between scream-breaths, her face became serene and peaceful. Then she began again.

Melissa needed someone to be with her to reap the full benefit of this procedure, and to protect her from hurting herself. Her inattention to her physical safety was alarming. I didn't like to be the one. Her unbridled raw release was too hard to witness. I wasn't calm or patient enough. After five or ten minutes of steady screeching, she would relax, breathe slowly and quietly, and her face would smooth out. When at last she opened her eyes, they were moist from her efforts. She would focus on whoever had been with her, and smile. That smile, tremulous, tender, fresh as birth, was what held us all. In those moments, we could see who she really was, who she could be, who she might have been.

Melissa frequently got "stuck" around the house. Before she could leave the bathroom, after brushing her teeth or taking a shower, she had to turn off the light seven times. Only problem was, she often lost count, or made a mistake, and then she would have to start over. Left on her own, it could take her as long as an hour to get out of the bathroom. If you tried to force her out, all hell broke loose. She would begin to shake and rattle, falling to the floor, the metal of her brace banging on the wall or the doorknob on her way down. I am sure these fits were voluntary, but they were terrifyingly effective, aware as we always were of her fragility.

One night, Melissa was particularly agitated, and screaming hadn't brought her much relief. She kept saying she wanted to SMASH! something. Maybe her HEAD! Maybe SOMEONE ELSE'S head! Maybe she would just go through a WINDOW! I had this great idea, or so I thought. Someone had gotten industrious, and cleaned out the basement. They had brought up a collection of glass bottles; old canning jars that had chips on the edges, gallon jugs from apple cider, even an old glass battery jar. These jars, ready to be discarded, were sitting in a box on the porch. I told Melissa to "WAIT! STAY THERE!" and ran to the porch. I lined the bottles up in the driveway, near the gashouse. I have no idea why we called it that, or what its purpose was. About four feet high, with a domed top just right for sitting on, it was a little hut with no windows, and only a low door on the back side. It was made of concrete, and was indestructible. I ran, turned on the hose, and filled all the bottles, one by one. Then I went and got Melissa. She came out as if blindfolded, leaning hard on my arm for guidance. I led her to the row of bottles shining in the lights from the porch on one side, and the tool shed on the other. I waited to see if Melissa would figure out what I had in mind. She looked at the bottles, at me, at the bottles, at the gashouse, cocked her head, and looked back at me inquiringly. I nodded. Melissa picked up a bottle and handed it to me. It was a one-quart canning jar with a nick at the mouth. She picked up another like it. We looked at each other, hefting the bottles in our hands.

"Oonne . . . Twoo . . . Threee!"

Simultaneously, we hurled our jars hard at the gashouse. They both hit, SMASH! on the sides, and a spurt of shattered glass and water leapt from each.

It wasn't until the last bottle was broken that I looked around and realized that splinters of broken glass lay all around the gashouse and us. Then I saw that Melissa was barefoot. A splotch of blood on her left foot told me that she had not miraculously been spared the consequences of leaping around in glass splinters. I turned my back to her, and told her to climb on. She was much taller than I, but so slight that she weighed less than the sacks of goat feed I was accustomed to carrying into the barn. Her arms clutched my neck as, step-by-step, I reached the porch, and she got off.

Melissa went home for the summer. One night, instead of slashing her wrists or setting fire to her house as she had done so many times in the past, she went out on her front porch, and tried screaming, as she had learned to do with us. The police descended on her suburban Cleveland home in minutes. Her parents, declaring that we had only made her *worse*! refused to allow her to come back.

Housing

As our numbers grew, we had to expand our living quarters. Since Peter had transformed a shed into a music studio/bedroom, half of the chicken shed had been similarly converted, and we had insulated the loft of the barn and replaced the windows, providing a large airy space for Laurel, Jeanie, and Clayton to live above the horses and goats. But we needed more space. So far, the upper part of the property had gone largely unused, except for the goats' grazings, and the few of us who bothered to ramble that far afield. Fletcher decided it was time to build a house for himself and Karen, and he chose a site up past the Jackson's.

The Jacksons had been there all along, although we had had little contact with them. Frankie was a solid country woman. Sturdy, and very dark, she must have been in her mid-forties although to me she seemed very old. She did not have a car, but walked by on the driveway deliberately and slowly twice each day, first down the hill on her way to her work as a housecleaner in town, and then back up the hill, passing within yards of the Main House. She surely saw us engaged in all kinds of odd behavior, but she determinedly looked neither right nor left, ignoring everything that accosted her. Stolid and expressionless, she swayed as she lumbered heavily from one leg to the other, seeming to rock more side-to-side than forward. Her legs were wrapped in thick beige support hose to help her varicose veins, and they hardly seemed to bend at all. Familiar as she was, the dogs never accepted her, and heralded each passing with a chorus of yaps and howls.

Delores, her eldest foster child at the time, was sixteen, and she was going somewhere. She was tart with determination. Rebelliously dressed like any other teenager, you would never have known she had to wash her hair in a bucket, with water she had carried up from the creek and heated on the wood stove, or that she had only one precious pair of stockings. She put those stockings on every morning at the bottom of the hill before her school bus arrived, and took them off again as soon as she disembarked in the afternoon. She did this defiantly, in the open, ignoring the possibility that we might see her. We were so insignificant to Delores that whether or not we saw her underwear was of no concern whatsoever. She had no time for us, nor was she curious. She passed with her nose high, as she went up and down the hill, hair as stiff and carefully arranged as meringue.

Marshall, Frankie's youngest and last foster child, was a latch-key kid without the key. At nine, his sullen moue was unrelenting. Woolly-headed and neglected, he drifted around getting into trouble. Frankie worked long hours, and seldom came home before dark. She did not allow Marshall in the house in her absence, because she was afraid of what he might steal or destroy. His pants were too large, as was his old flannel shirt, and his shoes had holes in them. He spent a lot of time hanging around his house tossing pebbles, but he also ventured into all corners of the property, and was not shy about entering empty buildings and taking a look around. For us, Marshall became the first suspect when anything disappeared or was mysteriously broken.

And then there was Jack. Jack was my nemesis. An insane German Shepherd kept on a chain outside their house, he animated my dreams for years. I had to pass by him on the way up and down the hill. Every time, he lunged, red-eyed and frothing, emitting the most horrific sounds as he choked himself against his own collar. He would throw himself forward again and again, the chain snapping tight at the last second and, each time, I imagined it letting go, sending Jack hurtling toward me. I could almost feel his hot breath on my skin. I used to creep by, hoping to escape his notice. But I never eluded him. Once, he leapt up just as I was passing. He threw himself with terrific force against his leash in one mad lunge for liberty, and the chain broke. Jack came charging crazily at me, fangs bared, mouth frothing, eyes crazed with the ferocity of long frustrated rage. . . or was that just another nightmare?

We went to visit the Jacksons, to let them know that we would be moving closer, whether out of respect or territorialism was not clear. Their red clapboard house, now that we looked closely, was in terrible disrepair. The roof had holes visible from the outside, the porch sagged, the outhouse tilted at a precarious angle and, in the yard, rusty skeletons of several old cars were grown over with vines. This, in addition to bags of garbage, old tires, and broken chairs made the house appear abandoned.

Entering the Jackson's house was a bizarre experience, even for us, inured to the bizarre as we were. In the little four-room cabin, they used only the kitchen. The other three rooms were piled, literally floor to ceiling, with things someone had been unable to throw away. Baby carriages, newspapers, old clothes, broken televisions, handle-less pumps, one-wheeled bicycles, and generations of junk resting in layers, a stratification of life. And the smell! The windows clearly were never opened—their access blocked by stuff. The powerful odor was of poorly washed bodies, old food, garbage, and an overtone of urine.

Three thin and lumpy mattresses lay in corners of the kitchen. Stacked on the small counter space were cans of Libby's sugared sweet potatoes, loaves of Wonder Bread, and jars of Miracle Whip. This world was as far from ours as the moon. Frankie greeted us and our plans with impassive neutrality, shrugging her shoulders as if to say, "It's your place, do what you want." Dolores dished out servings of her famous apple pie with a mixture of pride and resentment. As a relationship-building mission, it was a dismal failure. Egalitarian and inclusive as were our ideals, we could not seem to extend ourselves to the Jacksons, and we settled back to our old ways, politely ignoring each other, even though we passed more frequently now going up and down the hill. We co-existed uneasily for years, unwilling partners, but always aware of the other's presence. Sometimes when we were doing something particularly outrageous in the front yard, making pyramids, or dancing, or playing "Where Are You From," I would notice Frankie, frozen in the road on her way up, staring in spite of herself; or Marshall, peering between the buildings to see what we were up to. They couldn't join us, we couldn't welcome them, and they couldn't leave. The gap was too great. The will was too small. Our ideals of all-inclusive love and acceptance were all very well among the familiar, but here it felt unattainable. Like it or not, we found the differences between us and the Jacksons insurmountable.

• • •

Fletcher designed his house, and took great pride in the clean plan laid out on smoky blue architecture paper, and the economy of materials it would require. The structure was to be made of rammed earth. After reading up on adobe mixtures and different clays, it turned out that the red dirt right under our feet contained sufficient clay to make an excellent brick. This idea appealed to all of us. Fletcher devised a mixture to his liking, primarily comprised of our own Virginia dirt and a little sand, with straw added to give it structure, but no cement or other commercial adhesive.

We splurged, and bought a manual brick press, a bright yellow contraption reminiscent of a huge garlic press. It had a square compartment with a top, attached to which was a long handle. You filled the box with dirt, and then brought the handle down, which pressed the top of the box down onto its contents. You then had to apply pressure, by pulling down hard (Fletcher), or hanging (me) on the handle for several minutes. Releasing the handle and opening the box, out came a perfect square of rammed earth, a beautiful rust color, pressed smooth like cheese, fragile like bisqued clay.

We made the bricks one by one, and then lined them up on wooden racks. There they went through stages of curing and drying. We sprinkled them with water under the shed roof, then placed them out in the sun, where we turned them, as they slowly dried and aged, until Fletcher deemed them done. Then we carefully carted them in wheelbarrows up the hill to the house site. Even though brick-making was a popular job, it took months for us to make enough bricks to build the house

Once he began, Fletcher raised the house in record time. It seemed to grow by some organic process, and I saw him as a small figure that was pushed up from the earth by the house, rather than the force that raised it. In the beginning, he was standing on the ground, then he was straddling low brick walls, and finally, he could be seen spread-eagled on the roof, as if in surprise that this structure had emerged beneath him. And then it was done.

On the inside, Fletcher had left the walls exposed, showing the earthy coolness of the bricks. There was, of course, no running water or electricity, but Fletcher had built the house over a small spring, and in the kitchen floor there was a trap door on a leather hinge. Lifting it up by a rope handle, the cheerful trickle of cool water, pooling in a little cistern he had dug, was right at hand. Clever! Fletcher's kerosene lanterns were impeccably clean, wicks trimmed to give an even golden flame. His wood stoves were free of ash, and the well-cured wood was stacked near at hand. Everything was prepared, new and neat. The rammed earth house was a success.

Inspired, we continued, venturing further and further up the side of the mountain. Terry brought a teepee, Dennis set about building a cabin, and we raised several domes. Making the first dome was very exciting, almost magical. According to Buckminster Fuller and the *Whole Earth Catalogue*, equilateral triangles, arranged so that all sides meet, created a geodesic dome. It was an elegantly simple design, had great structural integrity, and needed a minimum of hardware. Plus, there was a lot of literature extolling the spiritual value of living in a dome. One could, it seemed, come into closer communion with the Earth and her various energies from within a sphere.

We received a shipment of four impressive black metal barrels, stamped with "Poison" and "Caution" signs, embellished with skull and crossbones. We were going to make our triangles out of a foam material created by combining two liquid chemicals, and pouring them into forms. When solid, the material was like Styrofoam, light and easy to handle, but durable. Carla expressed misgivings about using such toxic materials, but was assured that the substances became completely inert once combined and dried. If the *Whole Earth Catalogue* endorsed it, it must be okay.

The mixture went into the forms dark and clear, like honey. It then foamed and bubbled, and rose like bread dough. After drying over night, the stinking viscous liquid offered up light foamy triangles of a yellowish beige color, all the same size, easily hefted, yet robust. The dome took shape quickly, one triangle after another. Even Fletcher seemed to take pleasure in the order and regularity, and the fact that the project worked. We all pitched in on the final day, carrying the triangles up the hill, passing nuts and bolts, and raising the structure with our high spirits. Several triangle spaces were left empty for windows, and these Fletcher filled in with Plexiglas. Through one triangle, a hole was prepared for the stovepipe, and Fletcher built three steps up to the doorway. It was a wonderful house, open and spacious, but contained.

Carla moved in. I wasn't sure how I felt about this. It wasn't far away, it took maybe ten minutes to walk from the Main House to the dome. Part of me was thrilled. When she headed out for the night, I felt freed and independent. I could get up and read, or join the others in the living room, or do whatever I pleased without her knowing. On the other hand, I felt abandoned and a little bit afraid. If I needed her, I wasn't about to go out into the dark and walk up the hill to find her. It was the old problem. I didn't want her when she was available, but when she wasn't, I thought maybe I did.

Carla invited me to stay up there with her a few times, and the shape—being encircled by a round structure—was egg-like, or womb-like, and oddly comforting. She loved it. She wrote poetry, sitting by her window every morning, classical music crackling out from the radio, tapping on her black manual Remington. Some strange things happened with Carla while she was living there. She started knowing things, without knowing how she knew them. Oh, nothing huge, it was sort of like how she used to know when we were in trouble when we were away from the house, but it was still a little strange.

I had spent a frustrated hour looking all over for my book, although I hadn't told anybody. I had a bad habit of taking books with me wherever I went—up a tree, to the barn, out into the field, etc. and then sometimes I forgot where I had left them. This time it was really bad, and I was extremely irritated. Carla came down from her dome, walked into the house, and called me. "Come on," she said. I followed her curiously. She walked out of the house, hands in her back pockets in an attitude I liked. It was relaxed and humorous. She shuffled in her loose boots right into the back yard, and went directly to a spot by the fence where I had forgotten I had been sitting the day before because it afforded a good view. And there lay my book. Silently, she bent down, picked it up, and gave it to me, smiling mischievously.

Then there was the time that she had a visiting prospective member with her. She had taken him on a tour of the property, and they had ended up in her dome, where she made him a cup of hot chocolate on her wood stove. Just as the milk was getting warm, it started to pour. Rain always sounded thunderous in the dome, and the man had been upset, thinking of the walk down the hill to his car without so much as an umbrella.

"Don't worry," Carla had said. "It will stop." They went on with their conversation, drank their chocolate, and then it was time to go. It was still pouring. The man was distressed. He had been planning to meet some friends later in the day in a nearby town, and did not want to get drenched. Carla said, "Okay, okay, I'll stop it, just put your shoes on." The man looked at her as if she were crazy. She opened the door of the dome, and stood in her doorway looking out at the rolling fields, fairly steaming in the rain, green and verdant and undulant. She spread out her arms, raised her face to the sky, and said, "Rain . . . STOP!" And as if a switch had been flicked, it did. The rain stopped, the clouds lightened and parted, and rays of sunshine came through, showing a glorious rainbow stretching across the fields. The man was terrified. He scuttled down the hill, into his car, and was never heard from again.

Carla was a little unnerved as well. She hadn't been entirely serious, and had been as astonished as he, when it did stop. Later, she confided that she had tried it again a couple of times, and that she had about a fifty-fifty success rate, but only when she really meant it. Whatever it was that was going on with Carla and her psychic powers, a certain instability of energy seemed an inevitable consequence. In any event, it wasn't entirely a surprise when the dome caught fire and burned down.

We didn't even know it was burning until Dennis, on his way up to his little cabin in the woods, spotted the smoke. He instantly sounded the alarm, but by the time we all got up the hill, flames were already shooting out of several places in the dome, and a dense column of thick black smoke poured into the sky.

The dome didn't burn, it dematerialized.

"I knew it was bad stuff," Carla murmured, as she stood watching. The minute a flame touched a wall, it simply dissolved, bubbling and splattering as it went. We realized that there was nothing to do, no time to drag stuff out, no time to organize a water line, so we gathered in the spring snow in a large ring, far enough away not to have to breathe the toxic smoke, in awe of the power of it. We did call the fire department, but by the time the fire trucks manned by volunteers got there, it was over. Only the wooden platform the dome had sat on remained, blackened and charred. The fire, though quick, had been so hot that everything metal had melted, and other things had just combusted. Even the firemen were impressed. How had it happened? An errant spark from the wood stove? Marshall? Spontaneous combustion? An act of God?

In the rubble, I saw Carla's typewriter sitting at a crazy angle, letters pressed forward as if a fist had banged angrily on the keys. As quickly as we had raised this structure, and as smoothly, so had it disappeared. The dome, product of so much planning, intention, and cooperative effort, had been more ephemeral and transitory than we all thought. The making and the memory of it were more durable than their physical manifestation.

Carla stood, arms at her side, watching all her beloved possessions melt and sizzle. She did not seem entirely surprised. It seemed familiar to her, almost expected. I expected her to moan and protest, but she didn't. Instead, she seemed humbled or chastened, and clearly determined to start over out of the rubble. Something about living in the dome, wonderful as it had seemed, hadn't been right for her. There were times when Carla surprised me with her resourcefulness, and her willingness to learn from her experiences, even the difficult ones. That night, camping out in my room until she found a regular place to sleep, the odor of smoke strong in the room with us, she told me that while watching the fire she had decided that it was time to build a house for our family, and she wanted me to go with her in the morning to find the best site for it.

● ● ●

In the meantime, I decided to move out to the chicken shed and to share it with Catherine, a student who had been at Nethers for a couple of months. Half of the shed still housed the chickens, but there was a little room on the side with a loft and enough room for two. Catherine was a couple of years older than I. Her generally sad expression, and the long dark blonde hair that shrouded her cheek accentuated her round face and plain features. She was quiet and shy, rarely saying anything, actually, but I thought maybe if we lived together she would warm up. As always, I was on the look-out for a friend. I thought we might go out to the shed together in the evenings, build a fire and read or talk a little before getting into bed. I thought it would be wonderful, having our own little house, and engaged in fantasies of even sharing a meal out there now and then, or a batch of late-night popcorn, popped over the glowing wood stove. We moved our few possessions in quickly, and to my surprise, Catherine asked if she could have the bottom bunk. I had been hoping for the upper loft, but hadn't known how to approach the question. See? Instant compatibility! I skipped back to the house, congratulating myself on my choices.

Shortly after dinner, I realized that Catherine had disappeared. I looked all over the house for her, and she was nowhere. Looking out the window, I saw no signs of life in our shed. Surely she hadn't just gone out there without telling me! So I figured she had gone for a walk or something. After a couple of hours, when she hadn't reappeared, I reconsidered. Maybe she had gone to the shed after all. Setting out in the dark, I was trying not to make too big a deal out of it. So she had gone out without telling me. Big deal. Maybe she just wanted to be alone for a while.

When I opened the creaky door, I saw that Catherine was already under the covers, just her head visible, eyes open, staring up at the ceiling. It was all of 8:00, and freezing.

"Oh, hi!" I said.

I decided to build a fire, because I wanted to read. I went back outside and walked in the dark over to the communal woodpile, stacking logs in my arms, trying to find enough kindling to get it started. There wasn't any newspaper in the starters box, so I grabbed the only paper I could find—a limp piece of paper towel.

Our stove was the cheap kind, made of tin, sitting on rickety legs, gaps in the pipe a guarantee for smoke in the house. I stacked the wood carefully, starting with the smallest, most flammable pieces I could find, but a lot of it was green. Except for Fletcher, we just weren't good workers, and never gathered wood over the summer to give it time to cure before we wanted to use it.

Between the green wood and the sogginess of my limp paper towel, I was doomed. I managed to get a lame smolder going and a goodly amount of smoke poured into the air. Catherine expressed her displeasure with a heaving sigh. Just about the loudest noise that ever came out of her sour mouth. Climbing the ladder to my loft, I was suddenly furious. "What the FUCK was her problem anyway? It wasn't as if SHE had bothered to make a fire! Why in the HELL had she moved in here anyway, and WHAT was her PROBLEM?" I crawled under the covers in my dirty clothes, feeling the clamminess of my gritty blankets, hearing a rat scuttle away through a gap in the wall that separated us from the chickens. It seemed more pleasant in there, than here. I could picture them as I had so often seen them, feathers fluffed out, perched close to one another on their ledges, heads tucked into wings, the warmth of them wedged closely so that no one would pitch off in the night. No matter how contentious by day, no chicken sat alone at night.

For the few weeks that I stuck it out, Catherine never opened her mouth, but managed to convey a veritable diatribe of complaints with her silence. Like so many, she felt quite free from any dictates of friendly social congress. It was, apparently, quite unnecessary to say "Hello," "Good night," or "Good morning." So when I finally gave up and moved back into the main house, finding my old room thankfully still unoccupied, I felt under no obligation to tell her, or to say "Goodbye." I just left. I don't think we ever exchanged another word.

Sex Education

The best times at Nethers were when we were working on projects together. Building houses, ridding the lower garden of Japanese beetles in a single massacre, publishing the newsletter, or our occasional "sweats." Under Dave's direction, preparation for a sweat took forever. Two days in advance, we began early, fields still steaming with morning. Mark and Dennis went off in the red pickup to gather rocks from the ploughed fields, carefully avoiding river stones, which were reputed to become explosive under heat. (I had a secret desire to test this out.) Suzanne and Tim collected a truckload of wood for the fire. Laurel and Carla went to town to buy lots of fresh fruit. Dave, Ellen, Jeanie, and I went up into the forest. Dave and Ellen selected eight young, straight-growing saplings, and unceremoniously hacked them down, lopping off their greenery. Jeanie and I filled bags and bags with pine needles from the forest floor, our fingers getting sticky with sap.

Gathering back at the site, we prepared the fire. Suzanne and Tim stacked the wood in a square like a miniature log cabin. In the middle, Dave and Ellen lay down a bed of branches. Mark and Dennis placed a layer of rocks on top of that, followed by another layer of branches, then rocks, then branches, and so on, until the fire was taller than me. Then we sprinkled the whole pile with herbs and special plants of healing properties that Dave had gathered and dried, and finally we lit it. The fire burned for two days, fed in shifts, day and night.

We replanted the now-bare saplings in a large semicircle. Bending each one to cross in the middle, and burying the other end in holes we'd dug, we created a low dome. This we covered with layers of canvas, and then plastic (deerskins would have been preferable, but were not available). Someone rolled barrels of cold water down to the site, and set them up in a ring along the perimeter, while up at the house, others prepared huge vats of fruit salad.

Once we had to delay a sweat for several hours because our neighbor was working in the adjoining field. His land abutted ours by the lower garden and the pigpen, right where we had built our sweat hut. Most of the time, this was a very secluded spot, but three times a year, the farmer drove his tractor round and round the field. In the spring he ploughed, followed by flocks of birds greedily pecking at all the insects he exposed. Then he planted, and finally, in the fall, he came around to cut and bale the hay. The fall harvest was the most interesting for him—as this was when we were most active. He was consumed with curiosity about what we were up to.

He watched our preparations all day, and could not tear himself away. Darkness fell, and he continued to drive back and forth, back and forth across the field, his headlights now on, intent only on prolonging his observations. We tried to make it look as if we were just having a cookout, though what he was to make of the barrels of water and the sweat hut itself was anybody's guess. Suzanne suggested that we just invite him to join us. What would he have thought, if he could have seen us, listening carefully as the sound of his tractor finally faded away, then undressing as quickly as possible, laughing as we sneaked into the hut.

Finally, everything was ready. We all had fasted and prepared, each in his or her own way, for the past two days. Dave had rehearsed the Native American chants he had learned as a child, Jeffrey hummed the Hari Krishna and Eastern ones. Carla had been taking 1000 mg of vitamin C every hour to assist in cleansing her system, Laurel had been drawing little pictures every few minutes to develop creative flow, and writing poetry in her mind. I'd been too absorbed in the preparations, and in trying not to eat, to do much else. As dusk gath-

ered, we convened by the hut and doffed our clothes. I looked surreptitiously at the variety of bodies. Breasts and penises and pubic
hair, none of which I had, appeared in all sizes and colors. I felt terribly self-conscious, although I was aware that no one was looking
at me. That was both a disappointment and a relief.

I guess there was sex going on all the time, but nakedness was
not the norm. Clearly I knew nothing about a major part of life
here. Suzanne was the acknowledged expert. She was a big-boned
California girl, with coarse blonde hair, and large mobile breasts—
a blowzy, breezy, "here I am" gal. I was jealous of Suzanne. She was
big and confident, and she knew how to do everything. She could
cure all kinds of ills with teas or poultices, could cook anything,
had magical tales of mending puppy's tails with extract of golden
seal. She seemed afraid of nothing. Ample in size and volume, she
often teased, and then laughed unabashedly. Almost everything
had a sexual innuendo when Suzanne was involved. She had a way
of cocking her eyebrow, and saying "Oh!" that was positively lewd.

In late July she began her sex education classes, dubbed the Ladies
Aid Society, held usually in the kitchen in the hot afternoons. She
was nineteen or twenty at the time, an eternity older than I, an
initiate into worlds beyond my imagining. Her rapt audience was
comprised entirely of girls. I felt self-conscious and embarrassed,
being the youngest (it would have been impossible to induce Jeanie
to join us), and furthest from personal experience with the subject.
But nothing could have torn me away. Suzanne had a thick purple
candle named "Ba" that she used for demonstration, teaching us the
finer points of male pleasure. She sat on the kitchen floor, hiked up
her skirt, and placed Ba between her warm moist thighs.

"What Ba likes," she told us, "is this." Placing her palms around
the candle, she slid them up and down in a slow rhythm, fingers
carefully encircling the full width.

"And what drives him crazy," she said, "is this." She ran two fingers firmly along the "underside" of the candle.

"But what will make him your slave," she went on, "is this." She
leaned forward, and with teeth drawn carefully away, licked the

candle, circling the rim of it with the tip of her tongue, then licking the sides like a cat. She began rocking up and down, adding her hands to stroke places she could not reach with her tongue, taking the whole purple column of wax into her mouth and out, in and out. She stopped only when Ba, glistening and wet, threatened to come to life between her lips.

Suzanne also introduced us to the clitoris. Putting her hand on her own crotch, she instructed us to do likewise, describing the "little button" we would find if we rubbed around a little. Erica and Karen claimed to find theirs right off the bat. I never felt any "little button," but I was too embarrassed to try very hard.

One day the conversation turned to breasts, and there was a discussion of different sizes and shapes, sensitivity of nipples and aureoles. Karen put two oranges under her T-shirt on top of her breasts, and paraded around brandishing "double-sized knockers." It was quickly decided that grapefruits would be a better double, and the oranges were passed down to Rachel. Suzanne was given two cantaloupes, and everyone roared when Karen held two grapes out to Erica. Of course the attention had to shift around to me, and Suzanne got the biggest laugh of all as she handed me two matchbooks.

Shortly after this, we watched her seduction of Dave, the beautiful virgin, with awe and admiration. We were in the theatre having Drama Time when he first arrived, and hearing the sound of a motor, we all crowded around to look down from the attic windows. As soon as Dave climbed out of his pickup, his height apparent even from above, with his long, shiny chestnut hair, brown skin, and clear features, Suzanne's eyes widened in a mock swoon, and she said, "Oh, hot!" Erica, Rachel and Karen had all cracked up and said, "Go for it!" And she did. There was something almost predatory about her pursuit, on which she gave us running daily reports, at least until things really got going. He was, Suzanne confided, shy. Actually a virgin! But he was never meant to be, she assured us, this man was made for sex. But still, she wouldn't rush him. After a time, we began stumbling upon Suzanne and Dave pressed up against each other behind a door, or lying in a seemingly empty car, or clamped together in the telephone closet. Suzanne let us know that he wasn't ready for the real thing yet, she was still teaching him how to kiss. She would bump up against him with a kind of "oomph" that sounded disconcertingly horse-like. Finally, any resistance he might have had wore away, and they were off! They had sex in their bedroom despite the fact that they shared it with two other people, out in the field regardless of weather, in the hammock, the bathroom, you name it. We learned to heed that characteristic "oomph," and to come back later.

Perhaps because it was all so public, Suzanne and Dave's activities didn't have much impact. There was a general sense of amused tolerance toward them, and my main reaction was just to be a little put off by Suzanne's aggression. But it wasn't always like that.

One day, racing into the house from the bright sunshine, I ran up the stairs at full speed, yelling, "Dana! Come look!" wanting to show her that several of the chicks we had been waiting for had finally hatched. I swept open the curtain to her "cubby," full of enthusiasm and excitement. I dropped the curtain back just as quickly, and retreated down the stairs more quietly than I had come up, shame pulsing hot in my cheekbones.

Despite the dim light, the fraction of a second had been plenty long enough to register the two forms prone on the foam mattress, and to take in Mark's hand caressing the great pale dome of Laurel's backside, the rustling close between them and the soft breath of a moan from Laurel. It had been so unexpected, in the middle of the afternoon, in Dana's bedroom, to find them there. I was embarrassed, chagrined at my own pre-adolescent crush on Mark, now so sharply returned to my place as a child, nowhere near ready or wanting actual sexual experience.

Although, it was unusual to actually see people being sexual with each other, knowledge of other's sex lives was commonplace, and not particularly interesting. It was routine, like knowing a person's tastes in food, or spiritual preferences. There were two stable couples among the adults—Suzanne and Dave, Mark and Laurel. Certainly there must have been other more fleeting alliances (Ellen and

Jeffrey?) but they were generally discreet and attracted little notice. It was common for visitors to hook up with members for a brief time, and for visitors to become involved with each other. There was a rule that staff members could not sleep with students, but visitors were fair game. Many of the students were sleeping with each other, and were generally left alone about it. A couple of special Staff meetings were called when Mandy and Eric were found in bed together—he was only twelve, although Mandy at fourteen was known to already be quite experienced. Although Carla, Ellen, and Mark felt that the staff had a responsibility to chaperone student sexual behavior to some extent, it was very controversial, and even if they could have agreed on a rule it would have been impossible to enforce, so the matter was dropped. When Debra went on the pill so that she and Ethan could have sex, her breasts became huge. Of course she never wore a bra—no one ever did—and the heavy movement of her distended breasts was painful to watch. Dennis and Carol were known to have certain sexual difficulties related to being unable to relax. Once, they were given a six-pack of beer officially purchased to help them overcome their tensions.

Although I had not had the first stirring of sexuality myself, either physically or emotionally, I knew it all. I knew what cunnilingus was, and 69, I knew refractory periods and multiple orgasms. I knew French and soul in addition to butterfly kisses. I knew that scrotums sometimes moved on their own after sex, I knew impotence and premature ejaculation, vaginismus, yeast infections, and frigidity. I knew drops of seminal fluid could impregnate even if he did not cum (jizz, ejaculate, spew, spurt, gush, cream) "inside." I knew the hazards of vaginal sex after anal, and the best treatments for UTIs. I knew a cervical cap could make the tip of a man's penis sore, and that too much sex could be painful for a woman. I knew labia majora and minora, mons, pons, pubis, phallus, fellatio, cunt, testes, vulva, nymphae, and family jewels. All with my stubbornly flatiron chest, and singular lack of interest.

•••

Here in our sweat lodge, actually faced with all these bodies in the cool evening air, my knowledge rattled through my head irrelevantly, like a poem learned by heart in a foreign language.

Naked, we entered the hut through the narrow opening, one by one seating ourselves in a circle of fifteen people on the thick, fragrant pine needles, around a pit that had been dug in the center. Also naked, barefoot, and very careful, Dave and Tim removed rocks from the fire with pitchforks, and carried them into the pit. Once it was full, they too entered the hut, and closed the flap.

In the dimness of the hut, the rocks were white-hot, with a core of rose-colored heat in the center. They were translucent, mysterious, insubstantial, looking as if they would be soft and pliable if touched, and sweet if tasted—crusty on the outside, chewy and soft on the inside. I studied a rock on top of the pile, not far from me. It seemed a moment of danger. Was this a river stone? Would it suddenly explode? I could too easily imagine those searing bits showering over our naked bodies. Or was it just another trusty field rock, met regularly by generations of farmers, and tossed off to the side to free the field from obstructions? A stone, implacable and temperate, unaltered by shifts in location or a little fire? Or an unstable bomb of destruction, ready to deploy at any second? I wondered, too, if I were a river stone or a field rock. I felt sometimes as explosive and unstable as any dynamite, sensing all my burning splinters. At other times I was as serene and robust as a phlegmatic boulder. A moment of risk, exposed to unknown properties of my surroundings and myself.

Dave, his aquiline profile visible in the glow from the pit, reached for a bucket, and splashed a handful of water onto the rocks. With an angry spattering and rushing, a great cloud formed instantly around us, so thick it obscured those on the other side of the circle. At first, the warmth was welcome, as the ground was chilly, and the steam felt friendly, clothing my naked body. Dave started the chanting. "Je ram Je ram Je Je ramo." Gathering strength as we gained familiarity, the hut soon rang with the sonorous minor tones of ancient customs, long grown unfamiliar. As one ended, a new one was begun.

Jeffrey led: "Hari Krishna, Hari Krishna, Krishna Krishna, Hari Hari, Hari Ramo, Hari Ramo, Ramo Ramo, Hari Hari." And then Dave again: "Witchitata endora horenita horenita ene ene noa." The words themselves were gibberish to us, but their rhythm and the combined force of our voices made them powerful, and laden with meaning. We were singing to the earth, to our ancestors, to spirits and power, and to our own sweaty voices joining together. Eventually, running out of chants, we began on rounds. Never had "Row row row your boat" and "Ah poor bird," sounded so impressive. And then Silence. I could hear people breathing.

The air had now become so liquid and hot that it hurt to breathe. My nostrils narrowed sharply, and I could not catch my breath. Leaning down to press my face against the sharp, pungent smell of pine needles, I inhaled deeply and with relief, taking in the familiar smooth coolness of the forest floor. After a time, I sat up again in the harshly hot air, my hair curling around my face. When I raised my hands toward the roof, the heat up there was intolerable, burning my fingers. I had to get out.

Somehow climbing over people to get to the door, I stepped out into the night air, now shockingly cold. My limbs sent huge steaming clouds up into the darkness. Laurel, who had followed me out, danced, looking like she was wearing a filmy robe that trailed her every movement, rising from every inch of her. We each jumped into a barrel of cold water, or stood gasping for it to be sluiced over us, feeling it boil and hiss against our hot skin, as it had over the rocks in the hut.

The jolt of the cold water on my heated skin brought me back to an awareness of the night, and of myself. Suddenly cold, I returned for another round in the hot, dim enclosure. After each person had gone between the heat of the hut and the shock of the cold water several times, we all gathered around the fire. Burned down to a bed of shimmering orange embers, it emitted a welcome gentle warmth. We stood, arm in arm, swaying back and forth under the night sky, our fronts warm, backs pleasantly cool, in silent communion.

Suzanne put corn and potatoes into the coals, raking embers on top of them. Soon a wonderful aroma rose around us. Someone went up to the house to get the fruit salad, and we ate with our hands from the common bowl, squatting naked around the fire, and then slept in our beds, deep dreamless baby sleep.

The Knowledge

One morning, everyone woke up at three a.m., and all but two of us left half an hour later. Carla, Erica, Rachel, Suzanne, Dave, Mark, Ellen, Tim, Jeffrey, Karen, and all the others were supposed to be at the Ashram by six. I got up too, and watched them get together and eat a quick breakfast, conversing only in quiet murmurs. Suzanne, Dave and Mark had already gone twice, but both times had been turned away, their sincerity or dedication in question. This was their third and final chance to receive the Knowledge from Guru Maharaj Ji. They were nervous, and earnest in their desire to be received. Laurel was sick, and had to stay home. She was very disappointed, but it did solve the problem that of the entire group (not counting Fletcher), only I had elected not to go, and thus wouldn't have to be alone all day.

I wasn't sure why I had been so adamant about not going along on this adventure. Mark had been the first to meet the "premies" from the "Divine Light Mission" and they had invited him to attend "Satsang" at one of their informal evening gatherings. He was excited by them and what they had to say, and eagerly suggested that we go and find out more. I decided to go along—it sounded fun. Driving to town, we had gone as directed, to a house on the outskirts—the usual saltbox with the uniform hedges surrounding it, plastic squirrels chasing each other up the trunk of the maple tree on the front lawn. Inside, the living room was aglow with candles clustered on an altar covered by a brocade cloth, where we were supposed to put our offerings—the fruit and cookies we had brought according to instructions. We were asked to take our shoes off, and everybody sat on the floor on the very clean cream-colored rug. You could still see the vacuum cleaner tracks in the pile of the carpet. Two young men with a hectic brightness in their eyes smiled widely at us, their white teeth glossy in the candlelight. They talked for a couple of hours about getting the "Knowledge," being "Blissed-out," and "Serving Him" before we were released to go home. I had been bored silly, completely untouched by anything remotely spiritual or holy, and hungry. In the car, I wondered aloud who was going to eat all those cookies and oranges. No one responded. I had expected the usual banter and ridicule on the way home, but everyone was silent. At one point Mark, who was driving, said dreamily "Far out!" I looked at him in astonishment, realizing that this was not going to be the end of it. After that night, I was dismayed to see ever-larger groups going back again and again to Satsang, baking cookies to bring to the shrine, and actually dressing in skirts and button-down shirts. Now everyone had decided to get the Knowledge.

Not me. I hated the idea—I felt no need for a guru. It seemed irrelevant, just one more fad that had caught on, and would as quickly pass. Plus, I had a need to exercise my muscles of not going along, to know that I could stand against the current, alone if need be. Nonetheless, watching them all pile into the van in the mysterious pre-dawn darkness, excited and together, I felt left out and doubted my self-imposed exile.

It was a lonely day. Laurel was in bed the whole time, and I drifted around, climbing to the top of the pine tree to read *Moby Dick*, but unable to concentrate, heading out for a walk only to decide it was too much trouble, bored with playing solitaire, the piano or the recorder, not feeling like working on the hat I was crocheting. I couldn't seem to take interest in any of my usual pursuits. The weather was bad too, and finally I just sat on the window seat and stared out at the gray dreary day, taking some gloomy satisfaction in the match between it and my mood. That night I waited up late, hoping to see them when they all got home.

When they still hadn't gotten back by eleven, I finally went to bed, disconsolately climbing the too-silent stairs to my lonely room.

Awakening some time later, I heard the cars drive up. I jumped out of bed, threw on my jeans, and ran downstairs to watch everyone come back in. They were wreathed in elation. They looked exhausted, but their eyes were shining, and a couple of them were holding hands. They seemed to be moving slowly, floating, as if in a dream, or a trance.

"What happened?" I asked. "Did you all get it?"

"Oh, yes," Suzanne said. "It's wonderful."

"What's it like?" I asked.

"Oh, we're not allowed to say, but it is Wonderful! Amazing."

Feeling annoyed and even more left out, I went back to bed, determined to drag information out of somebody the next day.

But the following day was worse. Apparently, they each had pledged to keep a discipline of an hour of meditation twice a day every day. This was the first stage of practicing The Knowledge. But they had also sworn to keep the meditation techniques a secret from anyone who was not an initiate. They had been instructed that if ever they needed to meditate with a non-initiate (me) in their midst, they had to put blankets over their heads to keep the secret secure.

By the time I got to the living room, four people were already sitting there, shrouded like summer furniture. I went to sit with them. I tried to imagine what they might be doing, sitting there cross-legged, with their heads under blankets. I rolled my eyes back in my head, and bared my teeth. Did one have to make wild faces to receive The Spirit? Squint one's eyes to see The Light? They didn't seem to have anything under the blankets with them, nothing was being smoked or swallowed, no instruments played. What could they be doing? The only thing visible under the blankets were small movements of their hands around their heads. I copied their postures, and tried everything I could think of—pulled on my ear lobes and my tongue, stuck my fingers in my cheeks, rolled up my eyelids. Nothing happened.

After the meditation hour was over, I cornered Jeffrey in the kitchen where he was making dinner. Jeffrey was our most knowledgeable member spiritually. He had followed Sri Aurobindo for years, lived an abstinent and spartan life, and devoted himself to his spiritual journey. Although he sometimes made me nervous, Jeffrey and I had done yoga together early in the morning for about a year, and I felt he knew what he was talking about in such matters. Surely he could clue me in to what Guru Maharaj Ji was really all about.

"Jeffrey?" I said.

Silence.

"Jeefffrreeyy," I repeated.

He was measuring water into a huge saucepan, dreamily filling a cup at the tap and emptying it into the pot over and over. I waited until he was done, in case he had been counting.

"JEFFREY!" I yelled.

He looked over at me. "Hmm?" he responded.

"What *is* it?" I asked.

"What is what?" he returned vaguely.

"The Knowledge!" I answered.

"I can't tell you that," he said absentmindedly, now beginning to measure out cups of brown rice. "You have to follow your own path to readiness. Anyway, I'm not a Mahatma."

"Do you Know God now?" I persisted.

His silence was broken only by the metal spoon with which he was pointlessly stirring the rice around and around in the water.

"Jeffrey!" I demanded.

"What?"

"Do—You—Know—God—Now?"

"God?" he said distractedly.

"Yes!" I repeated. "God! Isn't that what this is supposed to be about?"

"Ummmm . . . I know The Way."

"So what is the way?"

Silence. Moving slowly, he began taking veggies out of the fridge, preparing to cut them up. Instead of piling several vegetables in his arms and carrying them over to the counter together like any sensible person would, Jeffrey took a separate trip for each. He opened the fridge door, looked absently at its interior, noticed the carrots, picked them up, closed the door, took the carrots to the counter, returned to the fridge, opened the door, stood there as if forgetting what he was doing, stooped down and took the broccoli from the bottom shelf, stood, closed the door, walked to the counter, set it down, moved back to the fridge, and so on, moving slowly, his gaze distant.

"What's the matter?" I asked snottily. "Are you so blissed out you can't talk to me?"

Jeffrey stopped in his tracks, a single onion in his left hand, and looked more or less in my direction. He sighed heavily. Finally, taking it slowly from the breast pocket of his shirt, he handed me a small photograph.

"Just look at this," he said, "and maybe some of the spirit will reach you. Then maybe you, too, will seek The Knowledge."

The picture showed a pudgy Indian kid—I had heard he was fifteen, barely older than I. He was draped in a gaudy embroidered shawl. His hands, folded sanctimoniously before him, were fat, and he had a fistful of golden rings on his fingers. His face looked pouty and sour, with mean little eyes, and a slack mouth. *This* was The Guru? The Bringer of The Light, the Giver of The Knowledge? He looked more like a kid to be avoided—spoiled and despotic.

Fed up with the whole thing, and not wanting to have to struggle again to get Jeffrey's attention, I stuck the picture directly back in his pocket as he stood staring vaguely at a head of cabbage, and went out to find Sun Bear, my new dog.

$$\bullet\ \bullet\ \bullet$$

That winter, Carla had suggested I go to a therapist. I had hotly refused, incensed that she would even suggest such a thing.

"But you seem so tense and lonely," she had protested.

I knew what she meant by tense. I had developed a habit of scrunching up my eyes, gritting the muscles in my jaw, clenching my teeth, and twisting my mouth in a horrible grimace. It felt awful, and I could only imagine how grotesque it looked, but I couldn't stop. The more aware of and upset about it I became, the more self-conscious I got, and the more I "had" to do it. Carla called it my "nervous habit," and bought me chewing gum to try to help me control it. Gum was enough of a departure from custom for me to know that she took it pretty seriously. I didn't know how seriously to take it myself. I knew I felt pressed a lot, that I was terribly ill at ease and unsure of myself. I was less clear about why.

Certainly there were things about my life that contributed to my discomfort—Carla was difficult, and I often got headaches when I was around her. Going back and forth between her and Daddy was jarring and disorienting, but I couldn't do without either of them. It wasn't as if there was a choice to make. Although he welcomed me for visits and vacations, there was clearly no room for me in my father's daily life on any long-term basis. Both he and Elaine worked ten-hour days as a matter of course, and they had a full social life of dinner parties, opera and theatre tickets. It wasn't just that I would have had to make that dread transition to public school, it was that I would so clearly cramp their style. And fundamentally, it was clear to me that I was supposed to be with my mother. I would have felt horribly left out if I left the commune although it exerted all kinds of pressures on me. It was hard to remain steady when those around me were so diverse, and there was so much chaos. I struggled always with the conflict of wanting to belong, but not really being able to—partly because of my age, partly my nature. There wasn't anywhere or anyone with whom I felt that I completely, safely belonged.

And then there was Toby, my still-missing, much-missed friend. One day, a couple of months earlier, Carla had come looking for me. I was way down the hill lying by the slowly seeping creek that was one border of our property, watching tadpoles. Hatched late in the season, they were almost frogs, now in that awkward phase where they had both legs and a tail. I was wondering whether they were going to make it into the colder weather. It had taken some doing for Carla to find me, and it surprised me to see her coming. She walked down the hill toward me, her face set in alarming lines. Sitting down in the tall grass above me, she asked me to join her on the hill, saying that she had some very bad news. In the time it took me to stand up and walk the two steps to sit beside her, I imagined every possible catastrophe. Something about my father, one of my sisters, or someone else I loved most. In that moment, it seemed that my loving someone put them at terrible risk.

It was Toby. My first reaction was a wave of relief that it wasn't Daddy, Rachel or Erica. Only then did I register who it was. Toby had been killed, Carla said. While deep-sea diving with his father, he had come up under the boat just a moment before its engine started, spinning him into the great propeller blades. Death was bad enough. This death, unimaginable. Except, of course I did imagine it—the irresistible suck into the prop, limbs, blood, water, his beloved father. Automatically, I looked down at my friendship bracelet. That slim nylon thread had now outlasted a certain grin that had been more tangible for me than any object. Was he still wearing his? Had he been, when . . . ? I swore again that I would never cut mine off, drenched by the cold finality that this time I was alone in my pledge. Toby's death stayed with me—I couldn't get used to the idea. I had always assumed that we would find each other again—we had said as much. We had been so easy together.

It certainly wasn't news to me that I was struggling, but it was humiliating to have Carla suggest I see a therapist, and I felt betrayed. Was there really something wrong with me? "Just get me a puppy," I had proposed. Carla agreed immediately, and we found a new litter of giveaways on a farm in the woods. I sat down among seven similar-looking pups as they gamboled and frolicked, mother bitch looking on tolerantly. I picked Sun Bear. Or did he pick me?

Sun Bear, his belly round as an olive, puppied over to me and plopped down in my lap with a homecoming sigh, resting his chin on my knee. And it was a done deal. I went through the motions of looking at all the other pups, but the choice was clear. Sun Bear was white with black and brown splotches over his face and body.

The thing he wanted most in the world was to be with me. He was friendly to other people, but I was his great love. He positively exploded with joy when I came out of the house to take him on a ramble. When I called for him, he came running, tearing across the field from whatever he had been doing, bunching his legs so close together that he looked round. From the right angle, it looked like he was rolling toward me. I would squat down to be on the same level, hold out my arms, and he would somersault right into me, not able to stop, not wanting to, knocking me over amidst puppy ears and arms and legs, and a lot of wet pink tongue. We would run and play hard, and then plop panting to the ground. He insisted on lying upside down in my lap, even after he got much too big. Not only was his tummy always round, but it was warm as a rock in the sun, warm as a friendly mitten, warm as a friend's cheek. We were very close. He loved me, and I him. Unreservedly. Seeing how happy I was with my puppy, Carla abandoned her idea of a therapist, at least for the moment.

• • •

I had long ago given up my beloved Wedgwood room. After Toby had gone, it had suddenly seemed less wonderful, empty rather than private. Now that I was back in the house, I found myself looking for alternatives. The trio of Rachel, Erica, and Karen had broken up when Fletcher had finished the rammed earth house, and Karen had moved up the hill to live with her dad. At some point, it turned out that I could share a room with Rachel. I was thrilled when she agreed to share with me. She was five years older, and I had always admired her, albeit often from a distance. Although she was my sister, our circles rarely intersected. She always seemed involved in mysterious grown-up things, and I usually felt like an intruder in her world. This was partly our personalities, and partly because she seemed to have bridged the gap between student and staff, functioning for all intents and purposes like the latter. Rachel was a singer, and she had read more than anyone else, naming books and their authors like a cast of her personal friends. She treated her precious things with such care, they took on an aura of rarity. She was not frivolous, either taking something seriously or not bothering with it at all. But here I was, actually going to live with her. I was flattered that she would even consider it, and imagined being able to talk with her while falling asleep, watch her brush her long red hair at night and maybe even borrow her books.

We were sharing a room meant for three. It was the biggest bedroom on the first floor, and it had two large windows, facing west and south, so the sun shone in all day. We took the two spots by the windows, placing our mattresses on the floor as usual, and arranging our things in apple crates. Nobody had furniture or bed frames—most of us slept on foam mattresses we bought directly from the factory. These were so light that we could move them easily and they were theoretically replaceable when something gross happened, like a goat getting in and peeing on them, or a dog chewing off a corner. Of course we never did replace any—there were too many more important things to spend money on.

Rachel put some of her books out on her shelf, and her Tarot deck wrapped in a sky blue silk scarf, along with her wishing stone. Bob had taught us about wishing stones. Each person, he said, had to find his or her own. A complete ring encircled the luckiest ones. If there were two rings, it was extra lucky. You wanted something small, he said, small enough to fit well in your hand and comfortably in your pocket. Rachel had found hers right away, a pleasingly round piece of milky white quartz with a single yellow circlet zigzagging its way all around. It took me a lot longer, but finally I found one too. It was an ugly shape, with a cone-like tip, but many lines encircled it and I thought it must have many levels of luck. Bob had taught us to rub our wishing stones along the sides of our noses, where there was, he informed us, a special oil that worked its way into every grain, gradually saturating the stone with our essence and making it shiny, while at the same time, we absorbed its magic. I had rubbed mine along my nose, and thought of all my wishes, and it grew shiny and smooth and a little greasy to the touch. I had lost it long ago, and seeing Rachel still faithfully nose-rubbing hers made me think of Bob, and muse on her ability to preserve things forever. She seemed so stable.

I had just begun keeping a journal—a practice common among us. Almost daily, I recorded my feelings about things, dreams I had, hopes and fears, important events. I found it comforting. Now, before going to bed, Rachel and I sat together, pens scribbling in our respective books, and it doubled the comfort. I went to sleep the first night in the glow of light from Rachel reading in bed, safe in our shared domesticity. I was very happy.

But there was space for one more person, so Jeffrey moved in. He hung a poster of Baba Ram Das and a photo of Guru Maharaj Ji in a gold frame over his bed, which he covered with a splendid bedspread of embroidered cloth. I wondered that he hung pictures of both his spiritual guides. I sort of thought you had to choose one or the other, but Jeffrey seemed comfortable with two.

His embroidered bedspread was black and yellow. Black stitching shaped a series of brilliant tiny yellow suns, and each one had a little mica mirror at its center. The whole cloth shimmered and rustled, and was rich, complex, and colorful. I expressed my admiration, and Jeffrey immediately pulled it off his bed, and handed it to me, saying that he would like me to use it as long as I wanted. This troubled me, but the beauty of the bedspread, and the thought of waking every morning under its bright wealth enticed me, and I accepted.

Jeffrey was difficult. He interested me, but he was weird. I liked our routine of doing Hatha Yoga together in the barn at five a.m. He taught me a lot of positions and breathing, and I was good at it. We did the Flamingo together, and the Cobra, the Cat, and the Peacock. Jeffrey wouldn't teach me how to massage my internal organs using my stomach muscles, because he said it wasn't safe for someone my age. But he demonstrated it for me. Standing bent over with his hands on his knees, pale torso bare, he drew his lean stomach in as far as possible, creating a huge hollow space, ribs protruding sharply. Then he moved his belly up under one side of his ribcage, over to the other, then down low on his abdomen. The mobility and articulation of his stomach was amazing. It looked as if he were rolling a ball around inside his skin.

Every now and then, Jeffrey would sit like a Yogi before a long roll of gauze coiled in water like a cobra in a dish. He would swallow the gauze, inch by inch, using only his lips to pull it spiraling out of the dish, into his mouth, and down his throat, until just a couple of inches remained visible. Ever so slowly, he then pulled it up again. This procedure, as gross as it looked, was supposed to cleanse his innards. No one could ever have been as clean as Jeffrey, but he seemed a little oily. He was a skinny man. A headband usually held his shoulder-length dark brown hair out of his face. He had a sharp nose, and very red lips, startling against pale skin. He meditated daily, and practiced a spiritual path of asceticism and self-denial. Knowing that from his sacrifices (giving me the bedspread) Jeffrey gained spiritual kudos, made them seem oddly selfish. I couldn't be sure whether he was lending me his bedspread because he wanted to, or because he liked me, or in order to get points for being generous and demonstrate his detachment from material objects. Something about it seemed vaguely dishonest, like I was helping him cheat.

Most mornings before we woke, Jeffrey went to a hard little mat in his spiritual corner and practiced his breathing in the Lotus Position while doing a headstand. He did this in the nude as Ron had done, now so long ago, but Jeffrey positioned himself carefully in the corner, so all we could see, should we awaken, was the line of sharp bony knobs on his spine ascending to the equally sharp cleft of his airborne buttocks. He took care to keep his back to us at all times, and we would have had to be really looking to see anything exciting. I wasn't much interested anyway, and somehow, I don't think Rachel would have bothered to look at Jeffrey too closely. She was an arbiter of good taste, and seemed to have little patience for excess or nonsense. Although tolerant enough, Rachel did not suffer fools gladly. She was not drawn to extremes, and would never have been attracted to Jeffrey.

The worst thing about living with Jeffrey was that he liked to experiment with different ways of waking me up. I was naturally an early riser, so there was no need for this—he was just amusing himself. I don't think he would have dared do this to Rachel, but he did it to Erica more than once. The sounds of the Breath of Fire were often the first things I heard, which was fine, but one morning early, I felt something tickling my foot. Despite my shaking and twitching, it wouldn't go away. Finally, I sat up to see Jeffrey with a feather, tickling my bare foot, which had been sticking out from under the covers. Another time, he blew in my ear until I awoke.

Yet another morning, I came to awareness with a jolt, hair on end. I sat up, startled for no obvious reason, for there had been no apparent noise or movement. I found Jeffrey sitting motionless in the Lotus Position (right-side up) two feet from my head, barely breathing. He was staring fixedly at me to see how long it would take me to become aware of his gaze. It felt like he had tunneled right through my skull.

That morning, I gave Jeffrey back his bedspread, and moved to another room. Even being able to share with Rachel wasn't worth that amount of weirdness. It was a well-established principle of communal living, that if you didn't like something, you left. I could have brought it up in Community Meeting, and no doubt would have received plenty of support, but I didn't want to make it into such a big deal. It didn't occur to me to just ask Jeffrey to go away, or to stop. He was exercising his rightful freedom. My freedom lay in leaving—a lonely freedom at that.

I had just wanted to be with my sister.

I idolized Rachel from a necessary distance. I knew she loved me, but she wasn't a companion the way my sister Erica was. She seemed preoccupied with different and more important concerns, like her music. She sang at the piano, at special occasions, and out on the porch with her guitar, her pure soprano sending chills up my spine. And she and Ethan recorded jingles to mark our day's events. These they piped through the house on a network of speakers inside and one loudspeaker outside the kitchen door. This was a tremendous upgrade from the old iron triangle used to alert people to meals, classes, or meetings. Rachel and Ethan set the word "Händewasche" to a fragment of Handel's Hallelujah Chorus, recording all four voices, and this was played right before meals instructing everyone to wash their hands. At nine p.m. for Quiet Hour, they played one of Ethan's harmonic compositions with Rachel singing "Now is the time for all to be quiet and say good night." They created a ditty for clean-ups that started "Oh clean oh clean," and ended "Oh scrabble in the dirt little piggies O." These wonderful little musical creations, each with multiple voice tracks and a combination of melodic approaches, made the house ring, giving our schedule polished structure. These were now our school bells, and they lent us legitimacy.

Ethan was a boarding student who had come to us when he was fifteen because he was too smart for regular school. He supposedly had an IQ of 170 or more, but he was flunking out. He was not much to look at: stringy shoulder-length hair of a mousy color, a lot of adolescent fat, and a face full of pimples. He was awkward and clumsy, and never sure where to put himself. His arms and legs never looked natural, as if he had consciously positioned them instead of just letting them be. When he was working with Rachel, Ethan became as excited as a child. His acned awkwardness disappeared, his fleshy hands found purpose as he skillfully recorded, switching tracks, swiftly pushing levers and buttons. I would hear them recording, laughing together, sharing musical camaraderie. I would listen to them from the hallway, scurrying away if it sounded as if they were coming out. I knew they wouldn't like to know I was there. I always assumed that Ethan was a little bit in love with my sister, even after he got involved with Debra. But Rachel was out of his league.

Ethan had several intellectual curiosities, but what fascinated me was his claim that he *saw* music. Every note, he said, was a different color, so he could compose visually. By mixing shades to a pleasing hue, he explained, he created chords. Melodies were developed similarly, by stringing colors in the air in a chromatic sequence that pleased his eye. Ethan brought with him a Moog synthesizer that was luminous with dials and a huge array of sounds. In his room, one of the tiny cubicles in the upstairs hallway, he would play a note for me, and tell me its color. The A above middle C was, he said, a dusky rose. The F# below, was dark orange. I closed my eyes, and listened to each note, straining vainly to see it. The persistently colorless darkness behind my lids disappointed me, yet I never stopped trying.

Ethan was also, perhaps foremost, a Telephone Hacker. For us, this was very convenient. For a long time, the pay phone in the hallway was completely free. Mark called his Nigerian host family from when he was in the Peace Corp; Erica, who dreamt of going to France, called an operator in Paris and asked about the weather in her schoolgirl French; and Carol called Moscow, trying to take a poll of the worker sentiments of the day for her study on the Russian Revolution.

With Ethan along on a trip, you never needed change to make a phone call. He had lots of tricks. He showed us that with certain pay phones, if you jiggled the receiver at the right frequency, you could fool the machine into giving you a dial tone, and open dialing. Once, standing in a phone booth, he sang lovingly into the receiver, an eerie high-pitched sequence of notes, and I thought for a moment that I could finally see the colors of the tones—a rainbow of orange and red, violet and green. I visualized them mingling down the lines with the colors of the telephone wires, mesmerizing an electronic brain somewhere that let him through, mistaking him for one of its own, and a prince at that.

We knew that Ethan was preoccupied with breaking through computer security systems just for the fun of it. He had no interest in the information that became available, the whole object was getting through. Someone must have realized that this could be risky, and Ethan was asked to do it only off the property. We knew he could tap into those square green metal telephone posts that were stuck into the dirt by the road. He used to set off across the field with a belt full of equipment; tools and phone receivers, and wires and clips, and a small reel-to-reel tape player. No one asked him what exactly he was doing.

The day the police arrived, our innocence was genuine. Somehow Ethan had given himself away. They kept him in jail for several hours, not quite believing that the only thing that interested him about breaking into classified government files was the fact that he could do so.

Not long after we bailed him out, the FBI offered Ethan a job.

Beautiful

"Hi, Beautiful," Alan said.

He always greeted me that way. An odd man, short reddish hair perpetually startled and standing on end, he always moved *quickly* and *urgently*. Alan did not feel bound by rules of polite conversation. Most of the time he simply declined to answer when spoken to, stalking rigidly out of the room instead. He often went days without responding verbally, so it had extra punch when he addressed me as "Beautiful."

Every now and then, Alan would rush into the living room, and abruptly sit down at the piano. His large hands could move with amazing speed, traveling the entire keyboard as easily as driving a toy car. He never used sheet music, or played the same thing twice, but seemed to have an infinite repertoire of compositions stored in his memory. All his unspoken words, as well as his silence and the charge behind his quickness sang eloquently through his hands. Pieces dark and complex, light and whimsical, contemplative and storied issued fluently from his fingers.

And he always called me "Beautiful"!

I didn't believe him. Not literally. I was all too aware of my child plainness. But I thought maybe he could see the future, and had noticed some promise I carried that escaped my eye. Alan also told me that I could do anything that I decided to do. He made me feel so . . . ambitious. Could I really??

I was in love with the piano. Having heard Bach's first two-part invention played by some visitor passing through, I thought it the most magical arrangement of sounds I had ever heard. Spending hours at the piano, I managed to pick out most of one hand by ear. I didn't know who had composed it, or what the music was, only that the complex intertwining of musical voices had captured my imagination, and I wanted to be able to play it. One day, after having heard me struggle to pick out the notes for weeks, Alan raced up to me, wordlessly thrust something into my hands, and hastily marched away. My music-reading skills were primitive, but it didn't take me long to hear that he had given me the music to the piece I was trying to learn.

It was so beautiful.

I could do anything I decided to do.

Alan's intensity drew me, partly because he strove to contain it within himself, and when it did come bursting out, it was in spite of his best efforts. He was brutally honest, seemingly incapable of social niceties, or politeness. If he said something, it was because he couldn't manage to prevent himself from doing so, and he meant it. So often feeling lost in the shuffle, I always felt real and appreciated with Alan. He gave me belief in perseverance, hope for my own evolution, and the means to do something I had decided to do. These were precious gifts. But they came at a heavy price, because it was Alan who ran over Sun Bear.

● ● ●

He had been driving the red truck up the road on the property, going too fast, not watching the dogs that were worrying the wheels and running alongside. A sudden swerve with those big hands, a foray into the wrong octave to avoid a deep hole had done it. A sharp jolt, a snuff of life, and that was it.

I felt nothing. It wasn't real—this false silence left where my best buddy had just been. Sun Bear lay in the road where the truck had flung him—no injury apparent except for a rim of blood around his lips. But his absence was deafening. I couldn't feel the loss, and I couldn't hate Alan, and I couldn't quite concentrate.

Alan put Sun Bear's body on a board, and carried the board to the spot on the hill I picked out. Then, refusing all help or company, I tried to dig that hole alone. The dirt was hard and rocky, and the shovel was too big for me, and I got blisters, but the hole wasn't nearly big enough. Alan came back, and I let him finish it for me. He helped me put Sun Bear down into it, and then I sent him away again. And then I hated him. I hated him for what he had done, and hated him more for being nice and trying to help, so I couldn't just blame him without restraint. I hated him because I loved him, and he had cost me dearly.

The first clumps of soil mingled with Sun Bear's beautiful white fur as he lay in the earth. I wished I had wrapped him in something. The sight of damp clods of dirt lying on him made him look so dead. I kept expecting him to spring up and shake himself clean as I had seen him do so many times.

I started shoveling dirt, and I covered his body up to his neck like laying a quilt over him. I couldn't cover up his head. I sat there for a long time, doing nothing. I was stumped. Eventually, Alan returned once more, and gently pushed me aside. Without another look, I left, and went back down the hill. Alan finished the job.

I knew I was abandoning Sun Bear. My roly-poly puppy who had never lost his pot-bellied sweetness. I wasn't even staying with him through his burial, letting someone else do it for me. But then he had left me. The one I had allowed myself to believe wouldn't go.

I went to the house, and took part in normal life, aware that everyone expected a reaction from me. My attachment to Sun Bear was no secret. They were disconcerted by my cheerful equanimity. The inquisitive surprise I saw in Suzanne's and Ellen's eyes made me self-conscious, knowing I should be acting bereaved. But I couldn't. I wasn't. I was supposed to cry and be sad, just as I was supposed to love everybody around me. Maybe I was, but maybe I was also relieved that I didn't have to worry about feeding him, or worry about him getting into trouble, or worry about him disappearing, or worry about him getting run over or worry about losing him. The worst had happened. Maybe I just wanted to pretend he was only a dog, and go my way.

Mostly what I felt was a need to get away, to escape notice, sympathy, expectation, and observation. The whole place suddenly felt like a pressure cooker—a hot pot—a teeming cauldron. I left the house, slamming the door on my way out, and tore down the hill to the road as fast as possible. Across the road, I climbed over the stile, landing abruptly in the neighbor's field.

I was on the lookout for bulls, trying to stay close to the fence while avoiding the brambles and the burrs that grew there. I skirted up the edge of the hill, passing by the cow graveyard. All the way up the hill, I could feel the eyes of the house on my back. Not, I thought with resentment, that anyone would actually notice my absence. My presence was as temporary and dispensable as anyone else's. Finally, I reached the top of the hill and went over the crest out of eyeshot of our little tempest world and, like a sigh, a weight was lifted.

By a grove of trees was a magical place where a small stream ran along a pebbly bottom. There, the wonderful tall grass was adorned with silvered tufts that Erica called "crickle fuzz." It looked silvergolden in the sun, and rustled comfortably in the breezes. After trailing my fingers in the water, touching a smooth pebble, chasing small minnows back into the shadows by a rock, I went and lay down in the tall grass. And knew myself to be completely invisible. Looking up, a shifting space of blue was framed by the tops of the waving grasses.

I fell asleep. Then awoke after a time, sun-pummeled, cold and stiff, and terribly sad. Sun Bear had loved it up there. We'd gone together many times, and he'd chased and snapped and burrowed and waded enthusiastically, coming up with idiotic expressions, his own private lunatic. It was inconceivable to think that I would never see him again.

On my way back, cresting the hill headed toward home, I could look down on the entire property. The Main House appeared mature and elegant from this distance. I could see the crazy garden, the goats around the barn. It looked so peaceful. How could it look so peaceful and be so disquiet? There were people milling out in the yard, two perched on the fence like magpies. They looked busy, serene, well-organized, and even a little mechanical. You'd never know from a distance what turbulence ran through the place like a swollen river.

I loved it and hated it. Loved the constant activity, the happenings. Hated the unrelenting uproar. Loved being a part of things, but hated not being able to escape them. I belonged completely—it was my country—and I was ever alien, looking out for my mother ship.

• • •

I asked my mother about that time on the phone yesterday morning.

"Do you remember my 'nervous habit'"?

"Oh yes, I felt *awful* for you. Where you aware of it?"

"*Aware* of it? It was the main thing I thought about. It was completely humiliating. There was nothing I could do to stop it."

"You poor thing. I didn't know how to help you."

"Well, I remember when you tried to get me to go to a therapist."

"Oh, really? I don't remember that, but you know I did consult a psychologist about you."

"Really? What did he say?"

"Well, after I told him all the things that had happened to you, he said 'What do you expect?'"

"What things?"

"Oh, my god, in the space of three or four years you left your home, moved far away from your father, were ostracized by your schoolmates, tore your face up falling off your bike, almost died getting stung by bees, had your best friend killed, and then your beloved dog."

"Oh, yeah," I say, realizing that I hadn't even put the bike accident and the bee stings in the book. Not that they weren't important, just that at least in memory, daily life on the commune felt more difficult than these discrete events.

"Maybe I should have made you see a therapist," she muses. "What do you think?"

"I don't know. I hated the idea. I suppose if I met the person and liked him or her, it might have been helpful."

"You would never talk about things. Do you remember when I read my poem to you for your sixteenth birthday?"

"Yes."

"Well, I had this hope, 'cause I talked about all these terrible things that had happened to you in my poem, that you would finally cry about them when I read it to you."

"That I would *finally cry* about them?"

"Well, yeah, you never did, you know."

Didn't I? Did I? Certainly if I cried it wouldn't have been with my mother. I grieved in my own hard way, with or without tears I am not sure.

But I clearly remember her taking me out to sit on the roof of our house for her to read that poem to me. It was summer, and she had surrounded the whole event with this air of importance that put me on my guard. I loved the poem, and her in the writing of it, but later when she told me of her hope that it would elicit some kind of emotional catharsis, release some reservoir of tears, I was shocked and furious at her intrusion.

What strikes me more now is how uncommunicative I had become. And how instinctively I sought solitude for my deepest sorrows or angers or upsets. And I wonder how I had transformed from a natural blabbermouth to such a withdrawn and reticent person with an over-developed sense of privacy and a crushing super ego. Although she had lost her awareness of what I was feeling and experiencing, my mother was always available to talk. Why did I choose not to, and if not to her, why didn't I talk to someone else? Like Erica, my secondary mother, or Ellen, who loved me? Something about the culture of sharing, expressiveness, and honesty had shut me up for good. I had stopped talking by the age of eleven. And it took a couple of decades to start me up again.

All of Carla's efforts over the years to reverse this trend had the opposite effect. Her poem reading was hardly her first attempt to unleash some torrent of emotion in me. I must have been thirteen or fourteen when my mother discovered Primal Scream Therapy. She left for New York for three weeks, having been given, she explained to me, a strict injunction against contact with anyone, including her children. She likened it to her fasting, a frequent practice of hers to which I had long grown accustomed. The theory behind fasting, as well as I understood it, was that digesting food placed a demand on "the system" that detracted energy from healing illness or injury. Fasting not only eliminated this drain of resources, but offered the body an opportunity to rid itself of accumulated toxins. This, she had explained to me, was why her tongue got coated during a fast (she eagerly stuck out her tongue as an exhibit, its pasty white coating thick and gooey) and her "B.M.'s" became dark brown and odiferous (she spared me a demonstration). The no-contact rule surrounding the Primal Scream Therapy was to help her focus her energies on healing, to purify her system, and to prevent her from distracting herself with current relationships. I couldn't help feeling a little insulted and hurt.

Life at Nethers without my mother went on as usual. I felt both freer and more lost. I realized in her absence that every night she had tracked me down to make me go to bed and to say good night, that she had noticed if I was missing from a meal or a meeting, that although I tried hard not to resort to it, she had offered a layer of protection or resource, the lack of which left me feeling exposed and tenuous.

There was one clandestine phone call, halfway through her treatment. I pictured her crouched in a stairwell, whispering furtively into the receiver of a pay phone. She sounded weird. She said she couldn't talk, but she wanted to tell me that she loved me and that she missed me, and was I okay? And that was it.

Was I okay? Three weeks was a long time. When she came home, I watched her from a distance for a few minutes before going to greet her, wondering and a little afraid to see what might have changed about her. She grabbed me and hugged me hard, then held me away to look closely into my face.

"I'm so glad to see you," she said. "It seemed like forever. How are you?"

"Fine" I answered.

"It was too long," she stated definitively, "but I think it really helped me."

"That's good."

She looked the same, except there was a sort of rarified sadness about her, a shadow of spent pain. She seemed quieter, gentled, chastened, even.

Primal Scream, it turned out, like The Knowledge, was something one had to continue to practice on a daily basis. To assist in her private sessions, Carla brought home with her a cassette tape of her colleagues screaming. Apparently all the participants had screamed together in a great darkened room (I pictured a basement), each on his or her own thin mattress, pounding pillows with Bataka Bats, moaning and sobbing, overcome with their infant-anguish at rejection, abandonment, loss, and fear.

Once a day, Carla headed off into the woods for an hour with her tape recorder and a pillow. She would return, subdued, with eyes moistened. One rainy day, she could not go into the woods, so she went into her room and shut the door, telling me she was going to "scream for a while." For the first fifteen minutes, I stayed as far away as possible. But then curiosity got the better of me, and I crept over to stand outside her room. At first I heard nothing but the hissing of a tape recorder, then diffuse sounds of people weeping. Then there was a man's voice crying clearly,

"Daddy! Daddy! Don't hurt me, Daddy." The voice was tinny and weak, but this did nothing to disguise its torment and fear. The back of my neck prickled.

"Daddy!" he went on, "Daddy!."

"DADDY!" my mother suddenly wailed from the other side of the thin door, causing me to jump back in alarm.

"Daddy!" wept the man on the tape.

"DADDY!" chorused my mother, "DADDY! WHY WON'T YOU
LOOK AT ME? DADDY!?"

"Daddy, Don't Hurt Me."

"DADDY LOVE ME, PLEASE LOVE ME, DADDY."

It took me several moments to sort out that she wasn't talking to
my daddy, she was talking to her own, the grandfather I had never
met. All I knew about him was that he had been a highly respected
judge in a small New Jersey community, that his wife had belittled
him, and that my aunt Lee had been his favorite. And here was
my mother weeping and calling out to him as a small child. It was
awful. I sort of wanted to cry myself, or maybe to throw up. I got
out of earshot as quickly as I could.

But this became incorporated into my mother's efforts to make
me emote and express, to "get it out."

"Why don't you go scream about it?" she would suggest when I
was upset about something, holding out to me her little tape deck
and pillow. "It really might make you feel better."

"Uhhh, no thanks," I'd answer. The thought of lying out in the
woods sobbing and pounding my fists into her pillow felt indecent.
And who would I call out for? My Daddy? Certainly. My Mommy?
Without question. And what earthly good would that do? Things
were as they were, and I didn't see any point in being melodramatic
about it.

23

What Bantam Roosters?

Back in Community Meeting. There was only one thing on the agenda. The rats. Again. But first, we were going around the circle checking in. Ellen started. She licked her lips and determinedly pushed her sleeves up to her elbows before speaking.

"I'm feeling resentful today—I am working very hard answering letters in the office, and I don't have any time for myself, and everyone else seems to be just knocking off and enjoying themselves."

Around the circle, several people nodded their heads understandingly and a couple of people looked blank.

"It's not that I mind working—I mean, I came here to work, really, and I think what I am doing is important, it's just that I don't feel appreciated for doing it."

The rule was not to respond to people during check-in unless asked to do so, and we waited quietly to see if Ellen was done.

"I guess that's it," she said. "I just needed to say it."

When it was her turn to speak, Amy sat up straight, her legs folded under her on the couch. She opened her hands, palms up, in a gesture of offering, "I just want to say 'thank-you' to all of you. I never thought I could feel this way. I love every one of you. This is such a beautiful place, and you are all such beautiful people. I dig it here so much. I realize that I have never been in a real living loving learning environment before. You've changed my life forever."

Amy radiated earnestness as she spoke. She had been with us for a week, during which she had thrown herself wholeheartedly into our activities. We had casually included her in the easy embrace of group life. She was pleasant and energetic, and unremarkable. Amy had planted her first row of beans, hammered her first nail, and milked her first goat. She had participated in a community meeting, played games with us, hugged a lot of people, and had many new experiences. She was dizzy with change. We nodded tolerantly at this familiar enthusiasm, accepted her thanks, told her how much we had enjoyed having her, wished her luck, and moved on to the next item on the agenda.

I looked at her wonderingly. She was not the first person to claim radical transformation from a brief stay with us. I didn't get that. Was it so easy to change a life? I could easily imagine changing location, or lifestyle, but that did not add up to the kind of dramatic alteration she was talking about. And how did spending a perfectly ordinary week with us bring about fundamental change? What had her life been like that a week in ours could transform her? Would it last?

What did this mean for me? Might I, too, be subject to sudden and radical change, when I stepped out into the unfamiliar? Was Amy particularly malleable, or was this the changeable way of things? Certainly I had witnessed many people undergo transformations, more or less before my eyes, but I had never thought that the same might someday happen to me. The thought made me uncomfortable. I had figured out that the only constant in life was change, but I had thought of it in terms of external change. I didn't like the thought that I might unexpectedly look down and find myself different, like Alice in Wonderland, with my feet far away.

After this, the meeting proper began. Few items showed up as frequently on the community meeting agenda as the rats. They were a terrible problem. Careless housekeeping, large bags of grains, flour, and beans, doors left open, and an absence of cats, all conspired to make us a highly desirable rat habitat. At first, we tried to ignore them. But they grew increasingly bold, running across people's beds at night, or sitting in full view, staring at us insolently. The noise they made was deafening. At night we could hear them chewing and gnawing, scampering and cavorting in the walls, and their destructive powers were alarming. The rats ate their way through the plastic garbage cans we bought to store grains, they chewed up sheaves of paper, they ate through telephone wires, and electric cables. I feared they were eating away the very foundations of the house, and imagined that one day, like a beaver's big tree felled in the wood, a great cracking and splintering would be heard, and the house would just collapse inward, leaving us staring in surprise at the sky through a few remaining timbers. We began to get serious about getting rid of them.

Rat poison. It seemed an obvious way to start. But a large faction of the community objected. For one thing, poison works slowly and painfully, and rats, although undesirable as housemates, had feelings too. Plus, Dave said they would crawl between the walls to die and leave a stink. And rat poison was environmentally objectionable, and a danger to other creatures. One long meeting later, we nonetheless set poison out in the basement and by the stairs outside, nowhere accessible to dogs, chickens or people.

My grandmother came to visit. We made a bed for her in the half-refinished attic, on the usual foam mattress on the floor. She was very brave, and went to bed without complaint, clutching her purse close to her person, as she did when she went shopping in New York City. But those furred thieves knew a treasure when they saw one, and as soon as she closed her eyes in uneasy sleep, two of them took the purse's handles in their front teeth, and were in the act of dragging it off toward their lair in the wall, when she awoke. Grandma threw her shoes at them, retrieved her purse, and woke my mother up, insisting that they get into the car and leave immediately.

The poison wasn't working.

Carla wanted to try Catch 'em Alive traps. This was pooh-poohed as inefficient, but a trial was agreed to. They actually worked pretty well at catching rats. But when we released them down by the barn, the rats simply turned around and headed home. It was clear that we had to take them further away. "What is the radius of a rat?" we asked. We tried one mile, then two, then five. Every time, no matter how many times we turned them around to confuse them, the released prisoners shot off at full speed in a direct line for the house. We knew where they were going. For a time, whenever anyone went anywhere, they would drop off several rats along their way. Once, Laurel took three with her when she went to Washington, D.C., and let them loose in Dupont Circle. I think it pleased her personal sense of displacement to do this. I don't know if those rats made it back too, or if news of new vacancies went out, but there was no decrease in population.

One morning, I was on my way downstairs in the dark to make breakfast. I hadn't put on a light because there were people sleeping in the upstairs hallway, and I didn't want to wake them. At the bottom of the stairs was a door that we kept shut at night to keep the heat downstairs. It was very quiet as I was sleepily feeling my way blindly down the dark stairway.

I didn't notice the rat at the bottom of the stairs until I stepped on it. I felt a soft squish under my feet, followed by shrill squeaks and the scrabbling of little claws on the floor. It was trapped, and so was I. I shrieked, threw open the door, and ran out into the hallway. But the rat in its panic had grabbed onto the bottom of my jeans, and was hanging on for dear life, squealing. I ran yelping down the hallway, shaking my leg for all I was worth, but unable to dislodge the rodent. Visions of it climbing inside my pants up my leg and onto my person, kept me in a screaming panic.

From somewhere came the idiotic notion that if I could put my leg into the toilet, the rat would drop off into the water. Forgetting that we had put bricks into the tank to lower the water level, I ran for the bathroom, awakening the room full of sleepers in the adjoining room. Once in the bathroom, people gathered groggily to see what the fuss was about. I suddenly realized my error with the water level, so I just dropped my pants. Perennially too large anyway, my jeans fell down loosely, covering the rat, and I escaped, leaving someone else to deal with it.

The Catch 'em Alive traps weren't working.

At that point, Kent and Carl, our two juvenile delinquents, took matters into their own hands. Without anyone knowing, they took several wooden broom handles and fastened knives and nails to the tips. One night, the two of them lay in ambush on top of the refrigerator and the cabinets, and waited until the rats came out. What happened next was all too clear from the blood splattered all over the kitchen in the morning, and the one small, mangled rat carcass outside the kitchen door. The savages themselves both developed rat phobias after that night, and paled at the mere mention of the rodents.

Fletcher said that we should feed the rats cottonseed, which would make the males sterile. Tim wanted to know whether that would work for people. We left dishes of it around, but I don't think the rats ever ate it. Perhaps Tim did.

Jerry brought Alice, his pet black snake. She was very friendly for a snake. She would wind herself comfortably on her favorite perch on Jerry's shoulders, twining around his neck and shoulders, and resting her head on top of his, facing the same direction. Jerry liked to wear her like this, particularly when visitors arrived. Unsuspecting folk would not notice Alice until her head moved, and she became alarmingly visible amidst the curly locks of her host.

Alice was relatively small, maybe two and a half feet long, when we put her in the basement to eat rats. It was warm and damp down there, and she happily slid off into one of those holes under the house. We never noticed a change in the rat population, but after some months, Jerry went down to find her, to see how she was doing. She had disappeared, and he wondered if she had taken off altogether. Wherever she was, she didn't seem to be eating very many rats.

Mark read an article that claimed that if you introduced domestic white rats into the territory of wild brown rats, a great war would ensue, and the whites would kill off the browns. Then, as you had used only males, they would die off within months. Discussion on this one was heated. Carla had read somewhere that lab rats carried a virulent strain of bacteria possibly transmittable to humans; Suzanne had a horror of the little pink eyes, and hairless tails of white rats. White rats were so . . . rat-like. Most of us were skeptical that laboratory-bred and cage-born domestic rats would be any match for country-fed wild ones. But eventually we decided to try it.

Nine white adult male rats were purchased, and let loose in the basement after Alice disappeared. This seemed a small army for the legions of their wild brown brothers, but the experts had attested to their fierceness. Tim and Russell wanted to christen them with the names of great warriors, thinking that would transmit extra powers. In the end, we just let them loose, because true to their reputation, they were already starting to scrap with each other.

The war was on! We could hear them fighting in the walls, day and night. It seemed that Mark's article had been right. After several days, there was quiet. It appeared that the fierce white warriors had, indeed slaughtered their wild foes.

"White man comes to America," Dave said.

Several quiet weeks later, someone unearthed a rat's nest in the closet. There, in their usual helplessness, were six little rat pups. But these looked different. Upon inspection, we saw that their skin was mottled. Splotches of pink and brown suggested that the warriors had not adhered to the informed medical opinion that domestic rats would not breed with wild ones.

The rats had won again.

We never found an effective way of getting rid of the rats. Their population waxed and waned according to season, year, and other unknown variables, but nothing we did seemed to have much impact. They eventually became a part of life—something we all hated, but with which we had to make peace.

• • •

My father's bedspread was finally done. I had worked on it in community meetings for almost two years, and it measured the hours spent there. It was enormous. I tied off the last knot with a sense of loss and apprehension. Spreading it out on the living room floor, I viewed it critically. I loved the richness of the unexpected color combinations, but minded that the colors changed irregularly. I loved the size and weight of it, and the fact that I had actually completed it. I was really quite proud, and began to anticipate my father's reaction with excitement. But there was one problem. It was filthy. Animal hairs stuck to it all over, many of my own hairs had gotten caught up into the stitches, there were smudges and dirt spots, and one place where I had spilled hot chocolate on it. It had a kind of sweaty, smoky, goaty odor.

Following Rachel's detailed instructions, I piled the whole thing into a tub full of cold water with soap, and started washing it. Instantly, the water darkened with dirt, and with all the different colors. I hated seeing the colors leaching out, afraid that it would leave the whole thing pale and faded. I washed it twice, and then rinsed it again and again. It was a sad-looking lump by that time, a sodden heap of yarn, and for a panicked moment I thought I had ruined it. I shouldn't have tried to wash it! I should have let Daddy worry about that! I should have listened to my mother who had advised against the wash. "He'll love it just like it is, because you made it for him," she had said. But I didn't want him to love it because I had made it, I wanted him to love it and to use it because it was beautiful.

I realized I hadn't thought this through. How was I going to dry it?? I knew I was supposed to lay it out flat, "block" it, and let it air dry, but where was I going to do that? It would take days! Rachel came to my rescue. Walking through the house, we determined that the attic was the best location, being warm and less trafficked than most, and hunted up some old sheets to spread on the floor. Together we carried the heavy dripping mass up the stairs, getting thoroughly soaked in the process. We then painstakingly laid it out, stretching it to its approximate correct shape and placing an odd assortment of boots, bricks, and boards at the corners and along the edges to serve as weights. It looked pathetic and drowned. Despondently, I closed the door behind me.

I checked on the bedspread hourly, and saw no change. In the afternoon, I impatiently pushed the weights off, because they seemed to be just making things worse, and I hated the way they looked. I had so wanted it to be beautiful. Then I just left and tried to forget about it.

Three or four days later, I screwed up my courage and went back. Slowly opening the door, it suddenly occurred to me that the rats might have found it and been chewing on it. I rushed in on the burst of adrenaline that thought produced, and saw, to my amazed delight, an almost dry, almost clean, and definitely beautiful bedspread. Some resilient property of the wool had pulled it back into shape and plumped the fibers again. The colors were still rich and wonderful, and kneeling down to sniff, I found it smelled pleasantly of soap. Taking off my shoes, I lay down in the middle of the bedspread, stretching out my arms and legs. It had worked! I had made something beautiful! I couldn't wait to give it to Daddy.

He inspected the package curiously. I had wrapped it in old funnies saved from some newspaper, wishing for real wrapping paper, maybe a ribbon. It made a huge bundle. Cautiously opening it and pulling away the paper, my father's mouth made that familiar "o" shape of surprise and admiration. He stood up and began unfolding the yards of material, clearly pleased and a little astonished. It bothered me only a little that what he said he liked best were the very irregularities that had offended me, but seeing it spread over their bed right away, and for years to come, never ceased to delight me. Emboldened, I ventured into sewing, discovered a talent, and began making clothes for everyone around me, not least of all my father.

24

Matt

In addition to her other jobs, Rachel had elected herself official mail carrier. Every morning at 11:15 she positioned herself in the field on a little hummock in sight of the mailbox. The mailman usually came by 11:45. In good weather, Rachel would take an apple crate out into the grass with her, and sit on it while playing the recorder, her abundant red hair shining and lifting in the breeze. Although Rachel was the official carrier, at the sound of the mail car—a beat-up old Pontiac with the U.S. Mail Carrier sign stuck in the rear window—a handful of people suddenly materialized and breathed impatiently down her neck as she gathered the armload of mail out of the box and walked up the hill, refusing to sort through it until she reached the porch. We would then crowd impatiently around the table as she carefully examined each letter, card, and magazine, and put it in its proper pile, or handed it to an eagerly outstretched hand.

The mail was a big event each day, and Sundays and holidays were decidedly sadder for the lack of it. Although the vast majority of the mail was related to school business, and most of that was bills, it still represented our only daily contact with the outside world. With no TV on the premises, and only the occasional newspaper, our isolation was quite intact. We had reason to think that our mail sometimes got read before it reached us. The postmistress's name was Lacy Orange. This was a name I loved, its delicacy suggesting something quite different from the fat, dour, arthritic old woman it belonged to. She knew a lot of details about us that we hadn't told anyone. I imagined her sitting in the tiny post office over a kettle of boiling water, steaming envelopes, and reading their contents, trying to make sense of us.

We didn't interact much with our neighbors—the nearest, not counting the Jacksons, was a half a mile away. Some were actively friendly, some ignored us altogether, but none were part of our lives. Most members of the commune had little contact with family or friends outside. Some people clearly came to Nethers to disappear, as Elias had. Many of our students were outcasts and misfits in their home schools and had few if any friends to be in touch with. Staff actively discouraged students from having too much contact with their parents, particularly when they first came, because it invariably caused dissonance and upset. I heard little talk about families or relationships outside our boundaries. Certainly from my own experiences of coming and going, the outside world faded quickly once I was back at Nethers. The immediate concerns were so in your face and pressing that outside matters dropped out of sight. And yet we were all drawn to the mail, seemingly waiting for some message or confirmation or word. Perhaps those who were in exile were looking out for reprieve; those in hiding, for discovery.

I got the very occasional post card from my father, who traveled a lot and sent me cards from Nairobi, Bolivia or Europe. Other than those, I couldn't expect anything, having next-to-no contact with other family members, and no current friendships outside of Nethers. I got caught up in the excitement nonetheless.

One day while I was hanging over the table as usual, watching Rachel dole out the letters, she paused, looked hard at a long white envelope, and then handed it to me. I received it with incredulity. Who could it be from? My name had been written on the front of the plain envelope in large letters, and traced and retraced repeatedly with a blue ballpoint pen, until it was more engraved than written, impressed deeply into the paper, then underlined and scored. There was no stamp, which meant that it had been hand-delivered. It was quite thick.

I knew right away that Matt, who had just been visiting, must have left it. His visit had been very strange. I had known Matt for several years. He was in his mid-twenties, an unremarkable-looking man, not large, but comfortably substantial, and capable. He had thick eyebrows, and straight blond hair, shorter than most, that tended to hang down into his eyes until he impatiently swept it back. He was quiet, but it was a warm quiet. Matt was a nomad, living out of his old VW van, traveling the circuit of communes around the country, staying in each place for as long as it felt right, and moving on when it didn't. He had been a regular visitor for years. Although he had never applied for membership, because we knew him he was allowed more flexibility to come and go than other visitors. He would stay a week, a month, or just a few days.

He had won my loyalty early on, with special attentions. He took me for drives in his van, which smelled of blankets, damp, and man—unfamiliar and peculiar, but pleasant. Before the pigs and my self-imposed vegetarianism, while Carla still had me on The Diet, we would drive to a nearby road stand where he bought me hamburgers and milkshakes in bold defiance. I would hop up into the front seat, high above the road, and look around at Matt's home-made bedroom in the back, where he had laid a foam mattress covered with an Indian bedspread. There was a box of books and a flashlight, a spare pair of boots, and a down vest. His clothes swayed on hooks by the door, and an empty beer bottle rolled around on the floor. I felt important "riding shotgun." It was exciting to sneak off with an adult to break rules. No matter that I didn't really like hamburgers anymore. It was our guilty secret, and secrets were thrilling.

I liked Matt, liked to go with him, and felt that I was special to him. The very fact that he had singled me out made me giddy and grateful. My only real beef with him was his disappearances. Oh, everyone disappeared—or could at any moment. I had learned that long ago, but I wished he would tell me when he was going and when he would be back. I thought of him out there, wandering the world, and wondered whether he ever thought of me. At least he always came back eventually, which was more than could be said for most people.

He had been gone for a year or so this time, and I had begun to wonder if he had finally disappeared for good, when he turned up. As always, he settled in immediately, coming into the house with no fanfare, and falling into our rhythm, picking up, unasked, on some job that needed to be done. I accompanied him out to the chicken shed to patch up new holes the rats had made, in preparation for shutting the hens in for molting. It was February or March, raw and blistering. Water had washed the red dirt of the driveway into ruts and rivulets, and then frozen. The grass was flat and colorless in defeat, matting the hills.

Squatting by the shed, we worked in silence and perfect accord. Together, we had gathered a pile of boards of all sizes to use for patches. Matt would select one and hold it against the wall, while I handed him nails one by one. I took pleasure in their biting coldness as they clung to my bare fingers. It was a game to see if I could have each nail ready exactly when Matt reached for it, positioned to go precisely from my hand to the board, to be nailed in with a few strong, well-aimed strokes of his hammer. Our rhythm was faultless and unbroken, my anticipation working smoothly like a sense of smell.

I often worked this way with my father when I visited him. Working together was the way we spent most of our time. Although Daddy was an artist, a scientist and an intellectual, he could also turn his hand to carpentry, plumbing, wiring, masonry, and any number of other practical skills. I could see him focusing his intelligence and creativity on a practical problem, and solving it with a combination of mind and memory. His father, my grandfather, had also been skilled with his hands, and I sensed his presence in my daddy's abilities. With Daddy, I learned how to help without being told what to do. I learned to sense where to be, what to have ready, the right tension on the rope, the right pressure on the lever, with no word exchanged. This was normal for me, as normal as how Daddy and I would slip out early in the morning when I visited him, me barefoot, he holding a mug of coffee in one hand, my hand firmly in the other. It was the foundation of our closest closeness. On that day with Matt, I missed him, my daddy, as only a thirteen-year-old girl can on a cold day with another man.

And it was cold. Matt, wearing only a vest, appeared to feel nothing, so I, out of some misbegotten sense of pride, stalwartly refused to don gloves or hat, and left my jacket open to the piercing wind, willing my teeth not to chatter.

As we worked, Matt became increasingly silent and distant, and I became increasingly hurt and confused. He glanced at me sharply from under his brows, but I could not understand his frowning look. I figured he was in a bad mood, or cold, or I didn't know what. Abruptly, he threw down his tools and stomped into the house, barely stopping to grab his backpack from the room where I had thought he was going to be staying, before he swung into his van, and was down the road with a splatter of gravel, without a word or a look for anyone.

I was shocked. I hadn't moved from my position squatting by the shed, surrounded by the tools from our unfinished job. My hands were cold. Despite myself, I started to cry. Here I had thought Matt and I were friends, and he hadn't even noticed I was with him. Obviously, he had other things on his mind, and couldn't even be bothered to help clean up or say goodbye.

I tried to finish the job myself, but lacked the strength to get those damn boards on. Plus, I was feeling too much like an idiot for thinking Matt had a special affection for me to be able to hammer a nail straight. The dismay of mistaken self-importance was sharp—one more lesson in insignificance.

And then, two days later, the letter.

I took it from Rachel's outstretched hand reluctantly, and ignored her inquiringly raised eyebrow, feeling self-conscious. Going around to the back of the house, I held it between my teeth while I climbed to the top of the pine tree by the door to one of my favorite private reading places. Near the top of the tree, six branches stretched out from the trunk at the same level. There, I had found my place.

Head supported by a branch at just the right height, I could read there for hours undisturbed, and could rise periodically higher up into the wind and sky above me, by climbing up into the thin top-most branches that moved with the wind. I was close enough to the house to watch the life below me, and to know what was going on, but I didn't have to be a part of it unless I chose. No one ever looked up and saw me. Dozens of people went in and out over the course of the day. Some of them came right under my tree in thought or conversation, but they never looked up.

It took me a long time to open the envelope. It sat in my hand, ominously heavy and unfamiliar, and I wasn't sure I wanted to know what was in it. Finally I used a small branch to open the seal and took out the letter. It was written on odd scraps of paper, the first few pages torn out of a paperback book, the back of a check register, a receipt slip from a gas station. The writing was small and dark, wandering around the pages half-randomly, beginning without salutation, so I was not sure where it started. It didn't seem to matter:

I have had feelings for you for a long time that a grown-up man shouldn't have for a child. Sometimes when we are together, like this afternoon, I forget that you are just a kid, and I want to act like you are my own age, and do things that I know I shouldn't want to do with you. I am going away, and this time I won't be back. I don't think I will ever see you again. I keep going away, and trying to get my shit together, but every time I come back, I realize that I am just the same as before. So I won't come back anymore.

Maybe someday you will understand this letter. I know that some day you will meet a boy your own age, and you will discover the most wonderful things, and part of that will be the little hole between your legs, and the wonderful way it can make you feel. I know that boy can't be me, although I wish it could.

I hope you will forgive me someday. I don't want to lay a head-trip on you. I am trying hard to get my own head together straight, and don't want to mess yours up, like mine is.

Matt.

The back of my neck got hot, and I started to sweat. Embarrassment rose off me like steam, and the rank feel of it made me queasy. Shoving the pages back into their envelope, I crammed the whole thing into my pocket, dropped down out of my tree and took off across the fields, headed for the pine-forest. I sat on the fence that bordered it, grown over with honeysuckle and poison ivy, and faced the house for a long time.

Then I took the letter out and examined the front again. I imagined Matt sitting in his van in indecision for a long time, maybe right there in our driveway, tracing and re-tracing my name over and over again before finally leaving it in the box for me. All those excursions in that van to get ice cream . . . had he been thinking . . . ? Every time I hugged him hello or goodbye? Did everyone know about this? Everyone but me?? Is this why he kept going away and coming back? It was so completely unexpected, and felt so wrong. I had trusted him, thought he was my friend, thought we understood each other, and it turned out he had been thinking something completely different, something I would not have chosen. I had always thought of Matt as my special friend. Unlike with Mark, I had never wished I were older so we could have a different kind of relationship. I had been quite content. It had been such a relief to not have to say everything—to just know, like I felt I knew with Daddy. And it turned out I knew nothing. There was something humiliating about having been so clueless, and Matt's crude reference to my anatomy made me squirm.

Suddenly in a fury, I dug a small hole with my foot, tore the letter up into fragments, and put a match to the small shredded pile. The pages curled and smoked, and writhed in the pit with a lurid sinuous motion. I found a big stone, and dropped it unceremoniously on top, then dropped myself over the fence into the forest.

Its long, straight, shaded aisles, neatly aligned, seemed to lead off into another place and time. I lay down on the needles, and inhaled their damp sharp scent, gazing up at the feathered branches sifted by the sky. Hard as I tried with my constant forays into nature's peaceful impersonal corners, I could never escape the heat of my environment. I liked the heat partly, but sometimes it was too confusing. Sometimes, I wanted to just close my eyes, and not see so much. But my desire to be in the thick of things worked against that, and I ended up going back and forth. From the heat of the sweat to the cold dash of water. From the press of complicated relationships to the barren silence of solitude. Each extreme seemed heightened by the other, and I longed for a more temperate zone. But could not find one.

Certainly, I also longed for love. Everyone, it seemed, had love but me. I hopefully inspected every young male who arrived, and was invariably ousted by someone else. Erica was assertive and hypnotically pretty, while I felt shy and plain. Mandy had big breasts, while I still had none. Erin was an accomplished flirt, I was awkward and untried. Part of the problem was certainly that I did not know what I wanted. The thought of sex alarmed me—it wasn't that. But it was surely something. I wanted something. And only strange things came to me.

Jerry was a visiting prospective student. His teeth were surprisingly bad for someone so young. At fifteen, even without the graying influence of brushing with burnt eggplant, he had the teeth of an old tobacco-chewing man, snaggly and yellowed, with red swollen gums. His hair, cut in the shag-like style popular at the time, was a nondescript brown, and oily flat. His skin was pale, the face marked by abundant adolescent eruptions. He hunched over, his upper back curved in a sharp C so that his narrow chest was concave. And he had huge feet. He boasted that he could rarely find shoes big enough to fit.

We were all going to sleep outdoors. Jerry lay his bag down right next to mine. In the middle of the night, I awoke to find him stroking my face. When I did not react, he shifted over close to me, and brought his face into the opening of my bag, looming against the sky. I let him kiss me. No one had ever wanted to kiss me before, and I was curious. He brought his lips against mine, and pressed with a solid steady push. Then he exhaled a little puff of breath that went sideways across my lips, tickling. This dry mashing of lips went on for some time. Nothing happened or changed; I felt nothing except, after a while, bored and irritated. I finally rolled over and went to sleep.

In the morning, looking again, I could not believe that I had let this person near me. He looked at me and said nothing. No words had ever been exchanged between us. He was a total stranger. I suddenly hated him. Hated that he was the only one who had ever shown the slightest interest in me. Hated that he was so disgusting. Hated that he had just presumed to kiss me, hated that he had never spoken to me. Hated myself for allowing it.

Four days later, he applied for acceptance as a student. His existence humiliated me, and I did not want him in my home. But I knew, damnit, that blocking consensus on grounds of embarrassment was not fair. I was prisoner to my sense of justice. I said in community meeting that I hated him, and hoped he wouldn't be accepted, but I didn't block consensus, and he came. I studiously ignored him for months, dreading his approach, and loathing him for not approaching. I thought he was revolting, and if even he had no interest in me, what did that indicate??

• • •

My next adventure was a little better. At least Rob and I were sort of friends, and had actually spoken to each other first. The truck was full of new hay for the barn and he and I decided it would be fun to sleep together in the back. All night, we rolled around and around, first he on top, then me. Through all the layers of clothing and sleeping bags, I could feel a press of body and heat. Like Jerry, Rob also said nothing to me in daylight. I would look at him during meals, or in community meeting, and he would look back blankly, no stir of recognition. But for a week or so, every night, we would tacitly find somewhere to sleep, on the side of the house in the grass or upstairs in an empty cubicle, and all night we would press and press. We progressed to sharing the same sleeping bag, and I could feel his genitals through my jeans, and wanted to rub myself against him, but did not. Eventually, we just drifted apart. This wasn't love, was it?

I tried to reassure myself that my time would come, but I wasn't exactly convinced. I wasn't sure I had ever seen the real thing.

• • •

At this point, being with my father offered a blessedly asexual haven. Whatever He and Elaine did or did not do in this arena was blissfully out of sight and no erotic notice was taken of me. Sex was not visible, audible, or evident in any way, and seemed even strangely absent. We started traveling together. First, my father invited me to go with him to Wyoming for three weeks of fieldwork. Wyoming! (Where the hell was that?) I was embarrassed to ask. (What was fieldwork?) I was embarrassed to ask. Daddy planned their route west to be able to pick me up, and off we went, all three in the cab of the big blue truck (me in the middle) with a camper on the back, the dogs running after us down the dirt road in their traditional farewell. Wyoming turned to out to be a long drive, and field work turned out to be wonderful, camping for two weeks, following after my geologist father while he looked at rocks. After that trip, they took me with them to Colorado to learn to ski, we went backpacking in Switzerland, then in the Wind Rivers. All of this I loved; the camping, the driving, being outdoors for weeks on end. The three of us became more of a unit, the harmony of being together in foreign places strengthening our bond. Through all our camping trips, my father, Elaine, and I chastely shared a single tent meant for two. None of us were large people, but it was still snug, and I did wonder that they didn't want privacy. Nonetheless, on the (very) rare occasions that we actually stayed in an inn or hotel and my father booked two separate rooms, I felt slightly hurt and rejected. Still, where I had once appreciated being treated as an adult, I now enjoyed a child's innocence.

• • •

Dave and Suzanne went away for a week's vacation and came back married. As they came in the yard, their rings shone like beacons, winking and flashing, so we noticed them right away. They had wondered how long it would take for anyone to notice, figuring a month, a week, surely a day or two. But Dana, Jeanie and I were on the back porch when they arrived; we saw the rings immediately, Dana crying out loudly, "You got married!"

"Who got married?" asked Carla, sticking her head out of the office door.

"Dave and Suzanne!" we chorused, opening the door and going down the hallway loudly proclaiming the news.

Dave and Suzanne smiled sheepishly, and nodded their heads. Married! It sounded quaint and utterly pointless. I was sort of taken aback that people still did that, thinking it had gone the way of stockings, bras, and baseball games, all things I thought of as obsolete historical artifacts. Suzanne, the queen of feminism, had actually gone so far as to take Dave's last name. We were very hurt that they had chosen to "elope," surprised—first, that they had decided to marry, and second, that they had not wanted to share this with us. We would surely have given them a magical wedding, homemade and lively with love. I couldn't figure it out, and resented their keeping something like this private. The beginning of their relationship had been so public, aggressively on display. For their privacy as a couple to suddenly take priority over their positions as members of the community felt odd. I think we all felt rebuffed.

Suzanne got pregnant almost immediately. She was meant to be a mom—she carried the added weight effortlessly on her large-boned frame, seeming to become more of herself than ever. As time went on and she got larger and more cumbersome, she groaned expressively when sitting down or standing up, but she still swung fifty-pound bags of rice or beans around like nothing, and she seemed to be enjoying herself heartily. Dave and Suzanne started attending natural childbirth classes, and they read up on different delivery methods—Lamaze, of course, and another one where the baby is born directly into warm water. Dave wanted to follow the Indian way, going off into the woods when the time was right, and letting Nature take her course again. But Suzanne buried herself in her herbal manuals, studying remedies for back labor and contraction pains, ways to speed labor up, slow it down, strengthen the fetal heart beat, tonics for the mother, herbs to help the placenta release, to let the milk down, herbs to bolster the father, to boost flagging spirits, to calm excessive energy, and so on. The plan was that they would have a home delivery (of course), but they would do it in the Main House instead of in their own cabin, because they wanted access to electricity and running water—amenities none of the dwellings outside of the Main House had.

We were just getting serious about preparing a birthing room right off the bathroom, when Nature took over without invitation. Almost a month early, Suzanne's water broke in the middle of the night, and she and Dave rushed to the hospital without telling anyone. They called the next afternoon, and Gabe had already been born by Cesarean section. Again, we were disappointed and disconcerted to be left out. Nobody had even noticed that Dave and Suzanne were gone. Somehow they repeatedly kept their important events away from us.

Three days later, they all came home, Gabe riding happily in a wicker laundry basket. I went to hug Suzanne in a rare moment of unambivalent love and happiness, and I clumsily clutched her hard around the middle. She flinched in pain, and turned away from me, and I felt both hurt and like an insensitive clod for not having realized I couldn't hug her right after surgery.

Gabe brought out the best in us. We lined up to take care of him, day and night. When Gabe was sleeping, we tiptoed around, foregoing the swearing and slamming of doors, lowered our voices, and did not play the piano. When Gabe was having a hard day, teething or gassy, he had an endless parade of different shoulders to cry on, different techniques for soothing, tireless legs for walking him around, bouncing him, rocking him. Never did new parents have so little to do. Dave and Suzanne had to ask to get their baby back, otherwise he would have been passed from welcoming hand to loving lap. When Gabe mastered something, a chorus was there to rejoice with him in his accomplishment. He was a delightful baby, wide-eyed, curious, and adventuresome. Gabe became like a model of how we could each be—loving, trusting, immediate with his feelings, honest and without design. He showed us the possibility of a state of grace we had only imagined theoretically possible.

25

Responsibility—A Weighty Rescue

My sisters Rachel and Erica both left for college in 1974, when I was fourteen. Rachel had stayed around an extra year as a full-fledged, official staff member, so even though she was a year older than Erica, they left at the same time. I was bereft. I might not have felt it as strongly if we hadn't all just moved in together. The solar-heated house, intended for my family, had only become habitable six months earlier. It was a funny house, all the way up the hill at the furthest end of the property. Shaped like a capital letter "B," the entire front was glass to catch the sun. One half of the "B" was designated for Carla, and the combined living room/kitchen, while the other half was divided into three tiny rooms for the three of us. When we were all under one roof once again, I began to rediscover my sisters. In those months before they left, we had spent hours together, talking, writing in our journals, fixing up the house, chopping wood for the insatiable wood stove, or carrying jugs of water for our use—there being no indoor plumbing or electricity. There had been this curiously intense pleasure in doing things together, in finding out that I did share more with them than with others, that there was something special about our being sisters after all. I felt more related to them than I ever had. Then they were gone and I was suddenly living alone in the house with Carla. Karen left at the same time. In a completely unexpected reversion to her family tradition, she had joined the Navy. We were all appalled.

When my sisters left, I took over their jobs of bookkeeping and check-writing from Rachel, and care of the goats from Erica. Doing these chores helped to keep me from missing them too much. Each day, in the still morning darkness, I'd clatter noisily out the kitchen door, kerosene lantern in one hand, milk-pail in the other. I'd shake the pail, making its loose cover rattle loudly. The racket served to awaken and accompany me in all the emptiness, summoning both the goats, and my own courage. The barn was so dark! Dark or light, one had to be wary and alert when entering the barn.

We had once advertised for a contribution of mosquito-eating geese, having heard that they could be an effective means of controlling unwanted insects. And sure enough, someone gave us a pair of young white goslings. They were cute as youngsters, hanging out around the house with the dogs, although no one saw them eat very many mosquitoes. When they were grown, they realized that the house yard was not the proper location for them, and migrated to the barn. And then they got very territorial and mean. They were big, with good heavy bodies, huge wingspans, and long necks ending in hard orange beaks. Going into the barn I had to be careful, because they would often lower their heads, stretch out their serpentine necks, and come at me at a run, hissing loudly. The first time this happened, I didn't take it very seriously until the goose bit me, hard, on the thigh. After that, I was more careful, kicking if they came at me, and keeping my eye out for an approach from the back. A lot of people were too scared to go there at all with the geese in residence.

• • •

I had begun to take more interest in the kitchen. I was supposedly still being given the freedom to be a child, but with Rachel and Erica gone, the antics of the students were less compelling, and I had less of a desire to be one of them. I wanted respect.

When I was very small, I had loved to lie in bed, listening to my mother moving around the kitchen. The fridge opened and closed, water ran in the sink, she answered the phone, and the rise and fall of her voice made me feel safe. I hadn't felt that way in a long time. I had lost the safety that makes childhood fun, and was left with the worries and the restrictions. I had to take care of myself—no one else was going to do it—and if I was mature enough to do that, surely I was mature enough to be taken seriously.

So I began trying to act more like an adult. Taking on jobs was a logical thing to do. It was also, I quickly learned, the only way to be sure something got done. Once I opened my eyes to it, however, I became aware of the never-ending list of things that needed to be done that exercised its own tyranny: cupboards to clean out, foods to organize, mold to curb, walls to paint, hinges to replace, broken boards to mend, brush to clear, weeds to pull, stones to move, rows to hoe, and on and on and on. Surely if I could just get the kitchen clean and organized, I'd be better able to manage the disorder of my life and emotions. If I could get the crusty grime scraped off the bottom of the fridge, maybe I would be less upset about the absence of harmony and agreement about bedtimes or how to get rid of the rats.

Horribly, as soon as I became aware of all that needed to be done, I felt it had to get done. It suddenly seemed essential that I combat the fundamental messiness of my surroundings. This was an impossible proposition. The very minute something was done, it began its immediate descent to coming un-done. Invariably, after scrubbing the kitchen floor, bringing back the whiteness square by square, a goat would get into the kitchen, or a group of gardeners would tromp in off the porch, leaving great clods of red mud behind them, or Suzanne would bake bread, dusting the kitchen with a fine layer of flour. It was as futile as building sand castles by the sea and hoping they would be there in the morning.

I quickly realized that no one was working very hard, and that I could count on no help. If I wanted to get something done, it was up to me to figure it out and do it. For any job more complex than cleaning, I rarely had the necessary tools, or strength, or ability. My father's well-equipped tool shed where he had drawn the outline of each tool on pegboard to show its proper location, seemed like a remote fantasy as I examined the one hammer I had managed to dig up after scrounging around in the tool shed for half an hour. Someone had used it to stir something—it looked like glue—and neglected to clean it, so the hook end was a solid blob of rock-hard something. It was heavy and off-balance, but I figured I could use it. I wanted to hang the hammock in the yard, and not having the proper screw hooks to go in the tree, I was planning to use nails. I got them in, but they didn't hold, repeatedly turning and depositing the hammock on the ground as soon as I hung it up. After struggling with it for an hour, I gave up.

But how did I end up being responsible for the entire kitchen at the age of fourteen? My own doing, but I hadn't realized what I was getting myself into. I had loved making spaghetti and sauce with Jillian, something we had done together once a week for as long as she had been a student at Nethers. We had a set routine, starting by getting out the two huge aluminum pots. Into one, we ran gallons of water, which we put on the stove to heat, both of us working together to hoist it up. For the other, we chopped and chopped, tomatoes, onions, peppers, adding spices as we went, stirring and tasting and singing together. After a time, the kitchen would get steamy, wreathed in the heady aroma of sauce bubbling reassuringly on the stove. Jillian and I had been peacefully compatible during those cookings.

Being in charge of the entire kitchen was a different matter. I planned the menus, made schedules and sign-up sheets for the preparation and clean-up of three meals each day. Once a week, I went grocery shopping at the local Safeway, spending $100 for a week's worth of food, which seemed like a fortune. Then, during the week, I filled in for any job that no one else showed up to do.

I spent hours poring through cookbooks, determined to find ways to enliven our monotonous diet with variety and interest. It was all so plain. Influenced by Daddy's gourmet kitchen, I craved elegance. Our normal fare consisted of rice and veggies, pasta and sauce, baked potatoes and broccoli, soup and salad, sandwiches,

scalloped potatoes with cheese and steamed spinach, bulgar, barley, red lentils, brown rice, beans and oatmeal. I thought for sure I
could bring new life to the table. Bill of the carob pudding was still
in prison as far as I knew, but his memory gave me hope. I certainly
did not have his skill or experience, so I turned to books—my normal method.

I found a recipe called Minnie's Baked Rice that sounded good.
A mixture of milk and onions, raisins, and . . . what was saffron
anyway? We had a surfeit of pumpkins that year, and I burrowed
for pumpkin ideas. Pumpkin soup, pumpkin bread, pumpkin
custard, stuffed pumpkin. I read each recipe with care, trying,
with my limited experience, to imagine the tastes of them, then
proudly writing them in the little squares of the chart I had made,
with reference to the cookbook and the page number. In the
store, I carefully found the special ingredients needed for each
new recipe, always substituting honey for sugar, whole-wheat
flour for white, and simply eliminating anything too expensive
or unfamiliar.

I waited anxiously to see what people's reactions would be to
my innovations. I waited to see who would sign up for the new
dishes I had thought of. Laurel signed up for Stuffed Pumpkin. I
was elated. But when she brought dinner to the table, she had made
scalloped potatoes, using the precious cheese I had planned for the
next night, and doing nothing to deplete our surfeit of pumpkin.
No one signed up for Minnie's Baked Rice, scheduled for Thursday evening. I checked every day, and the space stayed blank, along
with the one for clean-up afterward, as though that square repelled
people altogether. Finally, I had to do it myself, and the dishwash-
ing too. I started to make Minnie's Rice. It was the fourth day in a
row that I was filling in, and I was sick and tired of the kitchen. Ever
since I had taken over, more people were forgetting their jobs or not
signing up altogether, as if they knew that I would do it for them.
As if they knew . . . well, wouldn't I? Wasn't it true that I wouldn't
let a meal go uncooked, or the kitchen uncleaned? How had other
people dealt with this? I had wanted to impose some order and

some creativity on an unwieldy job. But maybe I was the only one interested in order. With a sudden wave of resentment, I longed to escape, to return to the child I was trying so hard to grow out of—or to be the child I had not been able to be.

• • •

The kitchen held its rewards as well. Bringing the milk in myself twice a day gave me more interest in its consumption. A lot of milk was wasted, because few people actually enjoyed its strong taste. It was used primarily for cooking, and for the dogs. I decided to try making cheese, because that required huge amounts of milk. Of course with cheese-making, you end up with quantities of whey, which I also hated to throw away, so I started making bread at the same time to use up the whey. This was deeply satisfying to my sense of economy. Daddy had taught me to make bread years ago, and although I had seldom attempted it on my own, I had a pretty good idea how to do it. I found a recipe that made sense to me, and laid it on the counter with the one for cheese I had dug out of one of Erica's goat journals. For days in advance, I froze half the take from each milking until I had over ten gallons. Heating it slowly in the huge aluminum pot, I tested the temperature on my wrist as I had learned to do for the baby goats when they needed bottles. When it was body-warm, I stirred rennet capsules into the milk. This caused me some discomfort. Rennet, I knew, was a product that came from the lining of a sheep's stomach, and I was still a strict vegetarian, not only refusing to eat meat, but rejecting any foods with other animal products like gelatin or anything made of leather. I had tried substituting for the rennet with Agar Agar—a product produced from seaweed, which also has gelatinous properties. It had been an unmitigated failure. So I decided that I needed to make an exception here—there just didn't seem to be any way to make cheese without bending my principles.

After several hours, the milk turned to beautiful smooth curds. With a huge knife, I cut through the whole mass, slicing in both directions to create a tidy crosshatch of trembling cubes in the softly gelatinous matter. Then, to break up the cubes further, I used my arms, up over the elbow, running hands, wrists and forearms deep through the silkiness. I closed my eyes and tried to think of all the different things that might feel like this. Brushing against satin sheets, bathing in a tub of custard, or being surrounded by a dense school of minnows. I imagined the slithery smoothness passing all along my naked skin—between my fingers, brushing my shoulders, my face.

The first pressing was easy. After I poured the whey and curds through the huge colander, I placed two wrapped bricks on top, sufficient weight to send the whey gushing out. This was warm and cloudy, redolent of goat and morning. When I added sugar and yeast to it to start the bread, it nearly exploded with growth, soon foaming enthusiastically. Leaving the curds pressing in the pantry, where they would go through a graduated series of ever-heavier weights over the next few days, I added flour to the whey, scoop by scoop, first stirring it in with my big wooden spoon, then scooping it out on to the countertop in a great gooey sticky mass.

Those great glops always seemed unmanageable at first. But gradually, kneading hard while standing on a chair to give me better leverage, I kept adding flour until it began to take shape. Eventually, I had two large mounds, smooth as baby cheeks, dark grains showing in the lighter dough like fine granite, slightly sweet to the taste, and pleasing to the face. I stuck my nose deep into the mass of it, and it gave like flesh.

Once, when no one else was in the house, I closed the kitchen door, and surreptitiously took off my shoes. After washing each toe carefully, I climbed up onto the counter, and danced in the bread, kneading it with my toes, rolling it between my soles. Arms spread wide, stomping in a rhythmic circle, some remnant of chant rose, close to a memory not mine.

Later, in the dining room, as the twelve crusty brown loaves were devoured with their usual shocking rapidity, I couldn't help smirking at what no one knew but my toes and me.

26

Another Kind of Love

When Andrea arrived, I studied her carefully. She had been a delib-
erate mystery, signing all her letters with a genderless "A," and being
careful never to give herself away overtly. She lived in Hawaii, and
because of the distance, could not come to visit first, so we took a
chance and accepted her as a student sight unseen, based on her
transcripts and letters. We had all gotten caught up in the intrigue
of her gender, and there were running bets, theories based on hand-
writing, vocabulary, and her stated interests. Asking was unthinkable, as that would suggest it would make some kind of difference.
She turned out to be a she, as most of us had thought. "A" stood for
Andrea. At seventeen, she was two years older than me. She had
long straight black hair and Asian features, just slightly reminiscent
of Lanny long ago. Unlike Lanny, she also had a square, squat little
body, low to the ground, with uncomfortably large breasts, and big
deep limpid eyes.

For the first couple of weeks, I watched her from a distance,
checking her out, waiting for her to emerge from her nondescript
pleasantness. She wanted to be a poet and wrote in her journal
incessantly with a silver fountain pen, which made her appear full
of meaning. She seemed pretty cool, and I started doing things with
her. I wasn't particularly taken with any of the other current students. They seemed less interesting than the previous generations,
or maybe being closer to them in age made them less fascinating
than when they were so much older than I. It had been a very long

time since I had had a good friend, and I was definitely on the lookout for one.

I invited Andrea to come to the barn with me for the evening milking, and she watched, silent but friendly, as I handled the goats, declining my offer to teach her how to milk. The next day she asked me did I want to take a walk? I agreed. As we went along the dirt road, we talked about her aged parents, her feeling that they did not even try to understand her. She felt she had to get away from them in order to be able to breathe, but was terribly sad that that meant she also had to leave her younger sister whom she adored and already missed so much. We talked about her beloved cats, while the tears welled in her dark eyes, and slipped, seemingly unnoticed, down her cheeks. I was a sucker for tears. I hardly ever cried, and when I did, it was brief and hard, no picturesque shimmering drops quavering on eyelids, and then gently spilling over. When I cried, my nose ran, and my eyes went red, and it got all caught up in my throat so I couldn't talk, but made horrid little gasping hiccups. So I sort of admired aesthetic tear-shedding. I figured those feelings were more profound than mine, certainly more elegant.

I was flattered that Andrea trusted me enough to share so much when we didn't really know each other. I did my best to be supportive, nodding my head gravely, trying to reassure her that her sister would be okay, and, at one point, taking her hand to comfort her. She grabbed on to my hand hard, and did not let go, so we ended up walking hand in hand. It made me think of Lily May. Her hand had been hard and dry like a root, resting lightly against mine. Andrea's hand was very soft, a little damp, and hot. It sort of clung to my skin, making me self-conscious, and unsure of whether to hold on or let go, imagining that I would have to actually shake my hand to separate it from hers. I was a little relieved when we got back to the house and unclasped our hands in a shared reluctance to be seen that way.

The next day I was in the upper garden weeding a row of sunflowers I had planted, thinking it would be fun to feed the seeds to the birds in the winter. Kneeling in the dirt under a warm late summer sun, completely absorbed in what I was doing, I didn't even notice Andrea until I caught sight of the toe of her brown shoe, hesitantly poised by a flower stalk. I got up, brushing off my knees, and wiping my hands on my rear,

"Hi," I said.

"I have to talk to you about something," she said.

"Okay," I answered, feeling intimidated and a little anxious. I put down my shovel and joined her on the bench between the two plum trees that Mark and Ellen had planted a couple of years earlier hoping for plums, not realizing that they were a decorative rather than fruit-bearing variety.

"It's just that I think I really like you," Andrea said, looking down at her knee as she swung her leg, feet brushing through the loose dirt under the bench. "And I don't like too many people," she continued, her hair covering her face. "And when I do like a person, I have to know that she won't let me down." She finished this almost sternly, swinging her hair back over her shoulder, straightening her spine, and glancing up to look me briefly in the face.

I wasn't sure what to say. It felt like half-invitation, half-threat. I couldn't believe that I was the one she had chosen to like. I was younger than she, I didn't know who Adrian Rich was, or Anne Sexton—her idols—and I didn't feel as deep as she appeared to be. After all, she was Hawaiian and Japanese and planned to go to Bennington College whatever that was. I was exhilarated that she liked me, impressed by her obvious intelligence, not to mention her discriminating taste, and thrilled to be chosen. In the end, I ignored my slight sense of discomfort and enthusiastically proclaimed reciprocal feelings.

There was something formal about the exchange, as if we had entered into an agreement or made a contract. There was no label for this pact, no definition of relationship that fit the feeling, but we had clearly arrived at a new level—or at least Andrea seemed to think so. Her expectations after our conversation were that we would spend all our time together, that we would not do things with other people, that we would share everything with each other, but tell nothing to anyone else, that we would hold hands all the time, and hug a lot.

At first, it felt wonderful. I launched myself wholeheartedly into the relationship, telling Andrea about my insecurities, my desire to be special to her, my fears that she would decide she liked one of the other students better. She not only echoed my feelings, but raised me one, proclaiming her jealousy when I spoke to others, or failed to include her in something I had assumed she would not be interested in. I could not believe it. I had so longed for a companion, and now, finally, I had one. I learned everything I could about her. She was a sort of romantic/tragic figure—her favorite weather was right before a storm when the sky is lowering with clouds. She drew little ink drawings of cloudy skies, wistful crescent moons peeking out here and there. She had a terrible family medical history, filled with diabetes, cancer, and ulcers, and she proclaimed her conviction that she would die before the age of thirty. All of this made her seem vulnerable and fragile, and I, like a knight to the rescue, rose to shelter her. The one thing we could not find agreement on was the matter of boys. I shared with her my longing for a boyfriend, my impatience that this part of life had so far eluded me, my assumption that I would eventually settle with a man and have children. She stated that she would never be involved with a man, and had no intention of ever having children. I didn't know what to make of that.

Andrea loved me. Or so she told me at least fifty times a day, verbally, in the little notes she wrote and left for me everywhere she knew I would find them, in small gifts like Beatrix Potter books or small pretty boxes to keep things in. She demanded that I reciprocate, and if I did not proclaim my love and devotion frequently and convincingly enough, she could complain and ask me plaintively didn't I still love her? I felt wanted and needed and very important. I understood Andrea, and I began to sense that I was in a minority. I became protective of her, and dismissive of anyone who had something negative to say. I noticed that Andrea was particularly belittling in her comments about the male students, whom she regarded as immature and obnoxious without exception. I kept my own counsel, questioning my own affection for Nate with his quirky sense of humor, my appreciation of Sam's capacious appetite and seemingly unlimited energy. I figured my sensibilities were not as refined, and tried to see things more through Andrea's eyes.

And then she began getting upset with me. The first time, I was mystified. We had been going along as usual, and then one morning, inexplicably, she refused to talk to me. At first I thought I was imagining things, but it persisted, so I went right up to her and asked if something was the matter.

"What?" Andrea said, turning toward me a face masked with brightness. "Why would you ask me that?"

"I don't know," I answered. "It seems like you're upset with me."

"Why should I be upset with you?" she chirped, in a bizarre departure from her usual nearly inaudible husky voice. It seemed like a trick question, and I was stymied.

Trailing behind her as she went into the living room, I watched as my shy reticent friend greeted each person effusively, and settled cozily down on the couch, just inches away from Sam, whom I knew she disliked. What the heck was going on?

By the end of the day, I was frantic and spinning in my sense of helplessness. I had wracked my brains, unable to find anything I could have said or done that would have offended her. I was baffled by her unwillingness to level with me, she who had helped me to be more outspoken and communicative, actually telling someone what I was feeling in a straightforward way. I knew she was lying with every word and gesture throughout the day, but it was all so subtle and intangible that I could not call her on it.

After dinner, I disconsolately got down the milking pail and the lantern and headed for the barn without a word to anyone. As usual, she sneaked up on me. I was halfway through milking, somewhat calmed by the peacefulness of the barn, the quiet, the soft light, the goat Christie comforting in her warm solidity and predictability. Andrea must have made a movement, because I looked up, and saw that she had been leaning in the doorway for a while. Deciding to give her back some of what she had given me all day, I said nothing, but went about my business, moving the goats in and out past her in the doorway, and milking serenely, as if it were any other time.

After the last goat was done, I swept off the milking stand, took the lantern down from the hook, the bucket in my other hand, and went past Andrea out the barn and into the night. She followed me, took the lantern from me, and took my hand. Half way back to the house we stopped and sat by the driveway.

"I'm sorry," she said. "I know I have been a real shit to you today."

"Why?" I asked.

"I'm embarrassed to even tell you, it seems so silly."

"Tell me *what*?"

"It's just . . . it's just . . . Nate," she muttered, her chin practically resting on her chest.

"Nate? What *about* Nate?"

"You and Nate."

"What are you *talking* about?? What about me and Nate?"

"It's just that . . . " Silence. "It's just that I think you like him."

"Nate? Of course I like Nate. What does that have to do with anything?"

"No. I mean *like* like him, and it makes me feel sad, because I thought *I* was your best friend, and I don't want to stand in your way or anything, but I just couldn't stand it when I saw you two getting together. "

I had no clue what she was referring to. I had no memory of even talking to Nate, and certainly (regretfully) had no indication that we were or could be "getting together."

I assured Andrea of all this, dried her tears with the hem of my shirt, hugged and reassured her, and wondered what was going on.

I inadvertently hurt her feelings several times a day, and she would withdraw from me, sometimes blatantly ignoring me, looking through me, being exaggeratedly friendly to others, especially people I knew she hated. As if following a script, I would tease her out of her pouts, knowing just how to pacify her with remorse, extra attention and affection, with a drop of humor at just the right moment. Some of her complaints were incomprehensible to me, like the time she said she felt betrayed when I agreed to play Capture the Flag with other students when she didn't feel like playing. "It's just because you want to be with Sam," she accused nastily before dissolving into her usual tears. I bent over backwards denying it, reassuring her, resolving never to make her unhappy again. I certainly couldn't care less about Sam!

These emotional dramas took place anytime anyplace, and usually took hours to resolve. At the end, we would inevitably be locked in an embrace, standing with Andrea's arms wrapped around my waist, pressing her soft thighs against mine, and gazing imploringly into my eyes. I often longed to break her hold, but knew that if I did so prematurely, I would pay for it by having to go through the whole production again. I didn't want to hurt her feelings, but I was increasingly in a panic, nauseated by her possessiveness, her demanding, consuming, suffocating claim on me, and my seeming inability to extricate myself.

Carla, thinking she was doing something extra special nice for me, invited Andrea to come to live with us up at our house. Carla knew how much I missed my sisters, and how lonely the house was without them. She was delighted that I finally had a good friend, and wanted to welcome her. She issued this invitation to the two of us together, and my heart sank heavily as I realized that I was losing my last bastion of privacy. "NO!" I protested silently, while under the watchful eyes of Andrea, I expressed excitement and gratitude. That very afternoon she moved into Erica's room, next to mine, and the three of us "celebrated" with roasted chestnuts and hot chocolate.

It was sort of okay at first. It was nice to have company walking up the hill at night. Jack the dog was still there, snapping against his chain, and although I had gotten a lot better about it, I still got scared walking up the hill in the dark sometimes. Quickly, however, I began to miss my solitary trips up and down the hill. I was accustomed to spending a lot of time on my own, and it was exhausting to be with someone all the time. Especially this someone. I began getting more and more irritable and anxious. And then Andrea started climbing up into my bed.

My bedroom was tiny. The only way to have anything other than a bed in it was to have a raised loft. Although Carla was reluctant to have my bed out of her reach, she saw the logic in this, and agreed to let me have one built. Again, my bed was up against high windows, and I loved to lie on my belly and gaze out at the darkness, or the clouds racing over the moon, or the lights of the Main House shining below, as well as dim glimmers from the kerosene lanterns in the Rammed Earth House and Dennis's cabin visible through the trees. One night, Carla went away on some Future Village-related mission, leaving Andrea and me alone in the house. Claiming to be scared, Andrea asked if she could sleep with me. Still incapable of saying no, I agreed, unsure of why I was so nervous about it—people shared beds all the time, and it was no big deal unless one's bedmate snored or stole all the covers.

I climbed up the ladder first, claiming my side by the windows. Andrea climbed up after me. The bed was so close to the ceiling that there wasn't room to sit up, and she had to crawl forward onto the mattress. As she did so, the neck of her loose nightgown fell open, fully revealing her breasts. They were round, brown, large, and more or less in my face. I tried scooching over to give her more room, but she gazed down at me with her soulful eyes, and pressed her hand against my chest, pushing me to lie back on the bed. Then she lay over me, pressing her full length against me.

I finally got it. How stupid could I be?

"Um, I don't think you should sleep here," I said.

"Don't you want me to?" she asked softly.

"Uhh, I think I am getting a sore throat," I answered. "I don't want you to catch my cold."

"Oh, I'm not worried about that," she assured me, snuggling closer.

"You know," I said, "I move around a lot in my sleep, and I'm afraid you'll fall out."

"You don't want me to sleep here, do you?" asked Andrea.

"I guess I don't," I answered, finally being as direct as I could be.

"Why not?" she challenged.

"It doesn't feel right," I stated, sweating now.

"Fine!" she returned. "Fine!" sitting up too rapidly and cracking her skull sharply against the wood ceiling planks. "Goddamn it!" she shouted, whether about me or the pain in her head was unclear. "Fuck Fuck Fuck!" she chanted, not a customary user of profanity, while clumsily going down the ladder, out of my room and slamming my door, "FUCK IT, *FUCK IT.*"

In a dither of fear, clarity, embarrassment, and relief, I lay frozen in my bed, listening closely to the sounds, all too audible through the walls, of her rustling into her own bed and beginning to sob. All night, afraid to move, starting at any sound that might have meant she was coming back, I wished my mother was home, wished I had talked to someone about Andrea, wished I hadn't been so dense and stupid and blind. On the other hand, I was relieved to understand that the whole horrid suction cup vortex feeling hadn't been my imagination, or my inability to be a good friend, or something wrong with me.

At first light, I crept silently out of the house and down the hill, milked the goats, and then stationed myself at the parking lot to catch Carla as soon as she came home. I kept thinking Andrea was going to come down and find me and want to make up. I didn't want to make up, I just wanted out.

Carla turned into the driveway, surprised and pleased to see me waiting for her. Rushing over to the car and getting into the passenger seat beside her before she could get out, I sat in the car and allinarush explained that this friendship had gotten to be too much for me, that I thought I had stumbled into a one-sided romance and I didn't know what to do and would she please help me get out of it and above all make Andrea move out of our house? As she listened, Carla became by turns surprised, apologetic, protective and concerned. She got out of the car and marched determinedly straight up to our house, with me trailing reluctantly along behind her.

It was only late morning, although it felt as if days had passed. Andrea was still in bed, sitting up only when she heard the sounds of our entrance. Her hair was mussed, and her face puffy as she looked resentfully at the two of us. I left to go to the bathroom while Carla asked Andrea to get dressed and come into the living room so we could all talk together. Once we were settled in chairs with cups of Postum, Carla asked, "So, girls, why don't you tell me what is going on here?" I glared at her. I already had!

Andrea leapt at the chance to air her ills. "I don't know what Sandra's problem is," she stated bitterly, "I gave her the gift of my love and she threw it in my face like a little child." I was young enough for this insult to sting.

"I can hear that you are angry," said my mother brilliantly, "but I'm not sure I'm getting it. When we love someone, it doesn't place an obligation on that person to respond in exactly the way we want them to. When we really love, we give our love freely and openhandedly, without thinking about what we will get in return. Otherwise, it isn't really love, it's ownership, or possession, or an exchange arrangement."

Andrea and I both looked at her blankly. I knew she was trying to defend me, but the diplomacy was a little too thick. Why was she being so damned even-handed anyway? She was my mother, and I had asked for her protection and help. Suddenly my bulldozer mother is too discreet to be direct?

"I want you to move out," I said, without thinking about it. "I still like you as a friend, but I don't want to spend so much time together." Crying now, I continued. "I want to be free to do what I want with who I want without having to feel guilty all the time. I don't owe you anything, you know," struggling to talk, through my sobs and the tears that gushed so copiously as to surprise even me. "And I don't want you to send me any more letters, or hold my hand, or look at me. I just want some space!" With this, I got up, went to the bathroom for a wad of tissue paper, and left the house. Let Carla deal with it.

I didn't see Andrea for the rest of the day. When Carla came into the Main House, several hours later, she looked exhausted, but she nodded at me, "All clear." I went immediately up the hill to our house, needing to see that it really was empty, and it was, all trace of Andrea gone except for one sodden balled-up tissue by the neatly made bed. I knew she had left it there on purpose.

For the rest of the school year, Andrea and I co-existed with as little contact as possible under the circumstances. I don't think I was alone with her again all that time. I certainly never sought her out, nor she me. I felt, above all, tremendous relief and liberation, and dismay that the intensity of my longing for a friend had made me so determinedly blind to the obvious. Beware your own longing.

Break Up

I was away when it happened. Carla had dragged me off to stay in a cabin in the woods for a two-week "spring vacation." What made staying in a tiny, bug-infested A-frame with no running water, electricity, kitchen, books, people or entertainment a "vacation," was beyond me. Our own house was bug-infested, with no running water or electricity, and there was nothing novel or charming about that. My sisters, home for the break as independent adults during their sophomore years at college, were free to come or go as they pleased, which mostly meant go. It galled me that they were nearby, but I wasn't with them. They came to visit us in shifts for a day at a time, bringing a welcome break from the monotony and my prolonged tête-à-tête with Carla. It was Erica who brought the news, flushed with the weight of it, and its coiled potential for unknown change.

In our absence, Mark and Suzanne had unexpectedly announced that they were now romantically involved, leaving Laurel and Dave out in the cold. They had come out publicly and quite unabashedly, proclaiming their commitment to each other, and their termination of their respective prior involvements. According to Erica, Dave had already left, the place was rocking, and Gabe, our peaceful happy two-year-old, was now constantly wailing.

My instinct was to pack up on the spot and rush home, but Carla, for reasons of her own, refused to budge until our time was up—four more interminable days. Whether she needed to gather her resources for the coming emotional storm, clarify her position, or wait until the smoke cleared, I couldn't decide. I was in a fever to get back, thinking, I suppose, as children mistakenly do, that if I were there, I could hold the place together. Surely the passion of my determination would force things back where they belonged and we would continue as before.

When we finally got home, the place was desolate. Nobody was out in the yard, not even the goats were visible. I suddenly had the fantasy that the whole place was vacant, everybody having already decamped in my absence, or worse, that I had imagined the whole place à la Alice in Wonderland. But no, walking in the door, the first thing I heard was Gabe crying, a foreign prolonged weeping, and I knew we were in terrible trouble.

The new development shook the entire community. Tearful confrontations, the immediate disappearance of Dave, acrimonious accusations, and Gabe's distress, all spoke to the grave new difficulties we were in. Emotions erupted unexpectedly, violently, and frequently. A conversation about broccoli could abruptly bring on a sudden storm of tears or shouts. One might have expected the turn of events to have the greatest impact on the four people most directly involved. This was not the case, clearly demonstrating that we had achieved the connectedness we had liked to talk about as an ideal. It was as if the infidelity had been toward each one of us personally. Knowledge of past secrecies pervaded our awareness and our interactions, as if we expected to come upon Suzanne and Mark in passionate undress at any moment, behind every door. It wasn't only Laurel who engaged in the inevitable wondering about where they had held their trysts and when, who writhed at the newly discovered legacy of secrecy. This breaking apart of two couples and reconfiguration into one had unbalanced something fundamental in our structure. To survive, we would have to rearrange ourselves entirely. Could we?

We had always been relatively conservative about sex, engaging in none of the "free love," multiple pairings or scheduled rotation of partners practiced at our sister communes. The variations in constellations of casual couples had been discreet and sequential. But Mark and Laurel, Suzanne and Dave had been the two stable units for years now; they and Ellen had been the posts the house was built upon. Suzanne and Dave had even gone so far as to get married and have Gabe. Didn't that mean anything? Other communes would have laughed at us for being so quaint and old-fashioned as to be upset by such a simple (and natural) occurrence. These were no grounds for a commune to come apart at the seams! Everyone knew monogamy was wildly unrealistic! Far from earth-shaking or tragic, this was no big deal, par for the course.

But our experience was different. After encounter groups, marathon meetings, and countless tearful conversations, it became clear that emotionally, Dave was not the only cuckold, nor the only one who could not bear to stay. But neither did everyone want to leave immediately as he had done. There were three months of the school year left, all of our boarding students home for spring break were expecting to come back as usual. People were counting on us. What were we going to do? The paralysis of indecision held us all in thrall. Finally, at Carla's insistence, each person agreed that by the end of the week, he or she would decide whether to stay, leave now, or make a commitment to remain just through the academic year.

For me, this decision-making period was nightmarish. I had no decision to make. At fifteen, I couldn't go out on my own. While over the years I had occasionally flirted with the idea of living with my father, the prospect of getting myself into and then surviving public school as a high-school junior was prohibitive. My last year of formal education had been third grade. The disparity was fearsome. Algebra and geometry were not the only barriers. What about clothes and conversation, dates and ball games? Did people still do all that stuff? Years earlier, when Jeanie had chosen to attend public school, I had found the gap too wide to cross. Now it was immeasurably wider. I couldn't face it. Whatever anyone else did, I would be staying put with my mother until I was old enough to get away on my own. It was an agonizing wait. Each time I saw Ellen in the hallway, or Laurel, or Jeffrey, I imagined his or her departure.

Certain that if I could only find the right thing to say they would all stay, I found myself dumbstruck. Every conversation, no matter the apparent topic, contained my unspoken question, "Are you going?" I awaited each person's declaration like a prison sentence. And they decided, one by one, like lights going out.

First Ellen came and asked me to take a walk with her. Knowing full well what she had to say, I accompanied her reluctantly.

As we walked down the dirt road, she linked her arm through mine.

"Sandra," she said, "you know I love you very much, and I will always care about you. I have decided that I need to go on to do something different with my life. I've been here for five years, and I think it's time for me to go back into the world. I'm planning to leave when school is out."

"I know," I said glumly, although I hadn't, having held to the shred of hope that Ellen of all people might stay. I unlinked our arms and crammed my hands into my pockets. "I figured you'd go."

"What are you going to do?"

"What can I do?" I returned resentfully. "Stay in this fucking ghost town with Carla, what else?"

"Have you talked to your dad?"

"And do what? Go to public school at this point? Oh, please."

"I know this is hard for you. I'm sorry."

Finding, at the last minute, the grace to unbend just a little, I told her it wasn't her fault, and asked about her plans, pretending to be interested, pretending to hear what she said. I cut our walk short, said I wanted to be alone, and headed off the road out into the fields. From a distance, I watched her small figure walk back alone and hated myself for being so ungenerous. I hadn't even told her I loved her, or that I really really hoped she would be happy.

With Laurel, whom I loved, but not as intensely, I shed tears she handled lightly, for which I was grateful. She told me that she too would see the school year through, but that she had rented a house in Bethesda for herself, Jeanie and Clayton. They were already enrolled in school for fall, and she was looking at different options for herself.

By the time Mark and Suzanne cornered me together and told me brightly that in the summer they would be moving to D.C. to devote their time and energy to EST, I was able to get through the encounter with relative equanimity. Their cheerfulness was disgusting and I wanted nothing to do with either one of them.

Fletcher let it be known that he was moving to Arizona to be closer to where Karen was stationed. And indeed, each person announced his or her decision to finish out the school year and then leave.

Life went on, ostensibly as usual, only everything was different. Overwhelmed with anger and sadness and worry and misery, I, in my adolescent stinginess, withheld my feelings. I no longer spoke in the few meetings I consented to attend. I boycotted classes, meals, excursions, and other gatherings. I often did not bother to greet people, and wrote in my journal instead of talking to anyone. Even when coaxed to do so, I would not speak my heart to those who were hurting me. I would not deign to share with them my private feelings. I thought I would punish them that way, by withholding, refusing to participate.

This was my second divorce, and, much as I had fought against it ever being so, my second family, now lost as well. I don't think I had ever imagined that everyone could leave all at once. I was furious, and injured, regretting every resentment I had felt, every time I had wished they would all just disappear. I felt trapped in my abandonment with nowhere to go. To top things off, Carla, it appeared, almost welcomed this opportunity to re-set her course. For years she had been frustrated by the fact that while Nethers had flourished, her larger project of Future Village had gotten lost in the shuffle. She began brainstorming about how to use the break-up to redirect her efforts more toward her ultimate goal.

People became frustrated with me, and tired of urging me without success to be communicative, to share what I was feeling. I sure as hell wasn't going to share with them, I figured, and then have them all take off. Jeffrey requested bitterly through Carla, that I should deign to acknowledge his existence every now and then. This message made me feel awful, but I held to my resolve. Then one day in a meeting, Mark came right out and said that he was afraid of me. This comment, which wounded me deeply, especially coming from Mark, overcame my control and set loose a flood of tears that lasted through the remainder of the day. But even then, despite Mark's kindly jokes about cutting too many onions, I refused to talk.

We went on through the school year, made the necessary short-term decisions, held the graduation ceremony for our two seniors, published our last newsletter, and produced our usual annual play with the customary two performances for friends and family. "If we can do this," I often thought to myself, "if we can continue to function so well as a group, then why is everybody leaving??" To the last minute, I entertained fantasies that they would reconsider, and realize that they couldn't leave. Through the last two weeks, I began reciting to myself, "This is the last birthday cake, this is the last community meeting, this is the last dinner, evening, night, breakfast . . ." finally not knowing if I was dragging my feet or in a passion to hurry up and get this over with.

First the students left, having found places for themselves back at their old schools or in new places. Then the home community members left, several going together in the old blue van to catch buses and flights to their various destinations. Over the course of three or four days, the entire place emptied out, until only Carla and I remained. And then they were all gone, with scant or no goodbye from me. I felt that refusing to be involved with them was my best weapon. What I didn't know yet was that shutting down is a weapon that turns on the one who uses it. By withholding, I harmed only myself, as if love were an unrenewable resource, as if in loving even when we lose, we don't learn the better to love. I didn't know that love that flows freely is not lost, but circles around and comes back again to fill the heart, no matter the distance. In my tight-fisted clutching I was losing more than I needed to. In refusing to let go—to give anything—neither could I receive. They loved me. They would have talked with me, shared their thoughts and plans, listened to mine, made suggestions, and then written and called, even visited every now and then. I thought that if they really loved me, they wouldn't leave me. But they had to—they all had their own lives to lead and they weren't, in the final analysis, really my family. They were free to go. As an adolescent, I suppose I needed to be the one to push away. I was fifteen and hurt and angry, disconcerted by the intensity of my own feelings, and at a loss about how to deal with them, and at sea in my own life.

I went into the Main House after the last car had driven away, not at all astonished to find the place a shambles. I looked around in fuming amazement. Dirty dishes were stacked high in the sink and on the counter, the compost bucket was overflowing, newspapers lay strewn around the living room, and the usual layer of hair and scum had settled in the drain of the bathroom sink. Was it thoughtlessness or an expression of anger? If anger, was it at me? Carla? Nethers? I couldn't believe that I had been left to deal with the mess. And suddenly I thought about all the other chores. There were goats to milk, chickens to feed, the garden to take care of, the mail, the laundry, and countless other jobs I had never noticed—taking out the trash, watering the plants, mowing the lawn, getting hay bales down for the goats. I was furious, and very aware that I would have left things in exactly the same state, if I had had a chance.

The first day I just drifted through the empty rooms, sitting in one place and then another, knowing I should get started on all the jobs, but unable to. I was completely flattened by the enormity of the amount of work to be done. That night, I went back up to the house Carla and I shared. She had spent the day there at her typewriter, clearly in a creative burst. She made dinner for me, asked me what I had been doing, saying she had missed me, and hoped we could spend some time together the next day. Early in the morning, rejecting her company, I went right back down to the Main House, and opened the door to an echoing silence so unfamiliar and unbroken it was daunting. Stepping over the threshold, I felt I almost had to push against physical resistance.

I finally began cleaning. Starting from the top, going room by room, I cleaned and cleaned and cleaned, and, finally, cried and cried, sweeping people I loved out of my life, scouring out my pent-up anger, mopping the floors sprinkled with tears. I did the dishes, hearing the clatter of innumerable noisy and chaotic meals, scrubbed the kitchen floor and swept cobwebs out of corners. I vacuumed the living-room rug, reliving a lifetime of Community Meetings, I watered the plants and checked the water level in the furnace and scraped the mud off the porch steps. I thought about things that had happened, things that I had wanted to happen, things said and left unsaid, I thought about how much I loved some people and how little I liked others. Each chore, each room brought a different person or time to mind.

When it got dark, I went back up the hill to my house and my cheerful mother who had been busy all day writing letters and working on promoting Nethers as a work camp—a place people could come to work for a week at a time—which was her latest interim plan. I had no interest in her project. She knew what I was doing, several times said that I didn't have to do all that by myself, and did I want her to come so we could do it together. "No." I said, and went right to sleep, and straight back down the hill in the morning to clean some more. I emptied out cupboards, and piled trash, abandoned clothing, papers, and shoes in a big heap in the yard. I emptied and washed out the compost bucket, and the refrigerator, the mealy grain bins and old, fifty-pound honey tins. I went through closets that had never been cleared, drawers that had never been emptied.

• • •

"I had no idea," my mother said the other day, "that it was so painful for you when everybody left."

"How could you not have known?" Really. Could anything have been more obvious?

"Gee, now I wonder where my head was. I can't believe I missed so much." Her voice thickens, and I know that she is close to tears. I keep asking her if she would rather not have these conversations. I don't *intend* them to be hurtful, but clearly they are.

"Look," I say, "I'm *fine*, and I think we have a really nice relationship now, and most of the time I'm not particularly angry or bitter, so why can't we talk about it?"

"We can, it just makes me feel awful that I was so out of touch with what you were going through. I just never realized that those people were that important to you, I never thought of them as, you know, *primary*."

"Well, they were to me."

"I know that now."

"Didn't I tell you?"

"You never told me much."

"Oh, yeah," I remember. This still surprises me. I felt so transparent. My feelings felt so intense, I assumed that everybody knew what they were. Indeed, I strove mightily to contain them, and I guess I succeeded beyond my wildest dreams. In my own way, I was as out of touch as my mother.

• • •

Gradually, as the week went on, my tears dried and my attention turned around and I began to wonder where they were all going, what they would be doing, and what was going to happen to me. Supposedly I had two more years of high school before I would somehow miraculously be entering college, but it was unimaginable that I would be there alone with Carla for two years. What was I going to do?? When I was finally done cleaning, I went into the living room and sat on the window seat looking around at the orderly space, the unaccustomed smell of detergent strong in the air. Silence again echoed coldly from every corner.

The first few months, I spent a great deal of time down in the empty house, keeping the wood stove going, the plants alive, the floors swept, as if in readiness for someone's return. Some working guests came through, but they were nonentities as far as I was concerned, briefly there and gone, leaving no impact. As the solitude became oppressive, I began to migrate up to my mother's region. She appeared to be quite happily going about her business up at our house, and it slowly became more attractive. I gradually got the goats to dry up, as there was no one to use the milk and it was a chore I could do without. The chickens spontaneously stopped laying and wandered off into the fields. The gardens reverted to a wild state, coughing up the occasional uncultivated zucchini or cucumber, and growing a spectacular patch of purple thistle plants that soared eight feet into the air. The lawn went unmown, gradually losing any distinction from the fields outside the yard fence. And I finally abandoned my post, and climbed the hill to see what was there for me.

Carla and I, alone on the property, fell into a harmonious rhythm. We both rose early and spent our days following our own pursuits in our respective rooms. I had assigned myself a rigorous program of letter-writing and studying math. I took off for long walks in between, to write in my journal or lie on a rock and gaze at the trees. In the evening, we had dinner together, and then I read aloud while Carla did the dishes. We read *Islandia*, a family favorite, and her then-unpublished novel, *Somebody's Brother*. We read Shakespeare and Dickens, treating ourselves to hot chocolate by the fire on cold nights. Sometimes we would splurge and drive two hours to Charlottesville to go to the movies, watching double or even triple features. Once, with a conspiratorial giggle, we sat through four movies in a row. We stumbled out afterward, drunk on overstimulation, our minds reeling with images. We'd go eat ice cream to complete our immersion in modern culture and then crawl home to recuperate, silently sharing our relief as we turned into the dark drive and could again see the stars overhead. We were very close, only occasionally descending into the stormy raging battles that had always punctuated our relationship. We rarely had contact with other people.

Except for Steven. Steven, a local hippy, had been Laurel's lover after Mark left her. After everyone left, Steven continued to come around to see my mother. Or was it me? Exactly halfway between us in age, he proceeded to court us both simultaneously. And we, falling into some archaic mode of feminine competition, played right along. He was a musician who composed a sonata for clarinet, recorder and violin, our three instruments, and had us accompany a dance performance with him. I think he was sleeping with the woman who directed the dance company. "Sleeping" really, because we had learned from Laurel that he wasn't good for much in bed beyond "cuddling." In any event, having found some pretext to go somewhere alone with me, when he touched my breast, my first feeling was triumph that I had beat my mother. In the next split second, deflated to realize that he may have done as much or more with her, I pushed him away. Later, I told Carla that she could "have" Steven.

"It would be great for you," I told her. "You two should really get involved."

"Oh sweetie," she said, "I was just thinking how nice Steven would be for you as a first lover. I really think you should be the one."

The whole thing was getting way too weird.

I began to focus my energies on a feverish effort to apply to college a year early.

It had been Daddy's idea. With my permission, he started calling colleges and having them send me brochures and applications. Following my sisters' example, my stipulation had been that it be a small liberal arts college in New England. At first, the idea was preposterous. I would sit in the barn loft as the swallows flew in and out of the windows, and study glossy pictures of young adults with shiny hair and coordinated clothing, walking hand-in-hand across ivied campuses, sitting earnestly at desks, and energetically participating in class discussions. It was impossible to picture myself among them. But gradually, as I read more and got used to the idea, I decided to give it a try. What did I have to lose?

My mother was furious. It was hard to tell if she was madder at my father or me.

"WHY would you want to leave home a year early?!" she would shriek, when we got into it.

"Why wouldn't I?" I'd shout back. "There's nothing here for me, or haven't you noticed?"

"That's only because *you* won't *do anything!*"

There was truth to this. Carla was full of (utterly impossible) sug-gestions: "Why don't you go take a class in the high school? Why don't you join a drama club? Let's go meet some young people and ask them over!" Right. She had no clue. What in the world would I talk to "young people" about?

I hated her, and hated most how hard it was to imagine leaving her.

Having left off in math with third-grade fractions, I worked through programmed materials for hours every day, frequently dissolving into tears of frustration and self-pity and then hauling myself back out to continue, realizing that there was no rescue, and no way around it. Where Carla used to help me, I now felt that every equation was part of my half-guilty rebellion against her, and refused to turn to her. Nobody could do this for me, and giving in to the hopeless resentment I sometimes felt was just self-defeat-ing. I had to learn this stuff to make a respectable showing on the SATs—my first test of any sort for seven years—which I was hoping to take in time for applications.

• • •

Late in the fall, Carla and I saw a young man with a little silver-white puppy playing outside the general store. Unable to resist, I went over to see the puppy, and we learned that she had come from a nearby litter where there were eight more. Carla, knowing how lonely I was and concerned about how much time I was spending alone, asked me if I would like one. Instantly, I was in a passion of indecision, tears streaming freely down my face, while the young man looked on in confusion.

"Why don't we just go look at them?" Carla asked gently.

"Because then I'll want one," I wailed.

"But you can have one," she returned, puzzled.

"But then I'll love it," I sobbed, not really expecting her to under-stand, not sure I fully understood myself.

"Of course you will," she assured me.

We went to look, and, indeed, they were alluring, and one feisty fellow distinguished himself irresistibly.

"Do you want him?" Carla asked encouragingly.

"I don't know I don't know I don't know."

Unable to make up my mind to take the risk, unable to keep myself from wanting him, I couldn't decide. We left and went home, and I spent a day wandering around the property, as I hadn't done in the months since the place had emptied out. I had completely abandoned all my old haunts, which had served so often as escapes from the over-populated house. To my surprise, everything looked the same as it always had from out in the fields, from the pine forest, from the creek down at the bottom of the hill. Nethers the land was still there, largely unaffected by the loss of Nethers the people. I sat on the spot where Sun Bear was buried and thought about him and then about Ellen and Mark and Laurel and Suzanne and Jeffrey and Jeanie and Clayton and Amy and Fletcher and Karen and Dave and Peter and Bubbles and Mitch and Elias and Lynn and on and on. I thought about the fact that if I got the puppy, in the best case, he would die before I would. I thought about the fact that if I got what I wanted, I would be leaving in less than a year, and not able to take him with me. I thought about Daddy and Lanny and Princess Rose, my sacrificial dolly. And I thought about Toby. And I realized that I was better off for having had every one of them. And I realized that I didn't have to be so tight-fisted. And I realized that whoever left or how or when, I was still there every time, and I could count on myself for that.

I named my new puppy Byron.

• • •

Frankie Jackson was still there, now living alone in her tiny house. Delores had won first prize for the best apple pie in the county. Along with the blue ribbon had come a proposal of marriage that took her less than ten miles away, to another sharecropper's shack, much like the one she had grown up in. Marshall had been shipped off to reform school or some distant uncle, and Frankie lived alone, wearily walking up the hill at the end of each day, and not emerging between Friday evening and Monday morning.

On one of those snapping cold winter nights when the air is so clear you can see every star whispering in the sky, Carla and I were going up the hill to our house after a trip into town. Byron and I were ahead, impatient with Carla's slow pace. It was unusually cold. Out breaths surrounded us like a cloud, and breathing stung my nose. I could feel my eyelashes gathering ice from my own moisture. Byron had a silvery beard lengthening on his chin.

Close to the Jackson's house, Byron suddenly began to growl deep in his throat. He stood stiff-legged, the hair on his ruff rising, and rumbled the deepest snarl I had ever heard from him. Then he slowly advanced, growling the whole time. We reached the edge of the pool of light shed by Frankie's bright porch light and Byron halted, staring into the ditch at the side of the road, now furiously protesting.

Then I saw her. There in the ditch was Frankie. Her two grocery bags were sitting tidily side by side in the road, where she seemed to have carefully set them down, and she was in the ditch, lying motionless. Between her thick lips was a line of spittle, but otherwise, she looked normal. Her mask-like face was unreadable as always, but a sheen of now-frozen sweat was visible on her cheeks and forehead.

We knew immediately that she was dead. But how recent her death was, was unclear. Should we do mouth-to-mouth? Could we still bring her back? Carla and I stared at each other under a spectacular winter night sky, unmoving. Even Byron refused to approach her. His hair standing on end, his front paws braced against any forward motion, forced or accidental, expressed our sentiments exactly. As we looked down at Frankie, to us she was like the final ending note, the last unsettled piece put to rest.

I resolved that I was not going to mope around any more. I was going to get on with my life. I wasn't happy about what had happened, but it wasn't the end of the world either. It was time to find my way out as so many others had, and the only road I could see was college.

Reentry

On the date I was scheduled to take the SATs, Carla unhappily dropped me off at the local high school with my newly sharpened #2 pencils, and drove away, leaving me to enter those doors alone for the first and last time. The institutional smell was exactly the same as I remembered from my grade school in Baltimore, as was the hard little desk, and the round utilitarian clock high on the wall of the auditorium. I looked furtively at the teenagers gathered together, laughing and joking amongst themselves, casting sidelong glances in my direction. They looked completely foreign. I tried to ignore the dour-faced man and woman who prowled among us to be sure no one was cheating. I had decided to take the test early enough to have time to take it again if I really bombed, so I was relatively relaxed. I opened my book when instructed to do so, worked steadily until told to stop, and wasn't too unnerved by how little of each section I completed. I left that day feeling optimistic—maybe getting back into the world wasn't going to be so hard after all.

The test results, however, were abysmal. Even in English, which I had thought laughably easy, I had scored only average. But in math, I was the proud producer of a score in the 20th percentile. Daddy, clearly resolved to be encouraging, couldn't find anything to say when I called him.

I had four months before the next test date, and I determined to make the most of them. I put myself on an intensive daily regime of self-study and review, from which I did not allow myself to deviate. Suddenly I was in a panic to be accepted into college. It was no longer an option to not go the following year—it was a necessity.

Living alone with Carla had become effortless and scary. We didn't even fight anymore. We were in perfect accord, which was terribly disturbing although I couldn't exactly understand why. It felt timeless and suspended, like falling asleep in a snowdrift. Part of my mind kept shouting "NO!" while the rest of me was lulled by a sensation of comfort and safety. Sometimes I imagined that I would never leave—that we would remain thus forever, two eccentric women on top of our hill. We understood each other so well, were so compatible, and I could feel it getting harder for me to relate to other people. The effort to produce polite conversation became laborious and my preference for my journal over human company grew stronger. I knew that it was vitally important for me to break the spell and go. Now.

When the second test date arrived, I was terrified. I had taken innumerable practice tests, my scores in math had slowly begun to rise out of the sub-zero range, and at least the procedure was familiar. Studying English had been fun and I used it as a reward for doing math. Having always loved to memorize, I happily absorbed the word lists, and became a master at analogies. I took advantage of my mother's exceptional vocabulary as we left each other increasingly verbose notes and messages utilizing all the arcane verbiage we could muster. Still, this time wise enough to be nervous, clear about how important it was, I sweated through the whole thing, and by the end was nauseous and trembly.

The wait for my scores was excruciating. And then they came. Ironically, although I had managed to drag my math score up into marginally acceptable territory, it was my verbal score that had really improved, soaring up into the 99th percentile. This, in combination with my essay and reading list, and the fact that in 1977 there was a push for greater "diversity" in colleges, gained me admission to Wesleyan University in Connecticut and Hampshire College in New Hampshire in spite of my lack of a high-school diploma.

Determined to attend the most normal college I could get into, I decided on the first.

Late in the summer, a postcard came from Wesleyan. It read; "You have been assigned room 104b in Foss Hill. The name of your new roommate is Nirit Muhlbaum." There it was. The beginning of my new life. My roomie's name was beautiful. It evoked an image of a fairylike sprite with rippling dark hair, dusky skin, and big eyes who would be my friend and companion for four years. I imagined the room I would share with her, the confidences we would exchange late at night by candlelight, the things we would do together. Maybe I would sew her a dress. Maybe she would show me how to get my hair to wave like hers. I could hardly wait. I was scared stiff.

The weekend before I left for college, a couple of days after turning seventeen, I decided to go camping for two days by myself, with my dog Byron. Although I had spent countless hours in the woods alone, both at night and in the daytime, I had never ventured from the land immediately around me. Carla dropped us off at the head of the trail in the nearby National Park, and we agreed on a meeting place two days hence. The woods belonged to Byron and me alone. In my backpack, along with my sleeping bag I had dog food, matches, soup, bread, a book, and my journal. Byron had never so much as seen a leash, and it never occurred to me that I might need one. We were not owner and dog, we were mutual companions, together by choice, not obligation. He was delirious with excitement, frisking all around, tearing off into the bushes after a rabbit and popping out onto the path again an hour later. That night, Byron curled up at my feet and didn't move again till morning. I lay looking at the familiar stars, envying him his peaceful slumber, and wondered how I was going to manage college. What had I gotten myself into? I didn't even know enough to know what to worry about. There was nothing about this venture that I could picture—not living in a small town or a dorm or attending classes or interacting with a bunch of college students or being one. I thought about the things I did particularly well, and guessed they wouldn't come in handy much.

Not being the fastest goat-milker in the tri-state area, an expert tree climber, able to whip up twelve loaves of bread, or knowing a variety of ways to kill ticks was going to be of much help. I could sew any kind of garment, rid a household of lice, and feed thirty people on $100 a week, but the only applicable skill I could think of was typing. I had diligently continued in Carla's typing class for years, and was a passable "touch typist." I didn't know what else would be relevant. I did know that I would miss my dog, and my freedom, the open fields and dark nights. The rest was just guesswork.

I left early in the morning by train, with one big trunk. I had refused to let my mother take me to college, determined to go on my own. Carla protested emphatically. She had been planning to drive me up—but I was unbending. This was mine. I had pushed it through by myself, and needed to keep it fully my own. Partly I was afraid that I would lose my courage at the last minute, and partly I was preparing to go incognito. Carla, with her noisy proclivity for engaging people and imparting scads of personal information would utterly blow my cover, and I couldn't have that. No one was going to know more about me or where I came from than I wanted them to. I dressed carefully in my new white "painter" pants and flannel shirt. I wore my turquoise choker. My sneakers still seemed serviceable, although stained the inevitable red of our dirt, and my old puffy down jacket was sure to keep me warm even if the train was over-airconditioned. My straight hair, parted down the middle, was pulled up on my head, secured by a metal barrette as I always wore it to keep it out of my way.

Waving goodbye on the platform, I tried not to worry about what Carla would do, who she would talk to, what would become of her. She had decided not to rebuild Nethers, choosing instead to return her attention to her original project of Future Village. With me gone, she would be the only person remaining on the property, alone with four goats, now wild, and my beloved dog Byron. My urge to get away had been so fierce for the past months, waxing stronger as the time approached, that it wasn't until I looked through the window of the train and saw her actually standing on the platform that I focused on the reality of leaving her. And suddenly felt awash in sadness, remorse, uncertainty, guilt, love, hate and longing. Tears began streaming down my face just as the train rolled out, and Carla, of course, saw them. I just had time to see her expression of concern and pain, before she was beyond reach. I cried hard for the first half hour.

• • •

I had no inkling of what awaited me, but I had a small idea that it was going to be different. I was concerned that I would be too odd to find a place in the world. It was of vital importance to me that I appear normal. Could I pass? I tried to put my years at Nethers—my life—aside, and enter the world as a novice, throwing myself completely into making it there without being found out as the imposter I knew myself to be.

The trip was uneventful, and I arrived just at dusk, tired, rumpled, and apprehensive. I had been looking out for fellow Wesleyan students on the train, but spotted none. I figured they must be in different cars, or I had just failed to notice them. But when the train pulled into the station, amid several families and lone adults, I was the only young person to emerge. The college had said they would send someone to meet me at the train station, but I didn't see anyone. Lugging my trunk into the station—I had been too timid to check it—I looked around. Nobody.

I stepped outside, just in time to see a huge tank of a car pull up. Rolling down her window, a young woman leaned out and studied me.

"Wesleyan?" she asked uncertainly.

"Yes." I answered

"Hey! I'm Cheryl. Where's your stuff?"

"Wait a sec. I'll get it."

I ran back into the station, grabbed my case and went back out.

"Z'hat it?" She asked skeptically, standing by the now open trunk studying me, her chewing gum momentarily stilled.

"Yes."

I got into the car and we took off, radio blaring. I scrutinized her as best I could out of the sides of my eyes, but could barely speak. A lofty sophomore, Cheryl did her best to make conversation with me. She warned me about the "Freshman 10."

"Uh oh," I thought. "Here we go. What on earth is the Freshman 10?"

"Just don't fight it," Cheryl advised. "It's inevitable—happens to all of us."

What is this? I wondered. Some hazing ritual I should know about? But did I ask? Never! Stopping the car in front of the dorm, she helped me carry my stuff up the stairs to my room, saying something about calling her if I ever needed to. I thanked her and said goodbye, knowing I never would.

Room 104 was really two, an inner and an outer, each with its own window. Happy to see that "b" marked the inner room, I went about moving in. Ten minutes later, I was finished, having hung my two pictures, set out my books and my hand-dipped candle, and smoothed the wrinkles out of the beautiful bedspread Carla had given me from her own bed.

As far as I could tell, the place was deserted. Orientation wasn't until the next morning, and it appeared I was the only one on my floor to arrive early. I wrote in my journal for a long time, ate the leftovers from my lunch, and went to the cavernous bathroom, which contained ten stalls and sinks and showers, all shining clean. Brushing my teeth in front of a mirror, I looked at myself carefully to see if I looked normal. I certainly didn't *feel* normal. I crawled into my bed and turned out the light, for the first time seeing the reflections and shadows cast across the ceiling that were to become so familiar to me.

The next morning I dressed carefully in my favorite long skirt— one I had made out of woven blue curtains I had found stored in a box in the Main House. I brushed my hair and put it up as usual. I was holding a campus map in my hand, trying to summon the courage to go look for the dining hall, when the door flew open with a crash, and a large woman staggered in with a double armful of cushions, plants, rolled-up posters, and stuffed animals.

"Oomph!" she exclaimed. Straightening, she bellowed, "*FOUND IT* HUN, IT'S RIGHT *IN HERE!*" Turning, she noticed me for the first time.

"OH *HI!*" she roared, heading toward me. "Are you the roommate?"

Before I could answer, another figure staggered in carrying a standing lamp, a coffee pot, and a speaker. Nirit was dark as I had imagined, but there the similarities ended. Thick, brown hair falling straight to her shoulders was clipped back at her ears to reveal thick gold hoop earrings. Three gold chains surrounded her neck at graduated lengths, one with her name written in gold script, one with a Hebrew letter, and the third with a tiny heart, dangling right in the hollow of her throat. On her wrist was a charm bracelet jingling with an assortment of gold figures, tools, and animals. She was tall, small-breasted, with a slim upper body placed on large hips and heavy thighs. Standing next to her, I felt like a stick figure.

"Hi! Are you Sandra?" she asked, her gum smacking in her mouth.

"Yes. Are you Nirit?" I returned, still liking the music of her name.

"Yeah, but everybody calls me 'Rita,' nice ta meetcha!"

Just then her dad barreled through the door with her little sister in tow, and the family began fixing up her room. Nirit had driven up from New York City with two station wagons filled with her things. Her mother immediately started making her bed and piling it with pillows while her father tried to hammer nails into the cinder block walls. Finally resorting to tape, he hung posters of a baby panda, and a rainbow. They had brought a rug and a chair, a stereo and four speakers, an electric pot, electric shaver, an electric toothbrush, electric blanket, heating pad, clip-on light, standing lamp, and flashlight. Her mother began stacking piles of multicolored shirts and pants in the wardrobe and hanging endless dresses and skirts in the closet. Plants adorned the shelves and were draped over the doorways.

Hooks were stuck on the back of the door for Nirit's monogrammed terry bathrobe, and her slippers were placed under her bed. She had a phone that they plugged in and placed on the night table they had brought along. I watched from the doorway, spellbound.

When they were done, Nirit's mother turned to me and said, "Now honey, show us your room."

Tentatively, I opened the door to my monk's cell, and let them in.

"Oh!" she exclaimed. "When is your stuff getting here!? Poor thing, you just feel free to use anything you want of Rita's 'til it gets here, okay?"

Upon learning that this *was* my stuff, she fell silent, and looked at me as Cheryl had at the train station, with, I thought, pity and disbelief. There was obviously already something not quite right about me. And I had met all of two people. Dismay congealed in my belly.

College was, in a word, agony. Although I was vaguely interested, I could not focus on the wealth of academic learning offered to me. I could not wrest my anxious attention away from survival-level concerns. How do you talk to people? Can somebody please teach me how to shave my legs and armpits? I discovered with astonishment that all women had not burned their bras, that in fact my braless state was unusual. Where do you buy them? How do you know what size? People still go on *dates*? Why don't they ever ask me? What would I do if anyone did?? How do you know if someone is teasing you or serious? I was lacking the most basic understanding of social discourse, and felt entirely inept. The simple puzzle of whether to say "hello" when passing a stranger on the path haunted me through many sleepless hours. I wanted to be invisible. I wanted to be noticed. I could hardly breathe for worry.

Although I was as disciplined as ever—spending nine or ten hours a day in the library—while there I could barely keep my eyes open, and routinely awakened hunched over my stack of books, drool dampening my cheek. I went through tests and assignments like a zombie, certain of my doom. Most of my fellow freshmen were graduates of the best prep schools in New England. I had never written a paper. The only test I had taken since 3rd grade was the SAT. Facing my first English assignment, I called my mother from the pay phone in the hallway of my dorm, in the miserably familiar despair of not knowing how to achieve the impossible. She was as helpful as possible, trying to get me to tell her what I was supposed to write about, and to discuss the questions with her. But I was too immersed in my dread, too committed to disaster to be able to work with her. Finally hanging up, I agonized until two in the morning, and then sat down and wrote something, typed it up on the tiny manual Hermes Baby typewriter Daddy had given to me and went to class to turn it in. I didn't care anymore.

A week later, the paper was returned to me. Written at the bottom were several comments that I found helpful when I wrote my next paper the following week. Getting this one back, at the bottom were comments again, only this time, instead of "C–" I saw "C+." Only in that moment, understanding that "C–" was a C minus, as opposed to a C dash standing for "Comments," did I realize that this college used grades! How bizarre! I was torn between shame that I had done so poorly on my first paper, and pleasure at having raised it half a grade in one try. Overriding both was the confirmation of how little I knew about my surroundings—how much I was inevitably misinterpreting without even knowing it.

In mid-October, two-and-a-half months into exile, we had a five-day break. I longed bodily to be home. I had never spent so much time inside in my life, and I felt suffocated. I could see the leaves starting to change, imagine the smell of the air at home, and the silence. I yearned to feel space around me, to hear birds and insects unbroken by motors or voices. Although it was absurdly impractical, with my mother's encouragement I went home. Byron, waiting for me in the driveway, was overjoyed. And it was everything I wanted. For three unbroken days of golden sun, the hawks circled peacefully in the sky, and I simply sat and inhaled and cried. I spent a lot of time in the woods lying on logs looking up at the trees and the clouds and blue sky, taking one deep breath after another, willing the tears to stop.

Would I go back? Or should I forget the whole thing and just stay here where I was comfortable? Carla was gentle and supportive and loving. "Sweetheart, Sandra, you know you don't have to go back! You've done a terrific thing getting in, but maybe it was too soon. I'm sure we could get you a deferred admission for next year."

I knew it would make her happy if I returned. I could build Byron that dog house I had been planning, sew some dresses for my sisters, practice my book-binding and candle-making skills, read some novels. It would be so easy. It would be so peaceful. This felt like the real moment of decision because now I had some idea of the choice I was making. I had tasted the struggle it would take to be out in the world, and felt the despair of not knowing whether I could do it. My loneliness there was intense, more so than the months I had been isolated on this remote hill. Part of me longed to give in and forget the whole thing. But my stubbornness was stronger, as was some bulldog conviction that it would be worth it in the long run. I was pretty sure that if I gave in, if I listened to her siren song, I would not go the next year, or the one after that. Carla had already mentioned a campus-free college where you designed your own program, found local people to guide you in the subjects of your choice, and never required you to leave the safety of your own home, your own mother.

Running on sheer will, I forced myself back up to Connecticut, and dug in for the long battle. My solution to my social ineptitude and uncertainty in general was to sign up for an absurd number of courses, and do poorly in all of them. Gradually I found my feet, learned how to write papers and take tests. More slowly I carved out a tiny circle of friends I felt comfortable with. One of them was a misfit like me, half-Mexican, with her own version of unconventional mother. The other, inexplicably, had been second in her highschool class, and was completely at home at Wesleyan. Tall and beautiful, brilliant and accomplished, I had no idea what she was doing with us. But I counted my blessings. Without these friends, I would have foundered.

Every moment of the first two years was toil. Plagued by self-consciousness, insecurity, and awkwardness, I never spoke in class, and talked only to my friends. I never went to the dining hall alone, to a single party or social function.

The first summer I went home. But after my sophomore year, the sense of compression was overwhelming. This, combined with the fact that one of my two good friends was going to Spain for the year while the other was leaving for a job in New York City, led me to make my own plans. I went to Switzerland where I worked as a nurse's aide in a hospital for nine months, and from there to Israel where I volunteered on a kibbutz for eight months. Both of these environments were highly cloistered, in that way reminiscent of Nethers. But they were also very structured, offering a reprieve from the burdens of autonomy. Then I returned to Wesleyan, where I put my over-enrollment in credits to good use to graduate a year early, just before my twenty-first birthday. To do what?

• • •

After floundering for several years, I gradually began to feel more comfortable with myself and in the world. I went through a progression of dead-end jobs and relationships, went to graduate school, married, left the country, came back, found work I liked, went back for more graduate work, divorced, married again, adopted my two stepsons and then had a child of my own with whom I take the ultimate risk, by loving her unreservedly. A few years after I graduated from college, finally convinced that I wasn't coming back to live with her, Carla went to New York City for seven years and became a conservative rabbi. She then returned to her house on the hill where she continues to live alone and work toward social change. Rachel is a singer and a freelance writer, Erica a pediatric endocrinologist. Both have husbands and children and full lives.

Daddy died suddenly fifteen years ago. Missing him has been a constant thread throughout my life. I am grateful for our closeness and the many things we did together. I regret that I never learned to stand up to him. He died before I was confident enough to challenge or question him, which left our relationship unfinished and underdeveloped. My immediate impulse is to take the blame for this, but then he wasn't around that much. Sometimes I am angry and disbelieving that he just rolled over and let my mother do as she pleased. Wasn't he, a professor, worried about my education? Didn't he of all people know the hazards of my mother's disdain for convention? Perhaps if he had stood up more to Carla, I could have stood up more to him. My longtime impulse to protect him was based in how desperately I needed him, but I mourn the mature relationship we could have had, given the time. Most of all, I miss his delight in life—his active enjoyment of small pleasures. And I am so sad that I did not get to say goodbye.

I rarely get a chance to say goodbye to people. I used to think I liked it that way—the process of leaving was so painful that I preferred to play John Wayne, casually wave my hand and say "See ya'll" before turning my horse and heading off toward the horizon. Now I know better. Hard as it is to stand with the parting and say goodbye, it is less painful when I do. Even with casual goodbyes, there is always the uncertainty of whether we will see each other again. This urgency is very alive in my heart. I strive to say what I need to say to people as immediately as I can.

•••

In my work as a psychologist I have come to learn that my sense of not quite fitting in anywhere is far from uncommon. I believe one of the challenges of life, regardless of where we come from, is finding our "place," of coming to know and accept ourselves well enough to be able to be comfortable, accessible, genuine, and flexible. From my years in the commune I learned a tremendous lesson in tolerance, and in not giving appearances too much credence. I often sense the savage in people beneath the thin veneer of civilization, and can imagine how a person might unfold in an environment like Nethers.

Oddly, I am many things opposite to what I would expect from one who spent formative years on a commune, and I am reminded of the dialectic; how one extreme breeds the other. I am private and reserved to a fault—present document notwithstanding—which makes it hard for people to know me. I am ruthlessly disciplined, finding it no problem to regiment myself for work or pastime. I am deeply counter-dependent. It is very hard for me to let go of a fundamental, hard-won self-sufficiency. This is problematic in that it limits my range of intimacy. And perhaps it is only a fiction, representing more my need to think that I am fundamentally self-sufficient than the fact that I am.

And finally, I am crushingly over-responsible, with one glaring exception:

"I am so angry at you," says Carla, her voice thick with it, shooting what feels like a dark viscous spray through the phone wires and into my ear.

"I am *asking* you girls to put your heads together and pick out the date that you will all come to visit me. Or at the very least plan which week of the year you and your family will come."

I don't want her voice that close to my ear. The sound alone is an unwelcome intrusion. Truth is, I have no intention of going to visit her. I was just there, for heavens sake. Okay, so maybe it was two years ago. It feels like last week, and she is welcome to come visit us whenever she pleases. Neither my sisters nor I have ever gone to visit our mother on any regular basis, and we all allowed a decade or so to elapse in the early years before beginning to visit at all. Erica now tries to go once a year; Rachel and I go for big events. We all see Carla at least twice a year as she comes to us, albeit grudgingly. This has been the ongoing bitter argument between us all these years.

"It's just not *normal*," she has so often cried, "not to visit your *mother*, and not just for a day or two, but for a week minimum, at least twice a year. Everybody I know visits their parents. Everyone I know of my generation has their children visit them regularly."

She first hit me with this normal thing right after college. I had moved to Washington, D.C., to share an apartment with my sister Erica. Some months later, Carla stunned me by wailing into the phone, "I can't believe you never even came *home* after college."

"What??" I asked, incredulous, "*What?*"

"It is *normal* to come *home* after college."

Normal? Since when was "normal" in our vocabulary as a guiding principle? Which part of my early life exactly had been normal? How normal was *she?* It was like hearing a life-long fanatical atheist complain that we hadn't been going to church. It was like hearing a confirmed vegan bitterly demanding her rightful share of steaks (rare if you please). *Normal?* Mixed with my disorientation was pure rage. How *dare* she be such a freak and then act like she was any other parent? How *dare* she attribute the absence of normality to me? Come "home" after college? Home to *what?* A lonely depressed mother alone on the top of a hill in the middle of nowhere. No friends, no activities, no contact with the outside world, no plumbing, no electricity, and all manner of oddballs likely to appear at any moment. This was normal?

Long after I left, Carla continued to install modern amenities into her home; an oven, baseboard heating, a flush toilet, a bathtub, all ostensibly to make it more attractive for "when you girls come home," ignoring the fact that we didn't, or perhaps attributing our absence to a need for creature comforts. For years she refused to make use of our empty rooms, so we would have a place "to come home to."

At first, I was afraid to go back. It was only after I had been gone for a couple of years that I fully understood how narrow my escape had been. In hindsight, that last year alone on the hill with Carla had clearly been dangerous. It seemed to me that I could have lost my bearings altogether, and been unable to leave. My social withdrawal had been extreme and involuntary. By the time I left, holding up my end of a normal conversation felt strenuous and largely pointless. My ability to survive at college and in the world at large felt tenuous, and it seemed risky to go back. At the very thought, I could almost hear a sucking sound, feel the mud pulling at my shoes.

But as the years went on, and I became more rooted in my own life, I still didn't visit her. Partly I suppose it was out of anger and distaste, plus the fact that I saw her often enough as it was, and avoidance of the old disorientation that always accompanied my comings and goings from the Nethers world. There is certainly a dead spot here in my sense of responsibility. I know that my mother is at an age where the balance will soon tip, and her mobility will be limited. I don't know how I will handle that. Whether or not it is the universal moral wrong that she perceives it to be, I acknowledge that it is unusual that I don't go to see her. As is the fact that I don't feel terribly bad about it. Sometimes I think Carla unknowingly severed the chord of filial duty, and it cannot be re-joined.

The quality of my relationship with her, however, does not stem from a sense of obligation. My natural inclination is to call her every four or five days because I enjoy talking to her. There are many things I appreciate about my mother, and I let her know it. Despite life-long struggles with depression, loneliness, and more recently the inevitable challenges of aging, she remains active and deeply committed to life, creative, passionate, smart, lively, and striving always to be more the way she wants to be.

The importance of the Nethers years has a different trajectory for the two of us, in inverse relationship to the integrity of our nuclear units. As my own nuclear family gains strength, Nethers recedes into the past. In the early years, when it was replacing my family, it was paramount. For Carla, made more vulnerable by time, its fallout now becomes more important. I also realize that the commune, and the dissolution of her family that followed, was itself symptomatic, as it was her creation. If it hadn't been through Nethers, it would have happened in some other way. Our family was already, after all, partially dismantled when the whole thing began.

Remarkable as my circumstances were at Nethers, they had only a fleeting influence on me compared to that of my family: my mother, my father and my sisters. None of us talk much about Nethers now. When my sisters and I are together, it rarely comes up. We talk about our parents. The power of the nuclear family, in this instance, trumps the larger setting. Which is not to say that my years at Nethers didn't have a profound effect on me. They did, but at a more superficial level.

I often sing to my daughter a lullaby composed by Laurel for Gabe, still think the old in-jokes about roosters and cooking pots are funny, come up with odd bits of myth or wisdom, like how to get the smell of skunk off a dog's fur (bathe her in tomato juice). I have a loathing of wasted water, portion-sized packaging, and florescent lights. I can tolerate being dirty longer than most—camping for days on end without water for washing poses no problems for me—but I am happiest when I change my sheets often, as my intolerance for grit in the bed approaches obsession. I take active pleasure in a clean house, but I'm pretty sloppy. I crave the outdoors, and revel in long walks with Augie-the-Doggie. I become irate at my stepsons or my husband when they fail to pick up after themselves, leaving dirty plates on the table, trailing newspapers or clothing cavalierly behind them. They look startled at my intensity, not understanding that such behavior is a capital offence. When my stepson accuses me of being "anal" when I berate him for leaving crumbs on the counter or his pan unwashed (again), I have to laugh: my fastidious Daniel who showers daily and has a loathing of mice and spiders. But he's right—it really isn't that important.

I have not seen anyone from Nethers in over twenty years. News has trickled back over the years through Carla. Ellen went to school and became a physician's assistant, and eventually, a psychologist. Mark and Suzanne married, had several children, and went to do good deeds in Africa and other poor countries. Laurel went back to Washington, D.C., and became a well-regarded art therapist. Tim went to another commune. Ethan became a radio announcer, and rumor had it that he underwent a sex-change operation. Fletcher moved back to Minnesota. Karen spent several years in the Navy before marrying a fellow officer. Jillian became a dancer, Jeanie a lawyer.

We have all developed as individuals, absorbed by the world. As I raise my own daughter—now four—I wish for her a combination of a sense of safety and belonging, and the courage to walk her own path. My husband provides important ballast in convincing me that a moderate amount of carefully selected TV will not corrupt her brain, and sugar in small quantities is not lethal. When I imagine her in a setting like the one in which I grew up, I cringe.

The margin between freedom and endangerment is slim. I am very aware of how fortunate I was to have had eight years in conventional circumstances before being thrust into less protected ones. Although Nethers was hard and confusing, I had absorbed enough structure to ultimately be able to integrate the lack of it. Fanaticism of any kind is cruel, and the counterculture had its full share of fanatics. The wish to return to innocence came with the thought that by removing the barriers between adult and child, the children could be the bridge back to innocence. But the force of nature goes in the other direction, and many children lost their innocence devastatingly early. I often think I was fortunate not to have been molested. But in a sense I was. My exposure to sexual matters was premature, as was my close contact with extreme human peculiarities and, ultimately, the harsh reality of adults doing what was right for themselves as opposed to their charges. Perhaps much of my self-protectiveness comes from a too-early understanding of this ruthless human tendency for each to look after him or herself.

Several years ago, I could finally make friends with and appreciate my commune-born quirkiness. No longer afraid of discovery and expulsion, I appreciate the way it strengthens my tendency to be open-minded and non-judgmental. I like the irreverence toward organizational authority it engendered, and the enhancement of my do-it-yourself ingenuity. Although I would not choose communal life for myself as an adult or for my child, I appreciate many of the reasons that others did. Now domesticated, I can bring the wild back to my child.

Last year, my sisters and I did all return to Nethers with our families for a long weekend to celebrate our mother's 80th birthday. With husbands and children, there were fourteen of us in all.

When we arrived after driving for fifteen hours, I was shocked to see that where once there were open fields, there is now forest. The last time I had been on the property, there had been only saplings sprinkled across the hills. The road leading up to the house was now a tree-lined lane, in the darkness more like a tunnel. Where once I intimately knew that land in its every aspect, topography I visit in dreams not infrequently, it was now entirely unfamiliar.

The weekend was remarkable. We took walks, together planted the eighty daffodil bulbs I had brought, cooked meals, put on skits, and played charades as we used to do. Then we gathered in Carla's living room on the evening of her birthday. True to tradition, we had each written something for her, a poem, a story, or an essay, and we had gathered letters and offerings from old friends and fellow communards from far and wide and put them all into an album. Alex, my nephew and the family's youngest poet, started us off, and we went around the room until it was my turn.

Sitting forward in my chair as I prepared to read to my mother, my own daughter curled up against me, I was struck by the profound circularity of life, and I was glad to be able to be there and to feel love.

FOR CARLA ON HER EIGHTIETH BIRTHDAY

"Mommy, when will I be as old as Ariana?" asked Mirabel the other day on our way home from the park.

"Oh, honey, you'll never catch up with Ariana, she'll always be older than you."

"So how old will she be when I am her age?"

"Well, when you are twelve, she will be twenty," I replied.

"How old will Alex be when I'm his age?"

"When you are thirteen, Alex will be twenty-three."

"How old will Alex be when I am *your* age?"

"Oh my, let me see . . . when you are forty-two, Alex will be fifty-two." We both laugh at the absurdity of this notion.

"How old will you be when I am *your* age?"

"Oh jeez. When you are my age, I will be . . . Eighty!"

"*Eighty?!*"

"Eighty."

"That's a lot!"

This is not the first time I have noticed that the difference in age between Mirabel and me is the same as that between you and me, but somehow this conversation brings it into sharper focus. I realize also, that in my earliest memories of you, you are the age I am now, here at the dawn of memory for Mirabel.

Mirabel knows all the songs you sang to me, from "Baby's Boats" to "We Shall Overcome," she is accustomed to being expected to admire bedewed spider webs, golden sunsets and the underworld of puddles. She knows that milkweed seeds are really fairies on their silken steeds, sees promise of a rainbow in every sodden day, and reads the Morse of Lady-bug's dots. And I know, that just as these are gifts from my childhood to hers, they were gifts from your childhood to mine. That to this day you have sustained the magic and the wonder from your childhood means that we can simultaneously inhabit it. Certainly we are as different as we are alike, she from me, and I from you, and yet the connection, the string of gifts from one emerging awareness to the next; child become mother to child become mother to child, reaches across, so that we three children can play together across the small span of eighty years.

Acknowledgements

Warmest thanks to Casey Fuetsch for her fabulous editing and unflagging encouragement, and to Linda Ausse, LuAnn Killeen, Sylvia Levine, and Kay Seiler, each of whom read the manuscript at critical times and was unstintingly supportive. My deepest gratitude and appreciation goes to my husband, Richard Levine, who has championed this and all my efforts, and whose extraordinary depth of heart and mind never cease to amaze and delight me. I am lucky to share my days with you, Rarely Beloved.